The Career Trajectories of
English Language Teachers

The Career Trajectories of English Language Teachers

Edited by
Penny Haworth & Cheryl Craig

Oxford Studies in Comparative Education
Series Editor: David Phillips

SYMPOSIUM
BOOKS

Symposium Books
PO Box 204, Didcot, Oxford OX11 9ZQ, United Kingdom
www.symposium-books.co.uk

Published in the United Kingdom, 2016

ISBN 978-1-873927-87-8

This publication is also available on a subscription basis
as Volume 26 Number 1 of *Oxford Studies in Comparative Education*
(ISSN 0961-2149)

Printed and bound in the United Kingdom by Hobbs the Printers, Southampton
www.hobbs.uk.com

Contents

FOREWORD

The Career Trajectories of English Language Teachers

YVONNE FREEMAN & DAVID FREEMAN

This book fills an important void in the field of English language teaching. There are many textbooks available that provide information on language acquisition, cross-cultural communication, linguistics and English language teaching methods. Coursework and professional development on these topics can be found throughout the world. However, scant attention has been given to the complexity of the many different contexts that teachers of English language teachers find themselves in as they teach. Nor has there been much acknowledgement of the diversity of teacher backgrounds and experiences or the educational, historical and social context in which teachers find themselves. The challenges that English language teachers face need to be shared and their stories told.

Our own personal experiences reflect what many of the chapters describe. In fact, we have written about Yvonne's teaching journey and described how she developed her own approach to teaching through experiences teaching English learners in the United States and in several other countries. David and Yvonne, like many teachers in this book, can describe their teaching journeys as following *rivers of life* or *life histories*.

We both came to the profession of English language teaching from public school teaching. We received teaching credentials to teach English literature or Spanish to native speakers of English. However, the political climate of the USA encouraged us to try living and teaching in Colombia. This experience expanded our views of the world and of teaching. When we returned to the USA to teach again in public schools, refugee populations in our city immersed us in still a different world of teaching. We had to adapt to these students' needs, which were very different from those of our students in Colombia or our native English-speaking students in the USA. We found ourselves teaching multilingual multicultural students from countries including Vietnam, Cambodia, Thailand, India, Korea, Mexico, El Salvador, Saudi Arabia, Russia and China. And while we were teaching them English, they shared their experiences and taught us about their cultures and their perspectives on the world. After this experience we were bitten by the English as a Second Language (ESL) bug. We wanted to make English language teaching our life's work.

Circumstances have led us to live and teach abroad on different occasions. We taught EFL (English as a Foreign Language) and teaching methodology in Mexico, Colombia, Venezuela, Mallorca, India, Jakarta, Hong Kong and Lithuania. Each of those experiences taught us about ourselves and influenced our teaching and our understanding of the field of English language teaching. What we had learned in textbooks on language acquisition and second-language teaching methods was not enough. As we completed graduate studies, we combined the knowledge gained through education with our teaching experience to build a better understanding of how English language teaching is influenced by the context and the needs of the students and by the personalities, experiences, beliefs and backgrounds of the teachers.

We taught using different methods and approaches, including the audio-lingual approach, the notional-functional approach, the natural approach, whole language, and content-based instruction. When we reflected on our educational practices through self-study, we continually attempted to determine the effectiveness of different approaches in varied socio-cultural-political conditions.

Our careers followed a river that moved from public school teaching of English literature and Spanish to teaching elementary and high school in an international school, to ESL and EFL teaching of refugee adults, to teaching graduate students in ESL and bilingual education in California and along the Texas/Mexico border. Each experience built upon previous experiences and now, after over a half a century in the field, we can reflect and see how these experiences influenced not only our teaching but also our writing and our speaking.

Our own self-study has convinced us of the value of reflecting on our own teaching practices. What the chapters in this book, *The Career Trajectories of English Teachers*, do is to expand that understanding through reading the rivers of life of other teachers, teacher educators and researchers who have lived and taught in a variety of settings. The chapters tell readers about how each author came to their profession, the experiences that influenced them, and how the educational, historical, political and social contexts of different countries have influenced and continue to influence how they teach. These stories teach us much more than quantitative studies with all their tables and charts do.

Readers will learn the life histories of educators teaching in countries around the world. The authors recount English language teaching experiences in Turkey, the United States, Bahrain, Malaysia, India, China, Iceland, Chile, the Czech Republic, Brazil, Mexico, the United Kingdom, the United Arab Emirates, Thailand, Greece, Australia and New Zealand.

The chapters describe the career trajectories of teachers teaching students ranging from aboriginal peoples in remote villages to university students with advanced career goals. They investigate teachers who teach English with extensive backgrounds and those with very limited previous experience teaching language. Many of the teachers work in contexts where government mandates require teachers, even those with limited English ability, to teach English universally. The authors share their own stories relating experiences of teaching students at different ages and different levels of English proficiency.

There are common themes within the chapters; yet each trajectory is completely different. The scholars reflect on their own teaching lives, the influences different methodologies and educational practices had on their students, and the conflicts they have experienced when testing requirements and government mandates prevented them from implementing research-based best practices. Several authors describe how their students lacked communicative competence in English, yet when they tried to employ communicative approaches, they were hindered by tests that required students to know English grammar. Even within the USA, testing priorities keep teachers from employing the practices that would help their English learners succeed in acquiring English and doing well academically.

This book is an important one for present and future teachers of English as well as for teacher educators and researchers. It will resonate with educators teaching in different contexts around the world. It helps educators understand the world of English language teaching. The authors' stories are fascinating, and bring up problems in teaching English that are important to consider and often difficult to solve. However, each chapter provides pictures of English language teaching that can inform educators about the profession in ways that English language teaching textbooks seldom do. *The Career Trajectories of English Teachers* is a much-needed book that educates and, at the same time, inspires the reader.

INTRODUCTION

Crossroads in English Language Teaching

PENNY HAWORTH & CHERYL CRAIG

The Career Trajectories of English Language Teachers identifies, illustrates, compares, contrasts and provides informed reflective commentary on the diverse career trajectories of English language teachers, teacher educators and researchers in this field internationally.

The literature (e.g. Nias, 1989; Elbaz, 1990; Hogan et al, 2003) frequently depicts teachers' careers as a simple progression from novice to expert. Other research perhaps more accurately states that there are different levels of expertise in different fields and even experts can be novices in some fields. However, the career trajectories of English language teachers are particularly interesting, often including diverse accumulated employment experiences that span multiple national and international contexts. Further to this, their teaching assignments exceed the boundaries of teaching the English language as an academic discipline (Valdés, 2001) and extend to negotiating multiple literacies (Athanases, 2015), status, position and earning power in various countries and societies (Cummins, 1994, 2000; Fecho & Allen, 2003; Hadi-Tabassum, 2006).

As the status of English language teaching tends to be socially constructed, career trajectories within this profession can be influenced in negative, positive and neutral ways, and a single career trajectory can include strategic upwards, downwards and/or sideways moves. In responding to the changing needs of learners, English language teaching now extends beyond simply facilitating overseas travel experiences and/or teaching English language in one's home country. In the western world, international immigration has increased the need for English language teachers. In addition, globalisation has had positive effects on the status of English language teaching, with the field increasingly being linked to advanced academic study and enhanced work possibilities in diverse areas (Paltridge & Starfield, 2012).

Interestingly, the literature also reveals underlying tensions of being caught in the politically charged 'crossfire' (Cummins, 2000) of language policy and implementation (Menken, 2008) that may impact on teachers' career trajectories. For instance, Davison (2001) highlights how educational policies in Australia have eroded the status of English language teaching. Haworth (2008, 2009) notes similar effects in New Zealand schools where English language teaching is often undertaken by paraprofessionals, and positions tend to be part time and short term. In addition, Thornbury (2001) refers to 'the unbearable lightness' (p. 391) of English as a foreign language teaching, due to the phenomenon of international backpackers who are employed as English teachers simply because they are speakers of English rather than them having any relevant professional qualifications. Nonetheless, there is no doubt that many English language teachers, teacher educators and teacher researchers build satisfying careers that take an upwards trajectory, so we are especially interested in how that occurs.

This book provides a significant contribution to the wider body of scholarly literature on teachers', teacher educators' and teacher researchers' working lives and careers. Past studies have tended to focus on a single context. In contrast, this book provides a unique insight into the common themes and concerns in the profession nationally and internationally, as well as exploring how English language teachers, teacher educators and teacher researchers navigate their individual pathways to success, overcoming the contextually embedded tensions and challenges that exist in diverse national and international settings along the way. Despite the inherent tensions that exist in the field, it has been said that accounts of teachers' experiences are 'the landscape within which the work of teachers can be seen as making sense' (Elbaz, 1990, p. 32). Therefore, this book should be of interest to researchers, to those wishing to pursue a career in English language teaching, and to those who work as teacher educators in this field. In examining and comparing the diversity of career trajectories of professional English language teachers locally and internationally, as well as the critical turning points in their careers, a number of themes that appear to influence resilience in building a worthwhile professional career in this field rise to the fore.

In Section 1, contributors provide insights on their research into the working lives of teachers and teacher educators, and the local and international contexts against which their career trajectories play out. The authors' research methods draw on narrative inquiry, rivers of life, life histories, self-study, policy analysis and critical dialogic approaches. These chapters come from China, Turkey, the United States, India, Malaysia and Australia.

In Section 2, the focus shifts more towards socio-political contexts in teaching and teacher education, the experiences of developing identity in these contexts and the role of self-determination in constructing, reconstructing and co-constructing career trajectories in challenging contexts. Contributors in this section draw on cultural and linguistic autobiographical research in social and political contexts, teacher education programme analysis, emancipatory reflective practitioner research, community of practice, critical analysis of institutional practices, video case studies, narrative inquiry, critical incidents and rivers of life. These chapters come from Brazil, Mexico, the United Kingdom, the United Arab Emirates, the United States, Chile, China, Thailand, Australia, Greece and New Zealand.

In the final chapter, conclusions and reflective commentary on the field both now and in the future are provided, and an illustration of the unfolding nature of English language teachers' career trajectories is shared.

References

Athanases, S. (2015) Mentoring and Mediating the Interface of Multiple Knowledges in Learning to Teach Challenging Content, in C. Craig & L. Orland-Barak (Eds) *International Teacher Education: promising pedagogies*. Bingley: Emerald.

Cummins, J. (1994) Knowledge, Power, and Identity in Teaching English as a Second Language, in F. Genesee (Ed.) *Educating Second Language Children: the whole child, the whole curriculum, the whole community*, pp. 33-58. Cambridge: Cambridge University Press.

Cummins, J. (2000) *Language, Power, and Pedagogy: bilingual children in the crossfire*. Bilingual Education and Bilingualism, vol. 23. Bristol: Multilingual Matters.

Davison, C. (2001) Identity and Ideology: the problem of defining and defending ESL-ness, in B. Mohan, C. Leung & C. Davison (Eds) *English as a Second Language in the Mainstream: teaching, learning and identity*, pp. 71-90. New York: Longman.

Elbaz, F. (1990) Knowledge and Discourse: the evolution of research on teacher thinking, in C. Day, M. Pope & P. Denicolo (Eds) *Insight into Teacher Thinking and Practice*, pp. 15-42. New York: Falmer Press.

Fecho, B. & Allen, J. (2003) Teacher Inquiry into Literacy, Social Justice, and Power, in J. Flood, D. Lapp, J. Squire & J. Jensen (Eds) *Handbook of Research on Teaching the English Language Arts*, 2nd edn, pp. 232-246. Mahwah, NJ: Lawrence Erlbaum Associates.

Hadi-Tabassum, S. (2006) *Language, Space and Power: a critical look at bilingual education*. Bilingual Education and Bilingualism, vol. 55. Bristol: Multilingual Matters.

Haworth, P. (2008) Crossing Borders to Teach English Language Learners, *Teachers and Teaching: Theory and Practice* (Journal of the International Association for Teachers and Teachers [ISATT]), 14(5-6) (December), 411-430.

Haworth, P. (2009) The Quest for a Mainstream EAL Pedagogy, *Teachers College Record*, 111(9), 2179-2208.

Hogan, T., Rabinowitz, M. & Craven, J.A. (2003) Representation in Teaching: inferences from research of expert and novice teachers, *Educational Psychologist*, 38(4), 235-247. http://dx.doi.org/10.1207/S15326985EP3804_3

Menken, K. (2008) *English Learners Left Behind: standardized testing as language policy*. Bilingual Education and Bilingualism, vol. 65. Bristol: Multilingual Matters.

Nias, J. (1989) *Primary Teachers Talking: a study of teaching as work.* London: Routledge.

Paltridge, B. & Starfield, S. (2012) *The Handbook of English for Specific Purposes.* Malden, MA: Wiley Blackwell. http://dx.doi.org/10.1002/9781118339855

Thornbury, S. (2001) The Unbearable Lightness of EFL, *ELT Journal,* 55(4), 391-396. http://dx.doi.org/10.1093/elt/55.4.391

Valdés, G. (2001) *Learning and Not Learning English: Latino students in American schools.* New York: Teachers College Press.

CHAPTER 1

From Canada to Turkey with Places in Between: a quarter-century career of English language teaching

JOHN McKEOWN

SUMMARY Reflecting on an extensive and varied career in English language teaching (ELT), the author narratively unravels threads of professional change and personal growth as a teacher, administrator and consultant, through internal motivation and experiential adaptation, and found in reaction to pedagogic influences amidst the harmonizing of theory and practice. The reflective self-study demonstrates this ELT practitioner's dynamic shift in practice, re-focusing to e-approaches in ELT while advocating for critical friendship as a part of pro-personal development. Situating this shift of practice within an ELT environment where change is constant, the author uncovers a combination of sustaining professional strands found through involvement in educational reform, technological change and in communities of shared practice, and confirms the importance of opening pathways to intercultural dialogue in English language education.

When preparing this chapter, persistent themes emerged on my learning landscape that provide an anchor of unity and coherence to what may have previously appeared to be a patchwork quilt of successive ELT-related positions with increasing responsibility:

- developing technical-functional competence;
- aligning with certain groups (expert group, innovative group, technology group);
- making identity claims as a teacher, consultant, administrator;
- embarking on transformative learning (developing a new narrative that works better and challenges the old one);

15

- pursuing self-directedness with the enjoyment of trying something new and unknown;
- extending my leadership capacity.

Growing up in Thunder Bay, Canada, on the shores of Lake Superior, much around me was 'teacher': family, nature, people from all walks of life imbued with a Northerner spirit of resourcefulness. It was an isolated community of 90,000 people, without a passenger airport or a Trans-Canada highway connection until the 1960s, and I recognize that isolation had a significant effect. It was a rough-and-tumble place to grow up, and I had a vague sense that I would be more complete as a person participating in a wider, more expansive community.

During the course of my public schooling, I was interested in learning and supplemented my studies with lessons in sports and music. Teaching as a career did not seem appealing; even less so as I witnessed teachers who did not seem professionally fulfilled. However, each teacher left an indelible memory and I recall each one by name and subject, with an anecdote in which they connected with me as a whole person, not only as a student.

Family, friends and school counselors urged me to become a teacher. I coached skating and swimming, and assisted others with their lessons. But with an abiding interest in music, my ambition was to become an opera singer. During my journey to professional status, I took voice lessons and music theory at the local convent. Dedicated nuns persevered to expand my world-view, and set me on the road to the transformational power of art. Graduating from Lakehead University in 1978 with an Honors BA (Phil), I was initiated into the history of western thought. My imagination had been enriched and my world was expanding: I made a conscious decision to liberate my learning.

With degree in hand, I moved to Toronto and was accepted at the University of Toronto (U of T), where I was awarded the Associate Diploma in Voice. I had a fine, light tenor voice and excelled at Bach, early and contemporary music. I studied with superb teachers who extended my personal horizons. For seven years, I sang professionally and supported my singing habit by teaching voice privately, singing with the Canadian Opera Company chorus, concertizing, and teaching music theory and creative thinking at a recording studio. In this context, I was introduced to the work of Edward de Bono. In order to use lateral-thinking tools to connect with these aspiring rock stars in the studio, I connected with University of Toronto Schools, where I was encouraged to develop proficiency in the CoRT (de Bono, 1991) thinking program.

However, taking a dispassionate look one frosty Toronto morning at my various satchels for teaching and singing, I recognized that I was teaching more than singing, and loving it. I had become a teacher organically – without my even realizing it. That very day I applied for a one-year BEd program at U of T, and was subsequently accepted. In 1986, at age 30, I completed my teacher education program and upon graduation, took a position with the Toronto Board of Education, where I taught elementary school for 10 years. Toronto has been dubbed the most cosmopolitan city on earth, and each class was a polyglot of language, race and ethnicity. Without much preparation, I was tossed into an ESL context and loved that multicultural environment.

I sharpened my teeth teaching Grade 3 by creating a program with 'centers', in which students had choice in their learning. Change was taken one step at a time as part of an overall shift from a didactic model to more facilitated learning. With the support of the small and dedicated staff of George Miller Elementary School we arranged peer class visits, discussions and anecdotal sharing. Our respective teaching improved dramatically in terms of methods, empathy and interaction. The ongoing dialogue made explicit the expectations we had set and I gained clarity on how our improvements fit into a larger vision and strategy of improved teaching. As a novice teacher, I noticed in my school visits arranged by the Toronto Board of Education that there could be fossilization of practice if it was devoid of reflection, and that, on the other hand, a really good teaching staff could create better teachers.

This development of practice was acknowledged when I was invited to join the board's gifted and talented team. For the next five years, I worked exclusively with this student population, designing and implementing a middle school gifted program, and working peripatetically with student interest groups in math, science and French. It is difficult to put into words how excited I was to be part of an innovative team of six educators who had the ability, savvy and freedom to use more interactive methods of teaching and learning. We made space for reflection to think about what we were doing and why we were doing it, and had ownership of change. We were committed to our mutual growth as adult learners, and to enhancing the quality and efficiency of education in the classroom. I discovered that professional development was not something that was done to me but was a process wherein each team member had the opportunity to think about what they were doing, and to improve ways of teaching. This process translated into better learning conditions for our students.

Unfortunately, funding for this program ended, and I was assigned to teach Grade 1, a good match as I was intrigued by how students learn to read. I joined a team of three teachers who had developed an innovative Grades 1/2 program in which we divided 200 students into four different groups. Every afternoon, each one of us focused on art, science, math or design/technology lessons, experientially in rotation; a highly unusual collaboration at the time. With these seasoned colleagues (each with 15+ years of experience), we created a remarkable opportunity for our students. As teachers, we had increased our job satisfaction and the levels of enjoyment in our collegial work.

At that time, I did not have a specific educational career goal but wanted to work with skillful teachers. I'd become nimble at change, and a supportive team member. I began to see the ways in which knowledge was shaped by circumstances and people around me, and by personal, interpersonal, contextual and situational factors that shift over time. I was now a part of ongoing smaller group conversations that provided space to share what we knew, and in turn to hear different approaches. In retrospect, these stages of development seemed like porous boundaries rather than premeditated career moves.

Thinking critically about educational issues, I began to forge links between my practical knowledge and professional knowledge; my self-efficacy was increasing. Team professional development was engaging, satisfying, knowledge-generating and knowledge-unifying and stood in contrast to the professional development model of certification. For example, I gained Ontario additional specialist qualifications in music and special education, the established route for training. In contrast, I envisaged professional development (PD) as resolving problems of mutual concern, viewing my colleagues not as situated in hierarchy, but as people in relationship with one another, and as potential agents of change.

I started to examine broader educational issues that affected my classroom world and institutional stance. To expand my perspective, I embarked on an MA in the teaching of English at U of T, completed in 1995, part time, over three years. The knowledge that I gained was directly applied in my classes. In the process, I developed a frame of reference through which I could interpret and coherently organize meaning from a variety of sources, events and contextualized learning. I came to acknowledge that intuition plays a part in the process and that my developing intuitive expertise had depended on my conscious choices to study, to learn on the job, to demonstrate competence, and to stay open for challenges. The intellectual, affective and cognitive components of my teaching had become integrated.

During my graduate studies, it was suggested that I learn more about education in different contexts. I was accepted on a League of Commonwealth Teachers' Exchange Scheme in Glasgow, Scotland. Participating teachers exchange jobs, accommodation, pets, cars, etc., for a year. Coming from a Scottish heritage, I felt as if I had won the lottery. The year opened up boundaries as I witnessed, for example, using data to inform teacher practice and to improve student results. It was tough adapting to a different system but I developed resilience to changing conditions. Ringing in my ears was the sage advice of a Commonwealth League counselor who assured me that I would be heading abroad again, and that life in Toronto would not be sufficiently fulfilling.

Back in Toronto, I had to deal with the reality of reverse culture shock, not only professionally, but personally as well. AIDS was wreaking havoc. Many colleagues and friends passed away due to HIV-related complications. There was a terrible feeling of loss and sadness and I longed to be away from those painful memories. Furthermore, I had become what I term a 'progressive subversive' – that is, a teacher within a system who realizes its limitations and despite the odds, provides choice, autonomy and enriched content for students, and finds routes to professional growth. I began to identify ways in which teachers continued their development despite the systems in which they find themselves. As a result, I decided to explore knowledge communities (DuFour, 2004) in more depth.

My practice now shifted to the use of research to generate and provoke dialogue with self and colleagues. I began to gather data on how I was doing as a teacher, explaining to myself, and colleagues, why certain methods were more successful than others. My focus shifted to a culture of inquiry: from telling about what practices were better suited to learners, to sharing experiences. My teaching world expanded: at the 1998 international teacher recruitment fair in Toronto, I secured a position as an ESL teacher at the new Bilkent University Preparatory School (BUPS) in Ankara, Turkey.

At BUPS, we initiated a co-teaching model with two native speakers supporting each other in core subject lessons (English, math, science) with Turkish students who had little or no English language facility. We worked closely in tandem with Turkish staff delivering a Turkish Ministry of Education curriculum. It was a unique opportunity. I loved living abroad, and interacting with another culture. My learning focus converted to a knowledge-building cycle of shared practice – that is, engagement in the theorization of practical knowledge and in the practicalizing of theoretical knowledge (Tsui, 2007).

Quite by chance, a timely opportunity came my way as head of English at a school in İzmir. Once there, I realized that native talent, intuition or teaching skill are not sufficient to manage a 20-plus-member team. More leadership acumen was needed and, to that end, I enrolled in the International Leadership and Administration Diploma of the Principals Training Center. During these summer sessions, I learned more about pro-personal development (Bubb & Earley, 2007), encompassing a wider range of practical and theoretical interests, with more sustained levels of reflection and sharing of reflection. My research appetite was whetted and I felt ready to take on a terminal degree while working full time.

However, I could not find the right combination of factors to make further graduate study workable. Settling in Turkey made that goal seem even more remote, but I doggedly kept searching for the mix of necessary ingredients: manageable fees, minimal residence requirement, dedicated tutor. I was accepted onto a UK university EdD program, with a mix of distance/online and face-to-face learning. It may be informative to recall that in 2001, online education was in its infancy.

I whittled down my proposal: the factors in the creation of a learning community at Turkish foreign national schools. At that time, the family of foreign national schools where I worked was in the midst of institutional soul-searching, looking for ways to improve. To that end, they asked for and received substantial feedback from community stakeholders, and the foundation made their data available to me. Fortunately for the progress of my investigation, the board acknowledged the value of a participant researcher at the school and supported my study.

Throughout the process, I had an empathetic, experienced and reassuring tutor who played a pivotal role. Choosing a topic that highlighted local conditions and resources produced authentic results: as participant researcher I opened up the possibility of exploring local factors in context (Bennett & Bennett, 2004). Doctoral studies supported greater congruence between the institution, the workplace and professional learning, and the results were more strongly focused on the potentiality of workplace transformation. My practice was informed by research, and my shared professional discourse was deepening. I established what I now see as a dialogical process (Alexander, 2010), a renewable resource, in which familiar and tacit knowledge interacted with, and were shared by, newly explicit understanding.

To expand my administrative skill set, I undertook administrative duties for two years at the Luanda International School (LIS), Angola, an International Baccalaureate (IB) world-school, during the set-up phase, including setting up the authorization of the International Baccalaureate programs and accreditation by the Council of International Schools. My doctoral research on the creation of learning communities proved applicable. At LIS, we became a tight-knit group of educators who supported each other under peculiar conditions: we were a vibrant learning community. Living and working in Africa opened my eyes to the importance of education, and to the marginalization of people without access to education.

With this administrative experience, I was able to take on more senior managerial positions leading educational reform projects for an American educational service provider in Qatar and Abu Dhabi. Focused on educational reform initiatives, we were promoting a strong sense of a shared vision of the future linked to continuous improvement. Immersed in an Arabic bilingual working environment, and concerned with teaching English on all fronts, I recognized that I needed to have a more appropriate ELT qualification, and during 2008 successfully completed a CELTA (Certificate of English Language Teaching to Adults) issued by Cambridge University.

However, factors conspiring for change converged. That US company, along with several other international educational service providers, was not awarded further contracts. During this transition, the University of Bahrain's newly established Bahrain Teachers College (BTC) hired me as Assistant Professor of Education. Providing pre-service and in-service teacher education, I taught undergraduate and graduate courses. Appointed as faculty liaison for the teaching practicum (TP), I was given scope to implement the TP program, devised by the National Institute of Education, Singapore. I was immersed in a changing educational landscape with a convergence of technology and pedagogy, including the development of student e-portfolio and online TP documentation.

At the BTC, to move teacher education reform forward cohesively, faculty members were offered an opportunity to study at BTC for the Professional Certificate of Academic Proficiency (PCAP) through York St John's University (YSJU), UK. The experience had a sustained and profound effect on my practice in higher education. As part of the program, faculty from YSJU led on-site PCAP sessions. Also required was the submission of six journal reflections and an action research project. It was challenging: five of thirteen participants completed the PCAP. I quickly recognized that the program would push my learning and time to the limits as it was my first academic posting, and I had some hefty responsibilities.

I discovered the joys of critical friendship with a colleague in this program. We began discussing informally the work of McGregor (2006) and Biggs and Tang (2011), and how to incorporate them into our college teaching, particularly supporting student language learning. We became sounding boards for each other, sharing results and delving into the details of our action research projects. Our critical friendship blossomed through combining a common focus on improvement with continuous teacher talk about practice. We created a space where it was safe to take risks.

As a result of our collaboration, we co-authored and published several research papers, in which we developed the concept of educational cultural convergence (Diboll & McKeown, 2011a,b). Bonding was cut short by the eruption of the Arab Spring and the disastrous riots so ruthlessly quelled by the Bahraini monarchy. Rival faction riots at the BTC led to the indefinite closure of the universities. While the BTC offered many opportunities, we decided to take the *force majeure* option.

Through mutual friends, I was approached to work as an ELT senior lecturer at Mevlana University in Konya, Turkey. I was delighted to be back in Turkey. Those two years were spent teaching undergraduate classes in writing, speaking and research methods to prospective teachers. I had changed and could perceive – and this is of course difficult to measure – that my students demonstrated more enjoyment in their learning, increased engagement, and used their English with more confidence. I felt more self-assured about the direction of my teaching, particularly in addressing learner needs rather than learning outcomes. Writing, researching and presenting at international conferences with my co-author (Kurt & McKeown, 2012) augmented and added depth to my teaching.

After Konya, I accepted a position as deputy head of MEF International Schools in Istanbul. It was rewarding to be immersed in a collaborative, supportive culture, and in a more technologically sophisticated environment, as we initiated the use of e-tools to scaffold inquiry-based learning following the IB framework. As an administrator, I found that I had developed more technical administrative skills and had increased my expertise in managing others.

From MEFIS, I was recruited to my current position as director of the School of Foreign Languages at MEF University. With some sense of satisfaction, I find myself looking through the opposite end of the same telescope I peered into 25 years ago to envisage what this 'career' might look like. Following Huberman (1989), I started out in a discovery phase, became more experienced, found ways to open new horizons, and now am at the stage of passing on knowledge. I work with others to continuously improve current understanding by seeking information, building networks and solving challenging problems.

MEF University has adopted a flipped classroom pedagogical approach throughout all departments and the challenge has been to modify this method into a blended learning option (Halverson et al, 2014; Van Der Linden, 2014) for language learning in the foundation year English language preparatory program. Our preparatory team examined current research and practice related to the creation of a digital learning environment to support and enrich language development. Contrasting with what publishers, technology and service providers could offer for teaching materials in relation to student needs, the team created a unique blended learning option; the first of its kind worldwide.

Shifting to blended learning, we found ourselves at the intersection of technology and pedagogy. In conjunction with Oxford University, we are exploring the limits and possibilities of EMI (English as the medium of instruction), and investigating future scenarios of technologically enhanced learning environments. As technology changes, so too will our approach to curriculum implementation. Our shared goal is to refine our knowledge by mentoring, leading by example, developing contextualized and collaborative approaches to PD, and providing opportunities for autonomous learning. Together, we formatively evaluate the impact of changes in practice through reflection and multiple feedback loops, echoing the developments of my earlier career.

Moving forward in my practice and course design, I find I am using technology increasingly as the activator, with pedagogy as the driver. Continuing technological advances, particularly innovations in the delivery of ELT curriculum, provide new sustaining threads to my participation in educational reform, increasingly involving task-based teams working with unknown or untried circumstances. Living in different cultures reinforces my belief in the necessity for social cohesion, and for advocacy for intercultural awareness in an ongoing dialogue of diversity.

I have thrived on the pleasure of living in a wider world, and admit that I do not like getting too secure or too comfortable. My skill set has allowed me to continue to quickly adapt to changing work environments and challenges. I am *knowmadic* (Hokanson & Karlson, 2013), contextually applying what I know, thriving in non-hierarchical situations, and motivated to collaborate. As an international ELT educator, I respond to change, to moving on, and to not standing still: I live with the land, not on it (Said, 1994). My professional development continues with provocative and disruptive elements in which I leverage personal knowledge: old problems surface in new contexts.

My adaptation to cultural engagement has allowed me to participate in a culturally expansive dialogue to which I am thoroughly dedicated, and at which my publication and service have been aimed. Composing this chapter is a reminder of the power of reflection, the efficacy of teamwork, the shifting identities within ELT, the importance of critical friendship and the untapped potentiality of collegiality found in unsuspecting places, and with surprising people.

References

Alexander, R. (2010) *Dialogic Teaching Essentials*. National Institute of Education, Singapore. https://www.nie.edu.sg/files/oer/FINAL%20Dialogic%20Teaching%20Essentials.pdf

Bennett, J.M. & Bennett, M.J. (2004) Developing Intercultural Sensitivity: an integrative approach to global and domestic diversity, in D. Landis, J. Bennett & M. Bennett (Eds) *Handbook of Intercultural Training*, 3rd edn, pp. 147-165. Thousand Oaks, CA: SAGE.

Biggs, J. & Tang, C. (2011) *Teaching for Quality Learning at University*, 4th edn. Buckingham: SRHE/Open University Press.

Bubb, S. & Earley, P. (2007) *Leading and Managing Continuing Professional Development: developing people, developing schools*, 2nd edn. London: SAGE.

Curry, M. (2008) Critical Friends Groups: the possibilities and limitations embedded in teacher professional communities aimed at instructional improvement and school reform, *Teachers College Record*, 110(4), 733-774.

de Bono, E. (1991) *Lateral Thinking*. London: Penguin Books.

Diboll, M. & McKeown, J. (2011a) Building a Community of Shared Practice through Educational Cultural Convergence (ECCO), in *Languages for Specific Purposes in Theory and Practice*. Cambridge: Cambridge Scholars Press.

Diboll, M. & McKeown, J. (2011b) Critical Friendship in International Educational Reform: a journey to educational cultural convergence (ECCO), *International Mevlana Educational Journal of Research*, 1(2) 15-26.

DuFour, R. (2004) Schools as Learning Communities, *Educational Leadership*, 61(8), 6-11.

Halverson, L., Graham, C.R., Spring, K., Drysdale, J. & Henrie, C. (2014) A Thematic Analysis of the Most Highly Cited Scholarship in the First Decade of Blended Learning Research, *The Internet and Higher Education*. http://dx.doi.org/10.1016/j.iheduc.2013.09.004

Hokanson, B. & Karlson, R.W. (2013) Borderlands: developing character strengths for a nomadic world, *On the Horizon*, 21(2) 107-113. http://dx.doi.org/10.1108/10748121311323003

Huberman, M. (1989) The Professional Life Cycle of Teachers, *Teachers College Record*, 91, 31-57.

Kurt, I. & McKeown, J. (2012) Pathways to Cultural Rapprochement in Schools: becoming a global teacher through the use of the 'educational cultural convergence' (ECCO) model, *Mevlana International Journal of Education*, 2(1), 25-35.

McGregor, D. (2006) *The Human Side of Enterprise*. New York: McGraw-Hill.

McKeown, J. (2015) Liberating Learning: engaging students in English language learning utilizing digital technology. Paper delivered at the International Conference on English for Specific Purposes (ESP) and New Language Technologies: *Synergies of Language Learning*, University of Niš, Serbia.

Said, E. (1994) *Representations of the Intellectual*. New York: Random House.

Tsui, A.S. (2007) From Homogenization to Pluralism: international management research in the academy and beyond, *Academy of Management Journal*, 50(6), 1353-1364. http://dx.doi.org/10.5465/AMJ.2007.28166121

Van Der Linden, K. (2014) Blended Learning as Transformational Institutional Learning, *New Directions for Higher Education*, 2014(165), 75-85. http://dx.doi.org/10.1002/he.20085

CHAPTER 2

Unpacking Tensions: an autobiographical narrative inquiry into the cross-cultural teaching journey of a TESOL teacher educator

LIPING WEI

SUMMARY This chapter examines a TESOL (Teaching English to Speakers of Other Languages) teacher educator's career developments through storying and restorying her teaching experience in both eastern and western contexts. Using narrative inquiry, the researcher's personal practical knowledge is constructed and reconstructed as she intentionally and systematically inquires into the autobiographical narratives of her east-to-west teaching journey. In particular, this research brings to light a series of tensions the author has experienced, from being an EFL (English as a Foreign Language) learner and teacher in the East, to being an ESL (English as a Second Language) learner and TESOL teacher educator in the West. The tensions include: (a) learning language vs. learning about language; (b) official rhetoric vs. classroom realities; and (c) teaching one's best-loved self vs. teaching what one is told to teach. Through unraveling and illuminating these tensions, this research uncovers the nexus of not only where the personal and professional meet, but also where theory, practice and policy meet in a teacher's cross-cultural teaching journey.

Introduction

When teachers cease to be inquisitive about their practice, their practice ceases to be professional. (Samaras, 2011, p. 203)

As a TESOL (Teaching English to Speakers of Other Languages) teacher educator in a public university located in a southwestern state in the United States, I regard this quote as one of the mottos I cherish most. Looking back on my previous TESOL teaching experience in both China and the United States, I feel that this cross-cultural teaching journey has played a critical role in shaping my teaching philosophy and practices, though it is relatively short compared with many seasoned English teachers. This chapter aims to examine my development through storying and restorying my teaching experience in both eastern and western contexts. In particular, it will focus on bringing to light a series of tensions I have experienced, from being an EFL (English as a Foreign Language) learner and teacher in the East, to being an ESL (English as a Second Language) learner and TESOL teacher educator in the West. It is hoped that readers will find that this chapter goes beyond a mere reflection of my personal teaching journey by offering insights into the preparation and development of TESOL teachers in both EFL and ESL contexts.

Theoretical Framework

Two conceptualizations underpin this research: (a) self-study; and (b) a teacher's personal practical knowledge. The research is, first and foremost, grounded in the theoretical framework of self-study, and additionally rooted in the assumption that it is a teacher's personal practical knowledge that plays a central role in teacher development rather than the knowledge obtained elsewhere. The forthcoming section will elaborate on how these two notions have underpinned my autobiographical narrative inquiry.

Self-study

Self-study is understood as 'the study of one's self, one's actions, one's ideas, as well as the "not self"' (Hamilton & Pinnegar, 1998, p. 236). According to Clandinin and Connelly (2004), self-study is the highest form of research because it offers the closest look at particular contexts, and hence provides the greatest potential for change. It is particularly useful to examine who you are as a teacher, your teacher identity, the motivations behind your teacher goals, and the constraints and supports you have experienced in reaching those goals (Samaras, 2011). Berry (2007) outlined four reasons that compel teacher educators to embark on self-study research: '(1) articulating a philosophy of practice and checking consistency between practice and beliefs, (2) investigating a particular aspect of practice, (3) developing a model of critical reflection, and (4) generating more meaningful alternatives to institutional evaluation' (as cited in Ukpokodu, 2011, p. 439). My motivations fit the first two categories.

Another point worth mentioning is that '[w]hile self-study entails a personal inquiry, it is also interpersonal, interactive, and collaborative' (Samaras, 2011, p. 75). Self-study research involves not only my autobiographical narrative inquiry, but also interactions with students, and collaborations with critical friends. While examining my teaching experience involving both the East and the West, my TESOL teaching philosophy and the tensions experienced in both contexts are made explicit and meaningful not only personally and locally, but also socially and globally (Howe & Xu, 2013).

Teacher's Personal Practical Knowledge

A teacher's personal practical knowledge (Clandinin, 1986) is closely linked with the notion of teacher as curriculum maker (Clandinin & Connelly, 1992). In contrast to the prevalent teacher-as-curriculum-implementer image which treats teachers as 'mediators between curriculum and student outcomes' (Craig & Ross, 2008, p. 283), the notion of teacher as curriculum maker 'strengthens the view of teachers as knowing and knowledgeable human beings' (p. 283). Instead of implementing the curriculum mandated 'by virtue of (their) power, position, or formal knowledge base' (Craig, 2012, p. 91), teachers are encouraged to become agents of their own learning who act upon their own intelligence and knowledge. A teacher's personal practical knowledge, in Connelly and Clandinin's (1988) terms, is 'found in the teacher's practice' (p. 25). It subscribes to teachers being minded professionals, taking ownership of their personal professional accountability.

Methodology

Narrative Inquiry

This research employs narrative inquiry as the methodology, which uses stories as the portal through which human experience is interpreted and made meaningful both individually and socially. Reduced to its essence, narrative inquiry is 'the study of experience as story' (Clandinin et al, 2007, p. 22). It is also a 'personal experience method' (Clandinin & Connelly, 1994). Teachers bring their life histories into teaching (Goodson & Choi, 2008). Marrying narrative inquiry and self-study, Samaras et al (2004) employed the method to explore how teachers' personal experience, culture, history and learning experience inform their teaching 'personal history self-study method'. This research utilizes narrative inquiry as the method to undertake self-study, believing that it can best untangle the complexities of the researcher's cross-cultural career trajectory.

Data Sources

The primary data source of this research is the researcher's autobiographical narrative – namely, my education and teaching-related life history. Other types of data include my journals, teaching notes, course syllabi, students' reflective journals, and postings on Blackboard Learn. The conversations and emails with my critical friends have helped me to gain different interpretations and spark new ideas. According to Samara (2011), '[s]elf-study requires a transparent research process that clearly and accurately documents the research process through dialogue and critique' (p. 80). My critical friends group helped me to make the whole research process explicit to myself and transparent to others through critical collaborative inquiry.

Tools of Analysis

According to Clandinin et al (2007), 'narrative inquiry is much more than the telling of stories' (p. 21). Instead, it 'need(s) to move to the retelling and reliving of stories, that is, to inquiry into stories' (p. 33). Three analytical tools – broadening, burrowing and storying and restorying (Connelly & Clandinin, 1990) – are used for 'narratively cod(ing)' the field texts (Clandinin & Connelly, 2000, p. 131) in their transitioning to research texts. Through the use of broadening, my teacher development story is situated in my life experience as an English language learner and former teacher in the East and as a non-native TESOL teacher educator currently in the West. Burrowing allows me to gain a close-up examination of the particular tensions I have lived with in both socio-cultural contexts. Additionally, storying and restorying engages me in unfurling the breadth and depth of my career trajectory in a way that has not been possible before. Taken together, the three interpretive devices have enabled me to channel field texts into research texts that 'grow out of the repeated asking of questions concerning meaning and significance' (Clandinin & Connelly, 2000, p. 132).

Credibility

Like other forms of social science research, narrative inquiry texts 'require evidence, interpretive plausibility, and disciplined thought' (Connelly & Clandinin, 2006, p. 485). This evidence, however, is not built on empirical proof, or universal truth. Instead, what a narrative inquirer seeks to establish is 'not truth but truth-likeness or verisimilitude' (Bruner, 1985, p. 97), 'a compound of coherence and pragmatic utility,' as Bruner pointed out (1996, p. 90). Significance, then, is rooted in believability rather than in the absolute consistency or authenticity of events. Lyons and LaBoskey (2002) also suggested that for narrative inquirers, 'validity' rests on concrete examples of actual practices presented in enough detail so that the relevant community can judge the credibility and usefulness of the observations and the analysis of an inquiry. Therefore, the central focus of this work is to present 'something ... lifelike' with 'a real-life sense' (Bruner, 1986, p. 11). It is my hope that believable stories, convincing drama and credible historical accounts will make my experiences along my career continuum seem credible to readers of this volume.

Analysis

This autobiographical narrative inquiry into my cross-cultural teaching journey brought to light three tensions I have experienced: (a) learning a language vs. learning about a language; (b) official rhetoric vs. classroom realities (Nunan, 2003); and (c) teaching one's best-loved self (Craig, 2013) vs. teaching what one is told to teach. Teachers grow when placed in situations fraught with tensions. It is amid these three tensions that I have been able to continue to advance as a TESOL teacher educator.

Learning a Language vs. Learning about a Language

It is my firmly held belief that to be genuinely understanding of what it takes for a non-native speaker to learn English, it is indispensable that an ELL (English Language Learner) teacher possess a first-hand experience of learning a second or foreign language. The biggest lesson that my 20-year-or-so experience of learning and using English as a foreign and then second language has taught me is the huge distinction between learning a language and learning about a language. The following excerpt from my autobiographical narrative underlines this point:

> I was born and raised in a family highly emphasizing academic achievements. From a very early age, I was aware that excelling in academic study was vital. Self-disciplined, hard-working, and meticulous, I was always a top student, and rarely questioned my learning outcomes. However, English language learning was an exception. After years and years of committing English vocabulary and grammatical structures to memory, I still had a large difficulty calling them forth and bringing them under control as I wished. This deeply-felt frustration accompanied me to the U.S. where I chose to further my education. The language barriers I hence experienced turned out far beyond what I had expected before.
>
> I may show a relatively high degree of fluency in the academic areas I was familiar with, but beyond that I experienced a hard time communicating with people. In unfamiliar or impromptu situations, I usually am unable to respond verbally in an appropriate manner. Sometimes no matter how well thought out my viewpoints were, I had trouble articulating them while sustaining coherent use of structures in longer utterances. All types of errors occur when expressing somewhat complex ideas: awkward or inaccurate phrasing of ideas, mistaken time, space, person references, etc., especially when under tension. Though as a former English teacher I used to teach all the grammar and vocabulary knowledge to students, I even made mistakes with very simple grammar and vocabulary. This was very embarrassing and frustrating. My listening comprehension of other people's speech was poor, too, and always incomplete, due to fast speech rate, contractions, omission of certain sounds, heavy use of colloquialism, etc.

This autobiographical narrative excerpt clearly reveals my lack of ability to use English in actual communication, regardless of how many years I have been learning it and how hard I have studied. The following extract from my journals reflects how it negatively affected my academic study in the United States, among many other aspects.

29

At school, I find myself easily silenced in a group of people. Sometimes, I feel that I understand each word they say but just do not get what they mean with these words. When I get totally lost and have no hope of figuring out what they are talking about, my mind will go blank, and all my previous preparations will become meaningless. Even though I do understand them and want to express my opinions, I have difficulties getting into the conversation. I have to transform the ideas into language, thinking about what words to use and how to organize them into grammatically correct English. When I am ready, people have gone on to a different topic and what I wanted to say has become irrelevant to the issue under discussion. When I do get ready to say what I want to say at the right time, there may be people talking on and on, and I do not know when it is appropriate to take the turn. When I am hesitating, somebody else usually has jumped in and switched to another topic. I feel that I am always lagging behind.

Next, I present a journal entry that describes how my personal life suffered because of my poor communicative competence.

I know I should make American friends and integrate into American life, but it's easier to be said than done. The limit of my communicative competence restricts me so seriously. When among American people, I appear as a fool, unable to understand and respond appropriately and empathetically. I don't even remember how many times I have felt so stupid and embarrassed when everybody else is engaged in a lively talk and occasionally explode with laughter while I 'observe' everything silently as an outsider. I'm afraid I have gradually become numb and begun to resign myself to being silent all the time. Though physically in the US, my life is very insulated from Americans, but confined within the Chinese-speech community where I feel most at ease.

There has been a vicious circle. The more I am distanced, the poorer my communicative competence; the poorer my communicative competence, the more I am distanced. The consequence is that I feel I have never fit into the American life, and have never found a place that belongs to me. To overcome this situation, my communicative competence is the first and foremost issue to address. I always wish that if I had a stronger communicative competence in English and was not so apprehensive about communicating using English, I would very likely have made greater achievements with less pain and efforts in both academic context and non-academic aspects of life.

This experience spurred me to reflect upon my previous English learning experience more thoroughly, which was filled to the brim with all the moments of remembering lexical and grammatical knowledge and being tested on the mastery of knowledge while having very few opportunities to practice using the knowledge and translate it into actual ability. I realized that I had been *learning about English* – the knowledge that allows me to talk about the language – rather than *learning English* – obtaining the competence to use the language.

This tension is also clearly present in my international students enrolled in the TESOL teacher education program. I have had quite a number of students from EFL countries who are very experienced EFL teachers at university level in their countries. However, all experienced the language challenge to varying degrees and came up with the same realization. One student, Yao, in her journal wrote the following reflection:

> I studied English as my major in university, and taught university students English for 6 years. I was very confident in my English. I thought I knew it very well and never worried about it before I came to America. Then I found it is not true. I did know it, but what is the use of it? I can't use it! I still find it hard to communicate with Americans! It's embarrassing. This disappointment is something I will never forget in my lifetime. I think I should start thinking about how I will teach my future students. (Yao's journals)

Thanks to these experiences – my own and my students' – I have gained a deeper understanding of how the discrete phonetic, lexical and syntactic knowledge *learned* contributes to linguistic competence (Chomsky, 1965), but does not automatically transform to communicative competence (Hymes, 1971), which is essential in enabling learners to use English effectively in today's world of globalization with English as the lingua franca. All these experiences have played a fundamental role in shaping the core beliefs I have carried on to my practices as a TESOL teacher educator. I am more clear and certain that as a TESOL teacher educator, I want to instill in my students the concept that a language teacher should teach a 'language', not merely the 'knowledge about a language'. I therefore consciously stimulate my student teachers to ponder over the nature of language and the goals of language teaching. I hope they can realize that teaching a language involves more than teaching phonology, morphology, syntax, semantics and lexicon, as preservice language teachers are typically trained in. In short, the ability to use the language effectively for real communicative needs should always be the ultimate goal of language teaching.

Official Rhetoric vs. Classroom Realities

Many ELL teachers, when graduating from TESOL teacher education programs, may have been well prepared for the knowledge of second language acquisition theory, language teaching pedagogy, applied linguistics, etc., while probably least prepared for facing the disjunction between official rhetoric and classroom realities (Nunan, 2003), and this disjunction is not uncommon. What I encountered when teaching in the East amply spoke to this point.

Since the late twentieth century, in many East Asian countries, 'the official discourse on reforms of English-language education has repeatedly attributed the low quality of English instruction to the traditional teaching methodologies and called for new pedagogical practice' (Hu, 2005, p. 153) – namely, communicative language teaching (CLT). Criado and Sanchez (2009) even claimed that the 'official curricula all over the world include CLT as the predominant method in foreign language teaching' (p. 4). However, my classroom teaching experience revealed the opposite. An excerpt from my autobiographical narrative demonstrates how I struggled with the huge gap between the official rhetoric and my classroom realities:

> I made a lot of effort to establish a relaxed classroom atmosphere so students could feel free to engage in communicative activities. I also paid special attention to giving students positive and encouraging feedback. As long as errors didn't interfere with comprehension, I wouldn't correct them ... I tried every means to send students the message: Free communication is valued more than anything else. However, I soon discovered that it was of little success. Many setbacks were experienced in putting the principles of Communicative Language Teaching into practice, no matter how passionate I was about adopting it.
>
> The first difficulty stemmed from the assessment system that was in no way in alignment with CLT. Both the nation-wide tests (College English Test Band 4 and Band 6) and the university exams were largely focused on the discrete language points. Under pressure to help students meet the benchmark, I had to spend a considerable portion of class time teaching the textbook, working on reading comprehension, the language points at vocabulary and sentence level, etc., all indispensable for students to perform well on reading and grammar-centered tests, yet contributing little, if not nothing, to the development of students' communicative competence.

My explanation of the gap continued:

> Moreover, students generally did not have an intrinsic motivation to improve their practical language skills. Due to the lack of communicative needs in EFL contexts, students didn't see many practical benefits of developing communicative competence How to score high on tests was more instrumental and appealing for them. For the communicative activities I asked them to participate in, they appeared quite silent or passive, and reacted very negatively. I made every effort to look for more authentic language

resources to stimulate their interest, but there were not many, much to my dismay.

Also, the large classroom size was another obstacle to the enactment of Communicative Language Teaching. How to organize pair and small group work with a class of 50 to 60 students with a fixed arrangement of seating was really a huge issue. I so wished I had a chance to see how CLT could be conducted successfully in such circumstances.

Embarrassingly as it was, the last but not the least issue was my own insufficient English proficiency, which restrained me from teaching as communicatively as I would expect. I found I was even more comfortable explaining language points than facilitating interactions sometimes. Admittedly, CLT poses a higher demand on language proficiency of teachers.

As my autobiographical narrative unfolded, I experienced a variety of difficulties enacting CLT in the classroom, ranging from language knowledge–based texts, to overlarge class size, students' low motivation, teachers' inadequate English proficiency, and lack of real communicative needs and authentic language resources (Wei, 2011). I was not alone in suffering as a result of the chasm between the rhetoric officially advocated and the realities confronted in classrooms. Having investigated the English curriculum of seven Asia-Pacific countries and regions (China, Hong Kong, Japan, Korea, Malaysia, Taiwan and Vietnam), Nunan (2003) concluded that although CLT is 'enshrined in all of the documents examined, ... all informants, in all the countries surveyed, reported a huge gap between ministerial rhetoric and classroom reality' (p. 609). A large number of research studies have resonated with this finding, asserting that the official espousal of CLT has very little effect on the classroom (McPherron, 2008; Feng, 2009; Eisenchlas, 2010). Some research studies maintained that EFL countries should carefully study their English teaching situations and decide how CLT can best serve their needs and interests (Feryok, 2008; McPherron, 2008; Hu, 2010).

Having personally lived with this tension, I have come to profoundly recognize that there is not a one-size-fits-all standard. Just as the CLT developed in ESL contexts cannot embark on the same path when being employed in EFL contexts, there is not a single second language acquisition theory, language teaching principle, method or technique that can be applied equally well across contexts.

In one of the courses I offer – 'Techniques of Second Language Teaching', which leads students to explore a wide array of language teaching methods, the principles underlying each method, the techniques a certain method tends to use, and each method's strengths and weaknesses – I made it very clear at the outset and repeatedly stressed throughout the course that it is not the goal of the course to let students pick any language teaching principle or method. Instead, what I hope for is that students develop a comprehensive knowledge of language teaching methods and accumulate a large pool of useful techniques so that they can adopt and adapt them appropriately, flexibly and creatively in their respective teaching situations. One student, Anh, commented in her journal:

> Having been equipped with all sorts of SLA theories and language teaching methods, I feel that I am much better able to handle a complicated classroom. I don't identify with any specific teaching method. I want to use a mixture of them, that is, take an eclectic approach to language teaching. (Anh's journals)

Teaching One's Best-Loved Self vs. Teaching What One Is Told to Teach

The teachers' best-loved self' is a concept Craig (2013) introduced and championed from Schwab's original scholarship. An aspect of teachers' personal practical knowledge, this conceptualization also closely connects with the image of teacher as curriculum maker and with the image of teacher as curriculum implementer (Clandinin & Connelly, 1992). It contends that teachers should have discretionary spaces in their classrooms to enact their best-loved selves rather than simply being expected to act as conduits through whom the prescribed curriculum and directives pass.

Nevertheless, inevitably affected by the professional knowledge landscape and larger educational, social, economic and political milieus, to what extent can a person's best-loved self be immune to external influences and keep its integrity? Coming from the eastern educational milieus where education is more centralized, I am deeply cognizant of this tension. Here is how I explained this bifurcation in my autobiographical narrative.

> Every teacher had to abide by the school designated syllabus, textbooks, assignments, and examinations. We had very limited freedom to decide what we want to teach and how to teach it. All teachers were supposed to be on exactly the same page at exactly the same point in time. There was no way to get around it. A so-called specialist would randomly pick a classroom to observe and judge from time-to-time. The evaluation would be reported to the college administrators, which would have a great influence on our promotion. One comment the specialist gave me that I still remember until today was: I should make sure to stand in front of the class all the time so every student can see me, instead of walking around the classroom working with certain students occasionally.
>
> I felt I was not only implementing others' teaching plan, but also catering to others' propensities and desires. It was deplorable that as a teacher I was so vulnerable to reconcile what I perceived would work best for my students to the outside imperatives. There was not much 'self' in my teaching, let alone 'my best-loved self.' I

was not an agent of my own teaching, but an agent of someone
else, the school and beyond.

The biggest revelation that surfaced from this experience was: Teachers
should be allowed to acknowledge their best-loved selves as curriculum
makers and enact their personal practical knowledge. The curriculum and
instructional decisions made by those outside are less powerful, less
meaningful and less sustainable than the ones that are self-initiated, self-
motivated and self-valued. Instead of being passive receivers, teachers should
be active constructors, rebuilding what is told to them into something they
feel is more relevant, meaningful and suitable for their own classrooms, in
order for their teaching to make a real difference in students' learning
outcomes.

Six years later, as a TESOL teacher educator in an American university,
I found a similar tension happening to my students teaching in the K-12
school setting who had to compromise their best-loved selves to conform to
the image of teacher as curriculum implementer. One student, Maria,
described the tension in working with an ELL student in her class this way:

> I have a young boy in my 4th grade class who just came to the US
> from Mexico one and half years ago. He didn't speak any English
> before, and speaks only Spanish with his families at home ... I can
> see that he's gradually developing conversational language, but to
> master the academic language that will enable him to understand
> the grade-level content takes time. I want to transition him slowly
> and nicely, but I cannot ... Urged by my principal, I spend a lot
> more time giving benchmark tests. I feel that a large amount of
> important time was being stolen from instruction. Preparing
> students for tests is my major responsibility. I was so frustrated
> that funds were used to purchase a lot of test-preparation
> materials rather than to appropriate ESL materials that my ELL
> student needs badly! I felt very sorry that I couldn't provide this
> student the quality instruction he deserves! (Blackboard
> Discussion posting)

It is not uncommon that in-service teachers experience the tension between
practicing what they personally perceive to be morally right and fulfilling
what is prescribed by the school, school district, state, and the federal
government. Teacher educators are more often than not focused on the
particular things they wish teachers to know, but overlook the fact that the
real-world schools are infinitely more complex than the things teachers are
taught in teacher education and professional development. It is of crucial
importance to nurture preservice teachers as curriculum makers along their
career continuums, and the key is teaching them to develop and value their
personal practical knowledge. One way I do this is to ask students to
complete a language-teaching philosophy essay, where they pinpoint different

experiences that have emerged along their career trajectories as English language teachers.

Every student has his or her experiential knowledge of how language should be taught. As teacher educators, we should encourage students to activate this knowledge by examining their own language teaching and learning experience, and uncovering the attitudes and beliefs that embody their 'best-loved selves'. Although they may not be able to fully articulate what their personal practical knowledge is, they at least can feel it intellectually, emotionally, morally and aesthetically (Xu & Connelly, 2009) in their beings. This knowledge needs to be respected and built upon, not dismissed, or overturned. It is teachers' personal practical knowledge that sustains teachers to grow into teachers as curriculum makers who are more competent to maneuver the tensions experienced in teaching.

Concluding Remarks

Tensions, in Berry's (2007) view, lead to professional growth and learning. Personal practical knowledge lies at the heart of teachers' endeavors to mediate the tensions. According to Xu and Connelly (2009), 'it is what teachers know as persons, more than what they are taught, that is central' (p. 221). Based on my personal life narrative of a cross-cultural teaching journey, this research has allowed me to promote my personal practical knowledge and gain a more profound awareness of my development as a teacher educator. More importantly, it has contributed to the knowledge base of TESOL teacher education because it traverses both EFL and ESL contexts. Research studies have distinctly cautioned us that many teachers are not adequately prepared to teach ELL by their teacher preparation programs (Echevarria et al, 2006), nor is their professional development adequate (Mora et al, 2014). In addition, I hope this chapter sheds light on TESOL teacher development as well.

References

Berry, A. (2007) *Tensions in Teaching about Teaching: understanding practice as a teacher educator*. Dordrecht: Springer.

Bruner, J. (1985) Narrative and Paradigmatic Modes of Thought, in E. Eisner (Ed.) *Learning and Teaching the Ways of Knowing*, pp. 97-115. Chicago: University of Chicago Press.

Bruner, J. (1986) *Actual Minds, Possible Worlds*. Cambridge, MA: Harvard University Press.

Bruner, J. (1996) *The Culture of Education*. Cambridge, MA: Harvard University Press.

Chomsky, N. (1965) *Aspects of the Theory of Syntax*. Cambridge, MA: MIT Press.

Clandinin, D.J. (1986) *Classroom Practice: teacher images in action*. Philadelphia: Falmer Press.

Clandinin, D.J. & Connelly, F.M. (1992) Teacher as Curriculum Maker, in P.W. Jackson (Ed.) *Handbook of Research on Curriculum: a project of the American Educational Research Association*, pp. 363-401. New York: Macmillan.

Clandinin, D.J. & Connelly, F.M. (1994) Personal Experience Methods, in N.K. Denzin, & Y.S. Lincoln (Eds) *Handbook of Qualitative Research*, pp. 413-427. London: SAGE.

Clandinin, D.J. & Connelly, F.M. (2000) *Narrative Inquiry: experience and story in qualitative research*. San Francisco: Jossey-Bass.

Clandinin, D.J. & Connelly, F.M. (2004) Knowledge, Narrative, and Self-study, in J. Loughran, M. Hamilton, V. LaBoskey & T. Russell (Eds) *International Handbook of Self-study of Teaching and Teacher Education Practices*, pp. 575-600. Boston: Kluwer.

Clandinin, D.J., Pushor, D. & Orr, A.M. (2007) Navigating Sites for Narrative Inquiry, *Journal of Teacher Education*, 58(1), 21-35. http://dx.doi.org/10.1177/0022487106296218

Connelly, F.M. & Clandinin, D.J. (1988) *Teachers as Curriculum Planners: narratives of experience*. New York: Teachers College Press.

Connelly, F.M. & Clandinin, D.J. (1990) Stories of Experience and Narrative Inquiry, *Educational Researcher*, 19(5), 2-14. http://dx.doi.org/10.3102/0013189X019005002

Connelly, F.M. & Clandinin, D.J. (2006) Narrative Inquiry, in J.L. Green, G. Camilli & P. Elmore (Eds) *Handbook of Complementary Methods in Education Research*, pp. 477-487. Mahwah, NJ: Lawrence Erlbaum Associates.

Craig, C. (2012) 'Butterfly Under a Pin': an emergent teacher image amid mandated curriculum reform, *Journal of Educational Research*, 105(2), 1-12. http://dx.doi.org/10.1080/00220671.2010.519411

Craig, C. (2013) Teacher Education and the Best-loved Self, *Asia Pacific Journal of Education*, 33(3), 261-272. http://dx.doi.org/10.1080/02188791.2013.788476

Craig, C. & Ross, V. (2008) Cultivating the Image of Teachers as Curriculum Makers, in F.M. Connelly, M. He & J. Phillion (Eds) *Handbook of Curriculum and Instruction*, pp. 282-305. Thousand Oaks, CA: SAGE.

Criado, R. & Sanchez, A. (2009) English Language Teaching in Spain: do textbooks comply with the official methodological regulations? A Sample Analysis, *International Journal of English Studies*, 9(1), 1-28.

Echevarria, J., Short, D. & Powers, K. (2006) School Reform and Standards-based Education: an instructional model for English language learners, *Journal of Educational Research*, 99(4), 195-210. http://dx.doi.org/10.3200/JOER.99.4.195-211

Eisenchlas, S. (2010) Conceptualising 'Communication' in Foreign Language Instruction, *Babel*, 44(2), 13-21.

Feng, A. (2009) English in China: convergence and divergence in policy and practice, *AILA Review*, 22, 85-102. http://dx.doi.org/10.1075/aila.22.07fen

Feryok, A. (2008) An Armenian English Language Teacher's Practical Theory of Communicative Language Teaching, *System*, 36, 227-240. http://dx.doi.org/10.1016/j.system.2007.09.004

Goodson, I. & Choi, P.L. (2008) Life History and Collective Memory as Methodological Strategies: studying teacher professionalism, *Teacher Education Quarterly*, 35(2), 5-28.

Hamilton, M.L. & Pinnegar, S. (1998) Conclusion: the value and the promise of self-study, in M.L. Hamilton, S. Pinnegar, T. Russell, J.J. Loughran & V.K. LaBoskey (Eds) *Reconceptualizing Teaching Practice: self-study in teacher education*, pp. 234-246. London: Falmer Press.

Howe, E.R. & Xu, S. (2013) Transcultural Teacher Development within the Dialectic of the Global and Local: bridging gaps between east and west, *Teaching and Teacher Education*, 36, 1-11. http://dx.doi.org/10.1016/j.tate.2013.06.010

Hu, G. (2005) Reforms of Basic English-language Education in China: an overview, *International Journal of Educational Reform*, 14(2), 140-165.

Hu, W. (2010) Communicative Language Teaching in the Chinese Environment, *US-China Education Review*, 7(6), 78-82.

Hymes, D.H. (1971) *On Communicative Competence*. Philadelphia: University of Pennsylvania Press.

Lyons, N. & LaBoskey, V.K. (2002) Why Narrative Inquiry or Exemplars for a Scholarship of Teaching? In N. Lyons & V.K. LaBoskey (Eds) *Narrative Inquiry in Practice: advancing the knowledge of teaching*, pp. 11-27. New York: Teachers College Press.

McPherron, P.R. (2008) Internationalizing Teaching, Localizing English: language teaching reforms through a south Chinese university. Doctoral dissertation, available from ProQuest Dissertations and Theses database (AAT 3350759).

Mora, A., Trejo, P. & Roux, R. (2014) English Language Teachers' Professional Development and Identities, *Profile Issues in Teachers' Professional Development*, 16(1), 49-62.

Nunan, D. (2003) The Impact of English as a Global Language in Educational Policies and Practices in the Asia-Pacific Region, *TESOL Quarterly*, 37, 589-613. http://dx.doi.org/10.2307/3588214

Samaras, A.P. (2011) *Self-study Teacher Research: improving your practice through collaborative inquiry*. Thousand Oaks, CA: SAGE.

Samaras, A.P., Hicks, M.A. & Berger, J.G. (2004) Self-study through Personal History, in J. Loughran, M.L. Hamilton, V.K. LaBoskey & T. Russell (Eds) *The International Handbook of Self-study of Teaching and Teacher Education Practices*, pp. 905-942. Dordrecht: Kluwer.

Ukpokodu, O. (2011) Developing Teachers' Cultural Competence: one teacher educator's practice of unpacking student culturelessness, *Action in Teacher Education*, 33(5-6), 432-454.

Wei, L. (2011) Communicative Language Teaching in EFL Contexts: not a universal medicine, *NYS TESOL Idiom*, 40(4), 1-25.

Xu, S.J. & Connelly, F.M. (2009) Narrative Inquiry for Teacher Education and Development: focus on English as a second language in China, *Teaching and Teacher Education*, 25(2), 219-227. http://dx.doi.org/10.1016/j.tate.2008.10.006

CHAPTER 3

Everyday Priorities of Teachers of English Language Learners in the USA: a narrative of experience

JOHANNA BOONE, RAMONA MAILE CUTRI & STEFINEE PINNEGAR

SUMMARY In today's environment where teachers face pressures regarding reaching the needs of English learners, in a social milieu that accepts deficit views of teachers, and a professional landscape of high-stakes testing/accountability that can influence teachers' identities, the authors of this chapter wondered how teachers sustain themselves. The chapter examines the story of an experienced teacher and her unfolding career, focusing specifically on what guides her pedagogical decision-making as she negotiates a balance between meeting district/state mandates and finding satisfaction in her teaching. The authors explore competing stories that teachers might navigate in these contexts. The first author, working with critical friends (the other two authors), determined that her priorities center on relationships with students and helping students continue to progress. This study provides a glimpse into the priorities of teachers of English learners (ELs) in the United States who work for student success while living in a broader context of mandated change.

Introduction

I almost winced as I listened to Karen read out loud to me during her guided reading group time. The words came to her slowly, almost painfully, and many times she would notice the beginning sound and guess the word. I was constantly surprised that she was able to answer the comprehension questions even though her out-loud reading was mind-numbingly slow and inaccurate. Not for the first time, I felt tension between the time that I could give her and how much work I needed to do to really help her. I wished for more time so we could work on the foundations she needed to master for reading success, and wondered how I could make that happen. Truly being able to attend to Karen's individual needs as an English learner (EL), as well as those of several other EL students, and to the non-EL students in my class, seemed impossible and overwhelming. How could I ever help her and all of my other students progress at the rate that they needed to, in order to reach the mandated standards set by others? I could see Karen's growth and progress, but would they? Would the progress that I observed be enough to satisfy them and meet the legal mandates for progress and improvement that we were under?

This narrative, constructed from a personal experience that Johanna, the first author, had in her own classroom, reveals the competing stories (Clandinin et al, 2009) that she lives as a teacher of ELs. She stories herself as a teacher who is aware of, and works to meet, the needs of individual students. This way of storying herself is in competition with the narrative of needing to meet the mandates to help Karen and other students make 'enough' progress to reach adequate yearly progress (AYP) as demonstrated by scoring proficiently on high-stakes standardized tests. This narrative reveals Johanna's personal commitment to the success of each of her students, as well as the external pressure she feels to ensure that students are reaching authorized goals, rather than focusing on constant progress for individual students. The difficulties of reconciling these stories of her personal commitment to her students with the competing demand for quantifiable measures of student learning are common in education and cause internal tension for her.

The pressure of accountability mandates and fidelity to rigid direct instruction practices is felt by all teachers who work with ELs in high-poverty schools across the United States. As the number of EL students in the United States increases (National Clearinghouse for English Language Acquisition, 2011), the pressure to ensure that these students are given access to a good education, defined by making AYP on standardized tests, also increases (No Child Left Behind, 2002).

In spite of legislation making states, districts and individual schools accountable for the services provided for EL students, the demands and pressures for progress and improvement are increasingly focused on the individual teachers. School and district administrators seeking a one-size-fits-all panacea pressure teachers to implement with fidelity particular programs and practices, limiting their ability to make decisions regarding their students' learning. Such program mandates reduce teachers' autonomy to act to promote student learning, yet at the same time, they have ultimate accountability for student achievement.

Pressures on teachers to help students, especially EL students, achieve proficiency on high-stakes tests can take their toll on teacher emotions. Since teachers' emotions impact their choices regarding instruction and interactions with students (Hargreaves, 2005; O'Connor, 2008), emotions have practical significance for students. When teacher judgment conflicts with mandated practices, teachers may choose to accept, reject or resist them

(Hargreaves, 2005). Teachers' practice can represent political action, and it is played out in the ways in which they enact curriculum, or choose to give time and attention to the things that are personally most important to them (Zembylas, 2003; O'Connor, 2008). How do teachers develop, identify and live their priorities within the context of these competing stories, pressures and emotions?

Much can be observed and learned from the experiences of teachers working within these demanding parameters as they strive to live out the competing stories of focusing on individual student needs and meeting the mandates for student progress as demonstrated by high-stakes testing. The priorities that teachers reveal as they tell stories of their practice have the potential to provide a glimpse into 'what is happening in the day-to-day life of participants ... [which] helps make visible the structural and historically existing contradictions inherent in complex activity systems, like schools' (Gutierrez & Penuel, 2014, p. 20). Understanding teacher experiences in this context allows researchers to more fully understand teachers' lives and how these stories that have social, political and academic ramifications are lived out in schools. Such work can help researchers become wakeful to how teachers sustain themselves while teaching ELs.

Methods

Hamilton and Pinnegar (2013) used the adjective *intimate* to describe research that involves stories of experience. They posited that such research allows deeper understandings of issues under consideration, and can uncover knowledge that may not come to light with other methods. Defining the methodology for self-study of teacher education practice, Pinnegar and Hamilton (2009) state: 'We seek to select methods that help us better understand what we hope to examine and to reveal for readers where we looked, how we looked, along with the evidence from which we will develop our analysis' (p. 106). The authors of this study used self-study methodology to document and explore the lived priorities of teachers who teach EL students.

The US school studied has a student enrollment of approximately 560, with ELs, most of whom are Hispanic, making up 42% of the student population. In contrast with the student population, the majority of the teachers at the school are white, middle-class, English-speaking females, as is typical in the United States. As a school with a high population of students in poverty and a history of low scores on the statewide testing, this school is under pressure from the state, district and school administrators to show significant academic improvement for all students.

Three data sources contribute to this self-study: written stories, transcripts of audio recordings of story discussions, and interim texts. Johanna was involved in a larger study in which she collected and analyzed data from teachers about their implementation of best teaching practices for

ELs. During this time, she compiled stories of when she personally felt she helped and when she felt she had failed an EL student. Through this process, Johanna identified her own 'living contradictions' (Whitehead, 1989, p. 43). These stories are formed from the original data for this study.

Johanna wrote her narratives of experience and identified internal tensions and sought to remain open to them in order to better understand them. To facilitate this process, she turned to the second and third authors, requesting that they become her critical friends (Schuck & Russell, 2005). The second and third authors pushed her analysis of her stories and interpretation to deeper levels and helped to construct the research text.

As Johanna analyzed the data, she searched for themes and tensions, and identified overarching ideas to create interim texts. The form that these interim texts took varied, but over time the majority of them, with examples and evidence from her stories, emerged as the threads for her assertions for understanding. In an interactive process, she negotiated the text and her interpretations with Stefinee and Ramona, her critical friends.

Assertions for Understanding

Lived experiences, or stories to live by (Connelly & Clandinin, 1999), can be represented as threads in the tapestry of our lives. The two threads Johanna explored in this study are relationships and academic progress.

The Significance of Relationships

The first salient thread in the analysis is that of the significance of relationships. It demonstrates the importance of teachers' relationships with their EL students as they learn to teach and teach to learn and is indicative of teachers' priorities and what sustains them.

The following exemplar illustrates Johanna's experiences regarding relationships with students and families. She presents her story in the form of a vignette constructed from an experience earlier in her career.

> It was another day of early morning bus duty, and I was outside
> on the playground watching my students and children in other
> grades play before school. A couple of my own students came over
> to chat with me. One said that there had been a visit by
> immigration officials at his mother's work the day before, but that
> it was okay because someone had somehow known about it and
> tipped her off about it ahead of time, so she had not gone into
> work that day. I was thinking about what it must be like to live
> with that kind of uncertainty, and probably fear, as the mother
> and the child, when my student asked me, 'Miss Boone, are you
> afraid that they'll kick you out of the country?' I almost cried right
> there in front of my student. I was touched that my student
> trusted me enough to tell me about his mother, and that he

worried about me, yet I was also saddened and dismayed that the possibility of deportation was such a real thing for him and his family that he just assumed it was a part of everyone's life.

This story of Johanna's student telling her about his mother's avoided deportation provides a glimpse into her everyday priorities as a teacher of ELs. She cares about her students and their lives both in and out of the classroom and wonders how she can improve her relationships with them on a regular basis. In this story, she takes the time to listen to her student. He feels comfortable enough with her to talk about what is going on in his life. The level of confidence needed to trust someone with information as sensitive as the information about his mother's possible deportation shows a relationship of trust and caring. Her emotional response illustrates the level of concern and care that she has for this student. Her everyday priorities are evident in the way that she takes the time to listen to her student, and in the fact that he is willing to trust her with such personal, private information.

Reflecting on this story also makes Johanna wonder about her current and future students. Are there students currently in her class who are facing equally difficult circumstances? Has she been insensitive or impatient with students whose stories she has not taken the time to get to know? Has she made hasty judgments about students not working or trying, chalking it up to apathy, rather than to what is going on in their personal lives? What can she do now and in the future to help all of her students feel safe in her classroom even when things outside of it may be difficult? How can she further develop the relationships that she has with her students? And how does she balance the time required to get to know students with the increasing accountability that students and teachers face?

As she reflects on this story, many wonderings come to Johanna's mind, not only for her own practices, but also for her student's life. What if someone had not tipped off his mother about the immigration officials' visit? How would that have impacted her student? Would his mother have been deported? If his mother had been forced to leave the United States, would he even have been at school that day to tell her about the experience, or would he be on his way to Mexico with the rest of his family? If the mother had been required to go, and her student had stayed with other family members here, how would separation from his mother have impacted him? Would he have been able or willing to focus on school with such a huge personal burden to bear?

This story illustrates the importance of relationships between teachers and ELs. This narrative of experience allows teachers to see and assess how they are developing relationships.

Johanna's story of having her student tell her about his concerns about immigration authorities demonstrates how everyday relationships sustain teachers and are important to them. Relationships as a priority revealed in the story are evident in the safe, caring spaces she created for her students.

Perpetual Progression

The second major thread that emerged from Johanna's data analysis was that of perpetual progression. She used the phrase perpetual progression to refer to improvement and change that is realized or hoped for on an ongoing basis. This focus on continual progression points to teachers' desire to improve their ability to support student learning but also to position students so they can continue to progress.

Johanna's everyday priority of perpetual progression is evident in her personal story about a former student. Jose really struggled with reading. He came into Johanna's fifth-grade class at the beginning of the year and told her that he did not read, that he could not, and did not want to. During the school year he progressed from saying that he hated reading, to sneaking the book that she was reading out-loud to the class so that he could read it, and even setting a goal to improve in his reading fluency in order to earn a 'book pass' allowing him to choose any book as a prize for achieving his goal. The following constructed letter reflects a conversation Johanna had with Jose during his sixth-grade year (the year after Johanna was his teacher):

> Dear Jose,
> I was talking to Miss Hansen the other day, and she told me that you're not doing your best in class right now. We talked about how it makes us sad that you're making that choice, because we both know, and know that YOU know, that you can do better.
>   Remember last year when you decided that you wanted a book pass, so you worked hard on your reading and earned a book pass by improving in your fluency, and then earned another one by getting a great score on our end of the year test? I was so proud of you! Remember to do your very best! You can do amazing things if you decide that you want to, and you try!
> Love,
> Miss Boone

Johanna's everyday priority of focusing on students' perpetual progression is evident in the story of her interactions with Jose. Her concern for his progress is evident in the efforts she made during his fifth-grade year to help him progress. These included introducing him to interesting literature, working with him in small groups on his fluency, and motivating him with book passes. Jose's progress was disrupted by the summer break. He returned to his old negative views of reading and his reading abilities during this time. However, even though he was now in a different grade, Johanna continued to exhibit the concern she had for him. She did not stop caring about him and his academic achievement when he left her classroom. This story demonstrates how investing in students' ongoing progress is a priority for teachers and sustains them in the face of political mandates.

This experiential narrative is particularly significant, since Jose made huge leaps in his reading in her fifth-grade class but went into sixth grade evidencing the same attitude with which he had started fifth grade: He did not like to read, did not want to, and would not. When she saw him in the halls the year after he was in her class, she reminded him, as she could, that he could do better, and encouraged him to do so. This aspect of the story shows that progression is not always a steady state of forward motion. There are stops and starts, and at times painful backtracking, but as Johanna's story evidences, she, as a teacher, continues to push and prod students to achieve, using her skills, knowledge and time to enable students to progress. She takes action in the moment that will continue to push students to success.

Johanna's narratives reveal that she prioritizes relationships and progression in her teaching. She feels that forming and maintaining positive everyday relationships with all of her students is crucial to being a good teacher. Continuing to care about and help her students grow over time is an integral part of her everyday teaching. Also, changing her own practices over time is important to her, as she wants to be perpetually progressing.

Conclusions and Implications

Johanna, working in relationship with Ramona and Stefinee, analyzed her own stories of teaching EL students and uncovered that her overarching priorities were attention to the hearts and minds of students. As teachers take time to get to know their students, they build relationships with them and thus attend to their students' hearts. This attention to students' hearts benefits students emotionally, socially and academically. In addition, teachers attend to students' minds by intentionally helping them progress and succeed academically and by continuing to be concerned about students after students have left their classrooms.

Participating in this self-study of her practice shifted Johanna's paradigm of knowing. As a teacher, she faces the many pressures discussed in this study, and sometimes falls prey to a deficit view of herself. Johanna can see some good in what she does, but in the context of the high demands made of her, she often wonders if she is doing enough. Examining her practice with critical friends helped Johanna realize that while she may not be doing everything that could be done, she is prioritizing the things that are most important to her as a teacher of ELs. She is living true to the way that she stories herself as a teacher whose very identity is tied up in the care that she offers her students and the desire she has to help them progress to their maximum potential.

Another way in which Johanna's paradigm shifted throughout the course of this study included her recognition and increased advocacy through daily activity. Prior to this study, she did not recognize her daily actions as advocating for her students. However, the simple things that she does on a daily basis, such as taking time to get to know and listen to students, teaching them appropriate ways to act in school, responding with patience and humor, and helping them continue to progress truly do advocate for her students.

Recognizing this helped Johanna continue and increase these sorts of advocacy. Also, sharing the things that she and others prioritize in our teaching lives has helped Johanna advocate for herself and other teachers of ELs.

This study shows that while teachers feel pressure from school, district, state and federal authorities to have certain priorities regarding their EL students' achievement, teachers have priorities that are not acknowledged or encouraged by these entities. What matters most to teachers is in collision with what policy makers prioritize. Teachers prioritize relationships with students and perpetual progression, while policymakers prioritize achievement for all students on high-stakes tests. The moral wrestling between what they prioritize in their everyday teaching lives and what they are under pressure to prioritize by policy makers creates tension for teachers.

Teachers must strive to live these tensions as competing stories that teachers can balance in a practical way that does not erase the tension between the two stories but keeps it alive in a healthy way (Clandinin et al, 2009). This productive tension between competing stories is distinct from conflicting stories that are so disparate that teachers cannot attend to both of them, and that thus cause teachers to drop one or the other (Clandinin et al, 2009). As demonstrated in this study, an important first step for teachers is to identify their own stories by which they live so that their stories can healthily compete with the stories of policy makers.

Seeking to understand teachers' priorities regarding their EL students and how they balance these stories with the competing stories of policymakers leads to a deeper understanding of the ways that teachers help their students that are not visible in the results of high-stakes testing. This helps dispel a deficit view of teachers, and relieves some of the pressure that teachers are under, thus contributing to more positive teacher emotions and less burnout and attrition.

References

Clandinin, D.J., Murphy, M.S., Huber, J. & Orr, A.M. (2009) Negotiating Narrative Inquiries: living in a tension-filled midst, *Journal of Educational Research*, 103, 81-90. http://dx.doi.org/10.1080/00220670903323404

Connelly, F.M. & Clandinin, D.J. (1999) *Shaping a Professional Identity: stories of educational practice*. New York: Teachers College Press.

Gutierrez, K.D. & Penuel, W.R. (2014) Relevance to Practice as a Criterion for Rigor, *Educational Researcher*, 43, 19-23.
http://dx.doi.org/10.3102/0013189X13520289

Hamilton, M.L. & Pinnegar, S. (2013) What's in a Name? Exploring the Edges of Autoethnography, Narrative and Self-study of Teacher Education Practice Methodologies. Unpublished manuscript, Department of Curriculum and Teaching, University of Kansas, Lawrence; Department of Teacher Education, Brigham Young University, Provo, UT.

Hargreaves, A. (2005) Educational Change Takes Ages: life, career and generational factors in teachers' emotional responses to educational change, *Teaching and Teacher Education*, 21, 976-983. http://dx.doi.org/10.1016/j.tate.2005.06.007

National Clearinghouse for English Language Acquisition (2011) Graphs of the Increasing EL Population. *The Growing Numbers of English Learner Students.* http://www.ncela.us/files/uploads/9/growing_EL_0910.pdf

No Child Left Behind Act of 2001 (2002) Pub. L. No. 107-110, § 3122.

O'Connor, K. (2008) 'You Choose to Care': teachers, emotions and professional identity, *Teaching and Teacher Education*, 24, 117-126. http://dx.doi.org/10.1016/j.tate.2006.11.008

Pinnegar, S. & Hamilton, M.L. (2009) *Self-study as a Genre of Qualitative Research Theory, Methodology and Practice.* New York: Springer.

Schuck, S. & Russell, T. (2005) Self-study, Critical Friendship, and the Complexities of Teacher Education, *Studying Teacher Education*, 1(2), 107-121. http://dx.doi.org/10.1080/17425960500288291

Whitehead, J. (1989) Creating a Living Educational Theory from Questions of the Kind, 'How Do I Improve Her Practice?', *Cambridge Journal of Education*, 19(1), 41-52. http://dx.doi.org/10.1080/0305764890190106

Zembylas, M. (2003) Emotions and Teacher Identity: a poststructural perspective, *Teachers and Teaching: theory and practice*, 9, 213-238.

CHAPTER 4

Managing Context and Complexities: my career trajectory of teaching English as a second language in Malaysia

IDA FATIMAWATI Bt ADI BADIOZAMAN

SUMMARY This chapter outlines the trajectory of the author's journey as an English language teacher in Malaysia. The trajectory is shaped by a multitude of factors ranging from previous learning and teaching experiences, to cross-cultural experiences. The complexity of Malaysia's educational setting and its respective educational policies also significantly influenced the decisions made with regard to professional development. Therefore, the construction of teacher identity as part of the author's life trajectory is best described as a 'process of becoming' in which the emphasis on process underscores the importance of formation and transformation. This process of transformation is dynamic and complex as each formation of a stable identity is continuously challenged by the demands of teaching and learning, represented by the teaching context (i.e. new language policies, students' preferred learning styles and classroom management challenges). The process often results in conflicts which need to be managed through negotiation, reconstruction or even loss of identity as the author attempts to redefine her teacher identity. The chapter concludes with the fact that teacher identity construction develops in tandem with a teacher's own professional growth. More importantly, teaching is not a skill that can be acquired overnight, but a process of lifelong learning cultivated across different cultures of teaching and learning, as well as across various points in time.

Introduction

A teacher's career trajectory is imbued with transitional processes. A person's development as a teacher may involve various phases and transition points of their career cycles. Many factors will impact it, requiring teachers to constantly reassess and re-evaluate their positions against the uncertainty and variability of their disciplines, career possibilities, and also the changing circumstances of their academic institutions. In the Malaysian context, the impact of a long period of erratic language policies in the Malaysian education system on the teacher's career trajectory and identity is considerable. To understand the complexities of my lived experiences of teaching English in Malaysia, it is a useful starting point to provide a historical account of the formulation of language planning in Malaysia.

Historical Overview of the Malaysian Education System

Malaysia, once part of the British Empire, achieved independence in 1957. Malaysia has a multicultural, multilingual population of 28.3 million, comprising three main ethnic groups: Malays (53.3%), Chinese (26.0%) and Indians (7.7%). The non-Malay indigenous people make up another 11.8% of the population (Department of Statistics Malaysia, 2014, p. 3). The Malays and non-Malay indigenous people together comprise the *bumiputera* (natives of the soil) group and thus form the majority group in Malaysia.

Due to the nature and history of the country, the role of English has shifted frequently over time – in parallel with the focus of the education system (Foo & Richards, 2004). During British rule, there was an absence of uniformity within formal education in Malaysia. Under the colonial education system, separate schools offered different mediums of instruction and curricula for the main ethnic groups – Malays, Chinese and Indians. As a result, the colonial education system created severe social and economic disparities, which led to racial tensions (Subramani & Kempner, 2002). Accordingly, the ultimate objective of the education system post-independence was to create national unity (Rajendran, 2005). Education was seen as a medium that would facilitate the objective of national unity and thus, in 1957, all existing schools were converted to national or national-type schools. The national language, Bahasa Melayu (Malay language), was made a compulsory subject in these national-type schools, but English remained as one of the official languages of the country (Zaaba et al, 2011). This emphasis on English was to address the economic benefits of the country and regional demands (ASEAN) (Hashim, 2014).

During the period from 1975 to 1985, social and economic issues shaped the development of education. This was the period of the New Economic Policy (NEP), which was a socio-economic policy designed to achieve national unity and development through focusing on the eradication of poverty and the restructuring of Malaysian society. Since the prior British higher education model did not address national issues or the welfare of Malaysian society, this period saw education become a state-controlled system governed by the Ministry of Education (Ali, 2013). Tan and colleagues (Tan et al, 2011) summed up this top-down approach of the Malaysian education system as being 'highly centralised' and noted that 'education in Malaysia is a federal responsibility and so the education system comes under the Ministry of Education which functions at the federal level' (p. 138).

The last decade of the twentieth century witnessed a change in Malaysia's education policy, where English was reinstated as the medium of instruction in secondary schools and at the tertiary level. Unlike the change in the medium of instruction post-independence, which was principally driven by nationalistic sentiments, this more recent change in language policy (in 2003) was driven by concerns about globalization (Foo & Richards, 2004), the 'knowledge economy' and 'development-oriented nationalism' (Gill, 2006, p. 84). As a result of this controversial change, an immediate major restructuring of the education system was implemented. At the secondary level, new subjects were introduced (e.g. English for science and technology) and the medium of instruction for mathematics and science was changed to English.

In higher learning institutions, both private and public universities incorporated English as their medium of instruction, especially for science and technology-orientated subjects. English was elevated to the medium of instruction for science, engineering and medical courses since it was believed to have 'the highest capital linguistic value' (Gill, 2006, p. 84). In addition, many new public and private universities were developed. Intensive collaboration was set up with local and overseas universities, in order to provide more opportunities for higher learning. Amendments to the University College Acts 1996 also allowed universities to have greater autonomy to manage and operate their institutions. This was in line with Vision 2020, which was the government's vision to achieve developed nation status by the year 2020. Institutions of higher education 'play an important role in training the people necessary for the academic as well as the manpower needs of the nation' (Higher Educational Institutions Act 1996, as cited in Foo & Richards, 2004, p. 238). The Malaysian case provided an example of the dialectical relationship between global and local imperatives – the perceived need for English in pursuing national ambitions through internalization of education in the wake of globalization, on the one hand, and the necessity of preserving the status of the national language, on the other (Ali, 2013).

Teacher Career Trajectory

The language policies and the constant changes they bring may impact significantly on teachers in terms of their career trajectories and their ability to manage complexities and changes. This discussion will now turn to my own teacher trajectory, and how it was challenged and shaped by the demands of teaching and learning, represented by my teaching context.

The Apprentice Teacher

In Malaysia, teacher education for pre-service teachers occurs at two levels, with the training of non-graduate teachers in the teacher training colleges and the training of graduate teachers in the universities. Most programs offer concurrent general, subject-specific and professional preparation during a four- to five-year period. I received my education and training to be an English language teacher in Malaysia's oldest and most prestigious university, the University of Malaya. In 1998, I was enrolled in the Bachelor of Education in Teaching of English as a Second Language (TESL) for four years. The Honours program was designed to prepare those who are going to be English teachers with academic and professional training to teach at secondary schools in Malaysia. Subjects included Foundations for TESL Methodology, Linguistics for Language Teachers, Educational Psychology, Issues in TESL, Appraisal of Learning in Education, Language Testing and Assessment, and Sociology of Schooling, to name a few. The promise of employment upon completion of the studies and the inclusive financial assistance provided by the Ministry of Education made it a highly competitive program. Well-qualified English language teachers were also in high demand as there was a shortage (Ministry of Education, 1992).

In the final year of the program, the first 'real' teaching was done through a 12-week practicum in secondary schools. The opportunity to learn through our practicum experience varied not only because of the types of schools which were assigned to us, but fundamentally because of the conditions of the practicum: duration, actual teaching opportunities and degree of feedback from university supervisors and school mentors. It was during the practicum that I realized that theories do not necessarily reflect the multiple realities of the language classrooms. This was particularly evident in my lack of experience dealing with classroom management, institutional (and personal) adjustment and student discipline. The complexity of classroom realities faced during the teaching practicum challenged my personal competence and professional identity as a teacher. This was due to the fact that I had to negotiate the institutions' expectations and navigate the curriculum with my limited teaching/learning experiences. In other words, in these settings, student teachers had little room to develop their own practice and their teacher identity.

Moving from Teacher Education into Schools: the novice teacher

My novice teacher phase (Korhonen & Törmä, 2014) began when I was posted to a fully residential co-ed school, Sekolah Menengah Sains Kuching Sarawak. I was assigned to teach English to students aged 13 and 14 in Forms One and Two, respectively, and to teach English for Science and Technology (EST) and Literature in English to Form Four students, who were aged between 16 and 17. Being a fresh graduate, I was eager to start implementing all the things I learned during my undergraduate years – to put theories into practice. I soon discovered that the significant emphasis on exams and school rankings shaped the teaching of English in this particular school. A lot of extra classes were conducted to help students in mock exams and trial exams. Furthermore, the received curriculum did not allow me to tend to issues that I felt were important for second-language learners, such as communicative competence, sociocultural aspects of language learning and extensive reading (Hardman & A-Rahman, 2014).

Note that since language policies in Malaysia are centralized and are regulated by the Ministry of Education, all government schools around the country must deliver the same curriculum employing the same medium of instruction (Ali et al, 2011, p. 148). As a result, my beliefs about teaching and learning developed during the teacher training were a mismatch with the forced practices in my field placement. To illustrate, the exam-oriented environment resulted in English classes which focused on tangible skills that can be measured in examinations, and in an uneven emphasis on language skills (Tan & Miller, 2007). Consequently, instead of proficient English speakers, this system produced a new breed of students and graduates who can do well in examinations but have limited competency in using English (Shakir, 2009).

Tensions were further complicated by policies enforced on the school. To illustrate, one of the language policies in 2003 required science and mathematics to be taught using English as a medium of instruction. A collaborative effort between English teachers and their science and mathematics counterpart was formed through the 'Buddy Support Programme'. This buddy system required that 'English teachers ... be part of the resources to provide help in the teaching of mathematics and science in English' (Heng & Tan, 2006, p. 317). Competent English teachers were appointed as 'critical friends' to science and mathematics teachers in school. My short-lived experience of being a 'buddy teacher' did not end well, and the reliance on the scripted curriculum often resulted in confusion on the students' part. Furthermore, studies (e.g. Ali et al, 2011) have also shown that students from rural areas faced challenges in understanding the teaching of science and mathematics since they had poor English proficiency. In addition, learner differences can also make it challenging to meet the desired learning objectives. Factors such as different cultures of learning, favoured learning strategies, and those of a cognitive, psychological or experiential nature all shape the learning experience. That some students were very resistant to English being used a medium of instruction (Rajadurai, 2009, 2010) due to nationalistic sentiments also resulted in my disillusionment with the teaching profession.

Adapting to the school climate meant adjustments had to be made in terms of my core beliefs about teaching, goals and expectations. This process was not easy and often a site of conflict and struggle. In internalizing these adjustments, attempts at a strategic compromise (Lacey, 1977) often failed, as accommodating aspects of the school culture and my own goals for the teaching and learning of English in secondary school at times had no common ground in which to meet. For some beginning teachers, their tensions had severe consequences for their learning and functioning as a teacher (Pillen et al, 2013). In fact, literature has also identified that inability to adjust and lack of alignment of pedagogical beliefs has led to decisions to leave the teaching profession (Avalos & Bascopé, 2014).

Nonetheless, despite severe professional identity tensions, there were examples where tensions had positive consequences for my development as a teacher with regard to greater self-awareness and self-actualization. I became more aware of the dynamics of a teaching–learning situation (Tudor, 2003) and I triumphed delivering the 'right' ESL (English as a Second Language) pedagogy. This shift resonates with literature which maintains that professional identity tensions can serve as a positive resource for teacher learning (Pillen et al, 2012). In fact, I have also become more aware of the students' voice, the identities, goals and other individual differences that they bring with them into the language classroom. Although I did not realize it at that time, it took extensive engagement with practice to realize that teaching is very much a social activity and therefore dialogic in nature. Hallman sums it up aptly when she maintains that '[t]eacher identity must be theorized in a reciprocal relationship to other's identities' (Hallman, 2014, p. 3). Others here refers to students, administrators and the faculty.

Lifelong Learning and Teacher Change

The clash between expectations and personal goals on the one hand and the realities of teaching on the other was indicative of the teacher change that I was undergoing. The clash highlighted the fact that there were other factors and other influences that ultimately determined the quality of my teaching experience. In fact, having to juggle several competing goals highlighted not only the complexity of the teaching task, but also my inadequacies in terms of experience, knowledge and skills dealing with students with mixed abilities and varying educational backgrounds. This resonated with Pillen et al's (2013) study which found that tensions in the professional identity of beginning teachers are mostly accompanied by negative feelings, and involve internal struggles between aspects relevant to the teacher as a person and as a professional. The realization that I needed more knowledge and experience with regard to teaching led me to the decision of furthering my studies at a master's level in TESOL (Teaching English to Speakers of Other Languages), at Victoria University of Wellington in New Zealand. The emphasis on students' differences and sensitivity to a broader range of students (ESL and EFL [English as a Foreign Language]) made me purposely elect to study abroad in an English-speaking country. I wanted to improve my proficiency and teaching efficacy in the context of ESOL (English for Speakers of Other Languages) while being taught by experts in the field.

Since candidates for the Master of Arts in TESOL (MA TESOL) programme were required to already have at least two years' teaching experience in the teaching of English to speakers of other languages, it provided an invaluable opportunity to share experiences with experts in the field and also with fellow teachers from various parts of the world. These interchanges were instrumental as they contributed significantly to my knowledge construction of ESOL as a field, and as an instructor. They awakened me to the various issues facing ESOL instructors at an international level. We shared ideas of incorporating a student-centered approach in the fixed English curricula and raised concerns about the ever-increasing emphasis on standardized assessments. I also began to see the connection between research and teaching as something that was beneficial and essential to the teaching craft. It was at this juncture that my teacher identity became strengthened and distinguished with a postgraduate qualification symbolizing disciplinary expertise.

Reconstructing the Teacher Identity

Upon graduating with a master's degree, I embarked on a new juncture of my career trajectory as an English lecturer in a higher learning institution, Swinburne University of Technology Sarawak Campus, a foreign branch campus of Swinburne University of Technology (Melbourne, Australia) located in Kuching, Sarawak, Malaysia. Established in 2000, Swinburne Sarawak operates as a partnership between the Sarawak State Government and Swinburne Australia. This international partnership was part of the Ministry of Education's policy which aimed internationalizing higher education (Altbach & Knight, 2007) in Malaysia. The initiative behind the Sarawak campus is also part of a long-term strategy by Swinburne Australia to 'globalize its operations and provide its students with international living, working and learning opportunities' (Swinburne University of Technology Sarawak Campus, 2014).

As I was allocated to teach academic reading and writing at Foundation level to 18-to-19-year-old students who had just finished their high school, the challenge was presented in the form of catering to Malaysian students who were immersed in an Australian-influenced syllabus, which uses solely English as a medium of instruction. Although the literature states that the transition process is typically challenging for students entering a new academic setting (Hussey & Smith, 2010), the challenges were further exacerbated for Malaysian L2 learners who were not proficient in English. Those who wished to pursue engineering or business degrees not only found it hard to adapt to the new academic setting but also had to face several literacy issues which impeded their academic engagement. The majority of the students still preferred what was familiar to them, such as a teacher-centered approach and rote-learning during the lessons. Consequently, attempts to foster autonomous learning through communicative teaching approaches were not always well received (Che Musa et al, 2012).

At this stage, the contextual demands required me to reconstruct my teaching approach. I discovered that merging teacher training from an international (master's) and local (undergraduate) perspective resulted in a 'hybrid' approach that was able to sustain students' engagement, enhance participation, and gradually improve students' literacy and proficiency in English. In fact, incorporating student-centered activities for lessons which would not be evaluated through standardized assessments and introducing technology during teaching also encouraged students to become more autonomous learners. It became apparent that my teacher identity constantly shifted, be it of my own volition and or due to contextual factors.

My conceptions about teaching competency continuously evolved in tandem with the context in which I was embedded. The tensions faced at this point also became an impetus for me to embark on a research journey to better understand how best to assist ESL students in terms of their English-language competencies. As a full-fledged academic, my career pathway necessitated that I obtain a PhD qualification. Aided by the financial aid provided by the Ministry of Education, which aimed to increase the number of PhD holders in higher learning institutions in Malaysia, my career trajectory took a different course.

Navigating the Research World: becoming a research student

As a teacher, constant reflection, learning and being informed about the new approaches to teaching is important. In fact, although my student identity was predominant throughout my five years of study, the PhD journey was a pivotal factor for my teacher identity formation. I did my PhD in Education at Massey University, New Zealand in the area of TESOL. My trajectory of learning was also shaped and reshaped by various power relationships with supervisors and fellow postgraduate students. Having a strong network of support consisting of other postgraduate students also helped significantly in navigating and sustaining my PhD journey.

Triggered by my past teaching experiences, my thesis investigated the challenges faced by students in higher learning institutions with regard to learning academic writing and how this impacted on their engagement as part of their academic experience. Conducting research presented a steep learning curve and, as with all things, it also involved reconstruction and loss of identity as I now wrestled with cultivating the novice researcher identity. During the PhD journey, my investigation of the challenges that the participants faced as part of their literacy acquisition through the lenses of self-concept and engagement illuminated that the cognitive, affective and behavioural aspects, and the integration of these, should never be overlooked when attempting to understand and engage learners in the classroom (Badiozaman, 2012). Indeed, the thesis personally provided me with a greater understanding of self-concept and engagement in academic writing both as individual constructs, as well as in terms of understanding how the interactions and relationships between them have the potential to empower students towards academic development and achievement. The notion that student engagement is susceptible to internal and external factors within the learning ecology (Badiozaman, 2015) also meant that it was part of the instructors' responsibility to provide a supportive educational environment within which learners could learn.

While doing my PhD, I worked as an English teacher at the language centre of the university, teaching international postgraduate students who did not have the English-language competencies to enter postgraduate studies. Some of the units taught involved teaching academic writing and research writing skills. The two-year teaching experience not only helped my professional development, but also solidified my professional identity as an English language teacher in an international context. Although students were initially reluctant and hesitant about my position as an instructor because I did not look or sound like a native speaker, by relating to them as a postgraduate student and being emphatic towards their struggles (as I was also a second-language learner), my NNEST (non-native English-speaking teacher) identity was eventually accepted. By relating my lived experience with language learning to their own learning struggles, students' negative attitude towards me began to change and they began to perceive me as a bilingual role model.

The students' preference for a native speaker of English was also gradually diminished. It is likely that greater exposure in the university made them realize that the 'definitions of the term native speaker have become blurred in today's increasingly multilingual society and globalized world' (Moussu, 2010, p. 747). Having international students from various backgrounds further helped enrich the experience in the sense that I was a truly legitimate member of the ESOL academic community since I had now taught ESL and EFL students; as well as students in public schools and at the tertiary level.

Coming Full Circle

Upon receiving my doctorate, I returned to Malaysia and started working again at Swinburne University of Technology. With the qualification, I was entrusted to be the coordinator and an instructor for the MA TESOL programme at Swinburne University of Technology. Unlike in my early years of teaching, I held a more stable teacher identity that came with the PhD qualification and the international teaching experience. As a teacher educator, I am now very aware that the type of support that my student teachers need transcends that of providing them with pedagogical resources. The unique individual differences represented by the Malaysian students' diversity means that I have an obligation to assist my student teachers to value inclusivity and diversity, and achieve a positive sense of self, as part of their individual and social development, in the hope that they will eventually become positive and engaged members of the teaching community.

Reflecting back at how my teacher trajectory began, the journey was tumultuous at times, and the process of becoming was full of challenges, as well as successes. In tandem with the trajectory, my teacher identity became renegotiated and reconstructed across time and place. The formation of a teacher identity is clearly fraught with many complexities which were, at times, beyond my control since identity and competence are shaped and reshaped through active engagement in teaching practice (Williams, 2013). Some difficulties I faced when constructing such professional identity were due the linguistic environment and language policies in the Malaysian context. Within such a linguistic environment, the construction of professional identities is frequently played out against a background of rapid educational reform and sociocultural challenges. As a result, teachers are continually fashioning and refashioning their identities. This parallels Trent (2011), who maintained that teacher identities should be best regarded as multifaceted, constantly shifting and unstable. In my career trajectory, the language policies presented a possible discord and difficulties for the teacher.

Overall, this chapter has revealed that an English language teacher's trajectory includes a combination of personal, professional and contextual matters. It is inherently dynamic as it is shaped in interactions between the teacher as a person, his or her students, other teachers, and the school as a workplace, and by broader issues such as the personal environment of the teacher and the value placed on education in the national context. It is without a doubt a dynamic journey and a 'career-long process' (Korhonen & Törmä, 2014; Meijer et al, 2014). The teacher's identity, both personal and professional, is continuously reconstructed and the process is imbued with struggles, challenges and conflict, but can also lead to success, mirroring the never-ending complexity of language teaching and learning (Tudor, 2003) and life.

References

Ali, N.L. (2013) A Changing Paradigm in Language Planning: English-medium instruction policy at the tertiary level in Malaysia, *Current Issues in Language Planning*, 14(1), 73-92. http://dx.doi.org/10.1080/14664208.2013.775543

Ali, N.L., Hamid, M.O. & Moni, K. (2011) English in Primary Education in Malaysia: policies, outcomes and stakeholders' lived experiences, *Current Issues in Language Planning*, 12(2), 147-166. http://dx.doi.org/10.1080/14664208.2011.584371

Altbach, P.G. & Knight, J. (2007) The Internationalization of Higher Education: motivations and realities, *Journal of Studies in International Education*, 11(3-4), 290-305.

Avalos, B. & Bascopé, M. (2014) Future Teacher Trajectory Research: its contribution to teacher education and policy, *Education as Change*, 18(suppl. 1), S19-S32. http://dx.doi.org/10.1080/16823206.2013.877353

Badiozaman, I. (2012) The Relationship between Malaysian Learners' Self-concept and Engagement in Academic Writing in One Higher Learning Institution. PhD dissertation, Massey University, Palmerston North, New Zealand.

Badiozaman, I. (2015) Interrelated Influence of Internal and External Factors on Malaysian Learners' Self-concept in Academic Writing, *Asia TEFL Journal*, 12(1), 79-115.

Che Musa, N., Koo Yew, L. & Azman, H. (2012) Exploring English Language Learning and Teaching in Malaysia, *GEMA Online Journal of Language Studies*, 12(1), 35-51.

Department of Statistics Malaysia (2014) Population and Demographics. http://www.statistics.gov.my/portal/index.php

Foo, B. & Richards, C. (2004) English in Malaysia, *RELC Journal*, 35, 229-240. http://dx.doi.org/10.1177/003368820403500209

Gill, S. (2006) Change in Language Policy in Malaysia: the reality of implementation in public universities, *Current Issues in Language Planning*, 7(1), 82-94. http://dx.doi.org/10.2167/cilp083.0

Hallman, H. (2014) Teacher Identity as Dialogic Response, in Y.L. Cheung, S.B. Said & K. Park (Eds) *Advances and Current Trends in Language Teacher Identity Research*, pp. 3-15. London: Routledge.

Hardman, J. & A-Rahman, N. (2014) Teachers and the Implementation of a New English Curriculum in Malaysia, *Language, Culture and Curriculum*, 27(3), 260-277. http://dx.doi.org/10.1080/07908318.2014.980826

Hashim, A. (2014) English and the Linguistic Ecology of Malaysia, *World Englishes*, 33(4), 458-471. http://dx.doi.org/10.1111/weng.12107

Heng, C.S. & Tan, H. (2006) English for Mathematics and Science: current Malaysian language-in-education policies and practices, *Language and Education*, 20(4), 306-321. http://dx.doi.org/10.2167/le631.0

Hussey, T. & Smith, P. (2010) Transitions in Higher Education, *Innovations in Education and Teaching International*, 47(2), 155-164. http://dx.doi.org/10.1080/14703291003718893

Korhonen, V. & Törmä, S. (2014) Engagement with a Teaching Career: how a group of Finnish university teachers experience teacher identity and professional growth, *Journal of Further and Higher Education*, 1-18.

Lacey, C. (1977) *The Socialisation of Teachers*. London: Methuen.

Meijer, P.C., Oolbekkink, H.W., Pillen, M. & Aardema, A. (2014) Pedagogies of Developing Teacher Identity, in L. Orland-Barak & C. Craig (Eds) *International Teacher Education: promising pedagogies*, Part A, pp. 293-309. Bingley: Emerald Publishing Group. http://dx.doi.org/10.1108/s1479-368720140000022018

Ministry of Education (1992) *Teacher Education in Malaysia*. Kuala Lumpur: Ministry of Education.

Moussu, L. (2010) Influence of Teacher-contact Time and Other Variables on ESL Students' Attitudes towards Native- and Nonnative-English-speaking teachers, *TESOL Quarterly*, 44(4), 746-768. http://dx.doi.org/10.5054/tq.2010.235997

Pillen, M., Beijaard, D. & den Brok, P. (2012) Tensions in beginning teachers' professional identity development, accompanying feelings and coping strategies, *European Journal of Teacher Education*, 36(3), 240-260. http://dx.doi.org/10.1080/02619768.2012.696192

Pillen, M., den Brok, P.J. & Beijaard, D. (2013) Profiles and Change in Beginning Teachers' Professional Identity Tensions, *Teaching and Teacher Education*, 34, 86-97. http://dx.doi.org/10.1016/j.tate.2013.04.003

Rajadurai, J. (2009) The Interactional Experiences of English Language Learners in the Malay Community: a Malaysian case study, *International Journal of Language Society and Culture*. www.educ.utas.edu.au/users/tle/JOURNAL

Rajadurai, J. (2010) 'Malays are Expected to Speak Malay': community ideologies, language use and the negotiation of identities, *Journal of Language, Identity and Education*, 9, 91-106. http://dx.doi.org/10.1080/15348451003704776

Rajendran, N. (2005) Teachers Teaching Students from a Multicultural Background: the case of Malaysia, *Higher Education Policy*, 18, 361-374. http://dx.doi.org/10.1057/palgrave.hep.8300100

Shakir, R. (2009) Soft Skills at the Malaysian Institutes of Higher Learning, *Asia Pacific Education Review*, 10(3), 309-315. http://dx.doi.org/10.1007/s12564-009-9038-8

Subramani, S. & Kempner, K. (2002) Malaysian Higher Education: captive or post-western?, *Australian Journal of Education*, 46(3), 31-54. http://dx.doi.org/10.1177/000494410204600302

Swinburne University of Technology Sarawak Campus (2014) About Swinburne. http://www.swinburne.edu.my/

Tan, K.E., Lim, C.S., & Chew, C.M. (2011) Talking Mathematics in English, *The Asia-Pacific Education Researcher*, 21(1), 133-143.

Tan, K.E. & Miller, J. (2007) Writing in English in Malaysian High Schools: the discourse of examinations, *Language and Education*, 21(2), 124-140. http://dx.doi.org/10.2167/le663.0

Trent, J. (2011) 'Four Years On, I'm Ready to Teach': teacher education and the construction of teacher identities, *Teachers and Teaching*, 17(5), 529-543. http://dx.doi.org/10.1080/13540602.2011.602207

Tudor, I. (2003) Learning to Live with Complexity: towards an ecological perspective on language teaching, *System*, 31(1), 1-12. http://dx.doi.org/10.1016/S0346-251X(02)00070-2

Williams, J. (2013) *Constructing New Professional Identities: career changers in teacher education*. Rotterdam: Sense. http://dx.doi.org/10.1007/978-94-6209-260-0

Zaaba, Z., Ramadan, F.I., Anning, I.N.A., Gunggut, H. & Umemoto, K. (2011) Language-in-education Policy: a study of policy adjustment strategy in Malaysia, *International Journal of Education and Information Technologies*, 5(2), 157-165.

CHAPTER 5

My Career Trajectory as a Teacher of English as a Second Language in India: narrative self-construction through a dialogic lens

TARA RATNAM

SUMMARY This chapter sketches the complex recursive path negotiated by the author as she developed from a naïve beginning English as a Second Language teacher to a more mature and agentive one. The author uses narrative as a convenient vehicle for examining her self and how the development of the self proceeds. In explaining how her self as an ESL teacher, working in a particular sociocultural context in India, gets constructed in the story she tells, she found that a dialogic approach to story construction was more advantageous than a mere representational account. This is because a dialogic approach helped her articulate the relational aspect of her narrative (i.e. the interactional positioning that the self as a narrator of the story accomplished alongside its represented content). Using Bakhtin's concepts of utterance, voice and ventriloquation as analytical tools, she illustrates how the author's self develops at the intersection between the represented content and the interactional positioning of her autobiographical narrative.

My autobiographical narrative traces the trajectory of my development from a novice English as Second Language (ESL) teacher to a more mature social justice educator. As I recount episodes from my life, my past selves seem to vacillate between a vulnerable naïve voice and a more enlightened mature agentive voice. These primary types of narrated self, naïve and mature, presuppose two constellations of voices from the larger social world – namely, 'authoritative discourse' and 'heteroglossia' (Bakhtin, 1981). According to Bakhtin, authoritative discourse 'demands that we acknowledge it, that we make it our own.... We encounter it with its authority already fused to it'

(p. 342). It is monologic as it assumes a universal 'finalized' meaning. Voices of heteroglossia, on the other hand, represent a plurality of voices. They challenge and counter authoritative discourse, pulling away from its unifying tendencies. Heteroglossia is dialogic, as it is open to connect with other voices in dialogue, and therefore also open to growth and change. In my narrative, these two voices create a tension-laden path for me to negotiate, resulting in a career trajectory marked by cycles of regressions and progressions.

The question for my 'narrative inquiry' involves understanding how I position my storytelling self with respect to these two types of my narrated voices and with respect to my readers: how do I ventriloquate the two voices my narrated selves speak with, in order to position myself in the event of storytelling as a certain kind of person?

The autobiographical nature of the facilitative role of teachers and teacher educators (Russell & Bullock, 1999; O'Loughlin 2007; Lassonde, Galman & Kosnik, 2009; Hamilton & Pinnegar, 2014) makes narrative a convenient vehicle for understanding the self and other, and for acting on that understanding in new ways. Narrative form, as Gee (1985) points out, is '[o]ne of the primary ways – probably the primary way – human beings make sense of their experience' (p. 11; also Polkinghorne, 1988). Because of the centrality of story in comprehending the 'richness and indeterminacy' of our experience as teachers and teacher educators (Carter, 1993) involving moral responsibilities, political interests and emotions (LaBoskey, 2007; Kelchtermans, 2014), personal narratives are being seen increasingly as critical to the practice of teaching and teacher education (Connelly & Clandinin, 1988, 1999; Gudmundsdottir, 1995; Clandinin & Connelly, 2000; Olson & Craig, 2005; Elbaz-Luwisch, 2011; Syrjälä & Estola, 2013).

However, in explaining how 'we are at least partially constituted by the stories we tell to others and to ourselves about our experience' (Grumet, 1991, p. 69), what gets highlighted is their representational functions (Alvermann, 2000; Wortham, 2001). That is, in telling stories about themselves, teachers and teacher educators can foreground more productive practices and subsequently act in terms of these alternative practices (Cohen, 1996; Witherell & Noddings, 1991). Gergen and Kaye (1992) argue that this representational account of the power of autobiographical narrative is partial as it fails to take into account the interactional events between the narrator and audience to which the narrative is addressed (Grumet, 1987). The act of telling is at the same time a performance that positions the narrator in different ways with respect to the audience within the same story. I want to point out that this 'performative' (Butler, 1990) aspect of the self needs attention in any complete account of narrative self-construction (Cain, 1991; Harding, 1992; Hill, 1995; Schiffrin, 1996; Wortham, 2001; Abraham, 2014).

A Dialogic Approach to Narrative Self-construction

Wortham (2001) argues that the power of autobiographical narratives 'often comes from the complex relations across the represented and enacted worlds they create' (p. 13). In the autobiographical narrative I tell here, I explore how the representational and interactional functions interrelate in the construction of my career trajectory. This interrelationship, where social others are profoundly enmeshed with everything I do, figuring in even the most intimate depths of my thoughts (Stetsenko, 2009), can be understood in terms of Bakhtin's (1981) 'dialogism'. I use his concepts of utterance, voice and ventriloquation to analyse the positioning in my narrative and the parallelism between the positioning and represented content in it, and how these parallels between the narrated content and interactional positioning contribute to my self-construction.

Utterance

In Bakhtin's view, living utterance is formed through a speaker's relation to the other; by entering into dialogue with the other's words and expressions inseparable from the lived cultural world in time and place: 'Our thought is born and shaped in the process of interaction and struggle with others' thought, and this cannot but be reflected in the forms that verbally express our thought as well' (Bakhtin, 1986, p. 92). The utterance is not only related to preceding thoughts existing in other people's contexts and serving their intentions, it is also oriented toward a future world. This future orientation of an utterance comes from its inherent 'quality of being directed to someone, its addressivity' (Bakhtin, 1986, p.95). 'The speaker talks with an expectation of a response, agreement, sympathy, objection, execution and so forth' (Bakhtin, 1986, p. 69). Since an utterance forms itself in an atmosphere of the already spoken and at the same time is shaped by anticipated future response (Bakhtin, 1981), understanding of utterance requires one to analyze the speaker's position with respect to both earlier speakers and anticipated subsequent speakers.

Voice and Ventriloquation

Bakhtin's notions of voice and ventriloquation provide tools for analyzing these 'dialogic overtones' of utterance in an autobiographical narrative. As pointed out earlier, we inevitably use words that have already been used by others, words that 'taste' or 'echo with' the social locations and ideological commitments of various overlapping groups in the social world. Voice refers to words that index some social position, because these words are characteristically used by members of that group. Voices are inseparable from contexts. They invoke positions and ideologies from the larger social world, as the characters described come to speak like recognizable types of people.

According to Bakhtin (1986), every utterance contains 'two texts'. One is the represented or narrated content and the other, the narrator's interactional positioning with respect to the voices of the characters represented. He uses the term 'ventriloquation' to describe the process of positioning oneself by speaking through others' voices and reaccentuating them. It is a process through which a narrator adopts a position in the storytelling event or 'event of speaking' with respect to the types of voices that have been indexed while describing the 'narrated event'.[1] In an autobiographical narrative, the voicing and ventriloquation of the self produces a trajectory for the narrator, as the positions of past selves lead toward the self narrating the story in the present (Wortham, 2001).

Space limitations prevent a full analysis of my narrative. I restrict myself to an illustrative excerpt that forms a pivotal moment in my career and captures its central theme – namely, my development from a novice to a mature ESL teacher. In narrating this, I not only represent the central theme of my career, but also accomplish a change in my interactional positioning with respect to my past self as also with my positioning with the readers.

My Career Trajectory: a journey into the self

The following excerpt from my autobiographical narrative is about the early part of my career leading up to my transition into a mature agentive teacher from a novice. In analyzing it, I will identify the central voices and how I ventriloquate these voices, then show how this positions me with respect to my audience, the readers. The excerpt is divided into three episodes: (1) the certainty of initial beliefs; (2) fall from grace; (3) change in classroom practice.

1. The Certainty of Initial Beliefs

1. I plunged into the deep side of teaching straight after my MA [2] degree without any formal training.
2. The textbook was my armour, because throughout my school and college the thrust of teaching had been 'giving knowledge' and this formed the taken-for-granted purpose of my teaching.
3. However, even within this dominant transmissive cultural framework, my orientation to teaching was different.
4. This was due to the indelible impressions left from my early socialization at home.
5. These images are of my participation in games with my siblings at my mother's knees as she guided us, for instance, in patterning words out of the square cardboard pieces on which she had carved the alphabet.
6. What seemed as mere 'play' to me then can perhaps be restoried in Vygotskian terms as the 'leading activity' that created the ZPD [3] for our collaborative learning.

7. When I entered school, learning was not a burden, because I was well equipped with the cultural tools of literacy required at school, which I had appropriated largely from the fun games that my mother had played with us.
8. At the pre-university level, where I taught as an ESL teacher, my students too seemed to enjoy the activities I set for them and the questions through which I guided them in understanding the text.
9. Student contribution has been an important aspect of my class from the day I began teaching.
10. When one of my students commented, 'Miss, you make us feel as if *we* know everything', it affirmed my image of a 'good' teacher.
11. My days as a teacher seem like a song.
12. I did not suffer the tension that teachers with preservice training are wont to experience due to the gulf between their theoretical understanding and the reality of the classroom.
13. I was worse than my students in my eagerness to get away from college. However, this was not due to any distaste for teaching.
14. I was drawn by other interests. What happened in class hardly crossed my mind once I was away from it.
15. This is because I went away with the satisfaction of having done my job well under the naïve assumption that student learning was the direct result of my teaching.
16. To the English-medium students I taught, neither the English curriculum nor my teaching posed any new challenges, because they were already there where the curriculum expected them to be.
17. In teaching it, I had definite pre-specified outcomes towards which I led them efficiently.
18. I had no idea that I could stretch them further by exploiting the text for its dialogic possibilities and create space for students' meaning and self-expression.

During my early socialization, two types of voice can be identified – the voice of my home and the voice of the school. At home, my mother helped me learn through play and my father through questioning. Both of the strategies they used positioned me as an active participant investing in my own learning, and my parents as facilitators of my learning. However, at school as a student, I was positioned as a passive receiver of knowledge and teachers were positioned as 'knowers' in an environment characterized by a traditional transmissive culture. These two positionings (i.e. teacher as facilitator/ student as active learner and teacher as knower/student as passive learner) belong to two different ideologies. The former is aligned with the voices of heteroglossia and the latter with the institutionalized authoritative discourse. As a beginning teacher, I reproduced patterns from both these positions. They co-existed in my teaching without causing any dissonance in me. This is the narrated event. As a narrator, how do I ventriloquate these voices presupposed in my narrative to show the move from a past self? In the narrative I am positioned as a 'good teacher'. I am smug under this belief and do not experience any discrepancy between my value and my practice. As a narrator, I enact this complacent self for my readers (points 11-14 above). The topic sentence in point 11 above indexes this parallel between my telling and enacting by setting up the reader's anticipation of what is to come. Then in point 15 above, I slip out of this smug self and distance myself from my narrated self by using the evaluative indexical, 'naïve assumption'. I also step out of the narrative (points 16-18 above) to comment on the limitation in my teaching. My storytelling self which presupposes that my current self knows more positions my narrated self as 'naïve' and as aligning with the authoritative discourse of school. It indexes my past self as belonging to the social group of self-satisfied teachers. With this positioning of my past self as naïve and monologic, I open to question my narrated image of myself as a 'good teacher'. Through this implicit question, I invite my readers to add another layer of ventriloquation by the evaluative position they take with respect to the characters/voices represented in the narrated event. Figure 1 depicts the foregoing analysis. In this, and the other figures that follow, the 'narrated event' represents the salient characters and relationships of the narrative, while the 'storytelling event' shows the interactional positioning between the narrator and the characters and events in the story, as also between the narrator and the readers.

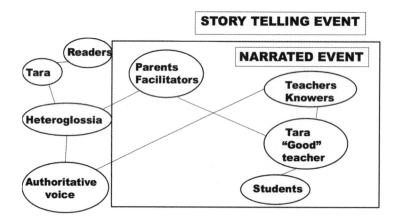

Figure 1. The certainty of initial beliefs.

In Figure 1, the narrated event represents my past self positioned as a 'good teacher' with respect to my students and the two voices of my socialization in my immediate surrounding, my parents and teachers. In the storytelling event, these voices are linked to the larger cultural patterns in the social world from which they derive – namely, voices of heteroglossia and authoritative discourse. My narrated self is aligned with the voice of authoritative discourse and the teachers who submit to this dominant voice, largely at a taken-for-granted level. This positioning suggests that my image of myself as a 'good teacher' may not be tenable.

2. Fall from Grace

19. My honeymoon days of teaching came to an abrupt end in the second year of my teaching.
20. The confidence that I exuded in the English-medium classes turned to despair, uncertainty and insecurity when I was given to teach sections of culturally diverse students from a vernacular medium of instruction.
21. In the beginning, I was very happy that I had an opportunity to help these 'poor' students from a rural background. I always had a soft spot for the 'underprivileged'.
22. As a young girl, I lived on a coffee plantation where my father was a doctor. His healing touch and human concern did not discriminate the 'lower-' class labourers (whose touch was considered pollution in those days) from the 'upper-' [4] class managers.
23. His democratic practices in a caste/class-ridden social set-up have left a strong impression on me.
24. In addition, the stories we were brought up on with strong heterodox voices such as the one about the social reformer Ramanujacharya and his inclusive practices had a special appeal for me.
25. However, these democratic voices lay dormant within me.
26. They did not disrupt my teaching practice, which was in line with the dominant authoritative voice, because the routine context of my teaching in the English-medium classes did not warrant it.
27. I did not experience any discrepancy between my value and practice in the first year of my teaching, where students positioned me as a 'good' teacher.
28. However, the vernacular-medium class was another context.
29. My efforts to involve the students there in learning activities were not appreciated by them.
30. In addition, the stubborn 'virtual position' [5] of 'English only' I adopted seemed to alienate them more, till one day a student made their cultural expectation plain to me: 'Pāta mādi, miss' (Do the lesson, miss). [6]
31. It made me feel like a toddler.
32. I was suddenly hurled into an unknown, unfamiliar world where I had to find my moorings.
33. The plight of my students, unable to make sense of my teaching, and of mine as their teacher, shouldering the responsibility of facilitating their ESL learning, jolted me out of my complacency, calling into question my self-image of a 'good' teacher.

34. It is painful to remember the deep sense of loss I went through then. I had to rebuild my identity.

35. I had to earn my students' trust by making them see that my efforts to involve them in the classroom processes were in their interest.

36. Despite spending hours with them both inside and outside the classroom, I returned home each day with a sense of incompleteness about my teaching.

37. The positive correlation between my teaching and student learning that I strove to achieve seemed an ever-elusive goal.

38. These students failed in large numbers and it hurt to see them bear the humiliation of being labelled as 'dull' and 'incapable of learning' by my colleagues and others.

39. I felt deeply implicated in the production of this failure.

40. My monologic stance and its impact on my students were mirrored to me by a student named Vasan [7], who was a victim of my teaching in these greenhorn days, when I held a thoughtless virtual position in the belief of providing students 'maximum exposure'.

41. Coming from a vernacular-medium background, he had found my classes very frustrating: 'It was very difficult to follow you. I was expecting at least 30% Kannada from you ... I could not participate in your class ... But in the history class, I used to answer questions.'

42. My cultural insensitivity and implicit authoritarian stance had closed off my access to the lived experience of my students and turned them away from me.

43. Looking back on this part of my career makes me squirm even now, although I've also come to judge myself less harshly for this, having learnt, from reading William Perry (1970) and Lev Vygotsky (1978), to recognize my behaviour as characteristic of the level at which I operated then with the cultural tools at my disposal.

44. I had to develop against the grain, both within me, in confronting my deeply embedded 'lay theories' largely invisible to my consciousness, and on the social plane, where these dominant cultural beliefs reigned supreme.

Episode 2 of the narrative describes how the routine context of my teaching was disrupted by subsequent contextualization. This is represented in Figure 2.

My naïve self, of which my narrated self was not aware in episode 1, is brought home to me by the subsequent context in which culturally diverse students (CDs)' expectation positions me as a novice (points 30-32 above). Besides, the conversation with Vasan (points 40-41 above), in which I am positioned as an oppressor and CDs as victims, also shows my culture insensitivity and its alienating effect on my students. This positioning made me aware of the gaps between my value and my practice. My value, which echoes with the democratic voices of my father and other more distant heterodox voices, was to empower the CDs and promote their learning. But my practice, which overlapped with authoritative discourse, became a hindrance to their learning.

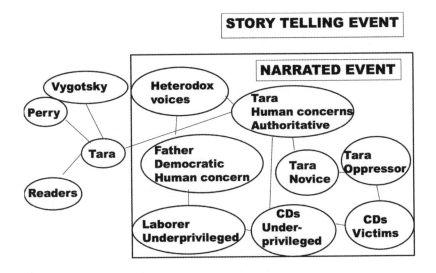

Figure 2. Fall from grace.

The development of this awareness in my narrated self is indicated in my questioning my position as a good teacher (point 33 above), the same doubt that the storytelling self had expressed earlier in episode 1. This awareness in my narrated self alters how my storytelling self accents my storied voice to establish closeness with it. There is also a parallel change in my interactional positioning with the readers. In the earlier episode, I had invited their critical evaluation of my narrated self by positioning her as naïve. However, here, I make a tacit plea to the readers to take a more sympathetic position, by positioning my storytelling self parallel to my narrated self. I am not merely a mature person in the present dispassionately recounting how my naïve self has developed greater awareness and culture sensitivity – I also enact this transition in my storytelling event: the pain of losing my sense of identity (point 34 above) and of losing my students (point 42 above). The words 'painful' (point 34 above) and 'squirm' (point 43 above), which appear in the present tense, indicate how this critical episode continues to affect me. I am closing the distance between the narrated and storytelling events not only by this enactment, but also by justifying this aspect of my career to the reader (points 43-44 above). With this, I also anticipate a less distanced relationship between my narrated self and the readers by positioning them as sympathetic audience.

3. Change in Classroom Practice

45. My practice and social relations with my students have come under critical scrutiny with my growing awareness.
46. From these students I have learned what culture sensitivity is and what inclusive education entails.
47. It is through an understanding of their ways of thinking that I learnt to link it to their new learning and make my teaching meaningful to them.
48. My focus now is on allowing students to find their voice from their multicultural location, and on using their mother tongue as a self-facilitating strategy to participate in this process.
49. This is very different from my earlier monologic/monolingual teaching practice which was focused on students' voice merging uncritically with the closed meaning that I represented.
50. Prashanth, who was a student of mine at this stage in my career, told me that my practice, which was cognizant of learners, had influenced the development of his own pedagogical practice.
51. Another student, Prakash, whom I interviewed around this time, pointed out that although my efforts to help students construct their own meaning were very unsettling in the beginning, they grew to find it useful in stimulating their thinking: 'Frankly ma'am, first when I attended your class, I thought what you were doing ... you don't know the way.... slowly we started understanding.... It is not just learning answers by heart. We have to think and answer. I found your class very difficult, first six months, very very difficult. Then I improved. I used to read, try to understand and express in my own way. That is good. If you plot time and interest, first of all, the interest would decrease, then it will go high'.
52. Comments such as these by my culturally diverse students reflect how my learning is contributing to bringing a closer affinity between the democratic values of social justice I cherish and my pedagogical practices.

Figure 3 shows the synchrony between my value and practice achieved by my narrated self through the changing interactional positioning with respect to my students. While the comments by Vasan and other CDs in episode 2 mirrored my initial authoritative position, the remarks by Prashanth and Prakash, coming later, seem to corroborate the changed interactional position I have accomplished in my social world and with respect to my students. This change has engaged me in a long journey of 'ideological becoming' (Bakhtin, 1981) beset by intense struggles to find a perspective among various intersecting voices available in my historical and cultural environment.

As a teacher, I reproduced authoritative monologic practices because of the ubiquity of these patterns in my cultural milieu. It wasn't until I intersected with contrary discourses that positioned me as an oppressor with respect to my diverse students that I questioned my own beliefs and asked myself afresh what is of value, good and helpful. This indeterminacy that turned me to further examine my context yielded insights for accomplishing new interactional positioning with respect to my students. A change in my position from an oppressor to a dialogic partner facilitated my access to the 'heartbeats' of my students and their access to mine (Barone, 1992).

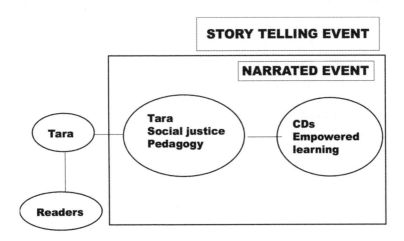

Figure 3. Change in classroom practice.

In the interaction between me and my readers I am positioned as a more experienced peer. This is indicated by the way my storytelling self is placed above the readers in Figure 3. My story of ideological becoming offers a possibility for them to transform their lives in an analogous way.[8] My story 'is read through the life of the reader' (Denzin, 1989, p. 26). Both narrators and readers 'conspire to create the lives they write and read about' (Denzin, 1989, p. 26). In the storytelling event, I position the readers also as narrators who enact an analogous struggle of their own by their 'actively responsive understanding' of my story. This 'actively responsive understanding' comes in the form of, as mentioned earlier, the readers' 'agreement, sympathy, objection, execution, and so forth' (Bakhtin, 1986, p. 69).

The Nature of Narrative Self-construction

From an epistemological point of view, my narrated self has moved close to the storytelling self in episode 3. However, this transition of my narrated self from a naïve and oppressive teacher to a more mature and agentive social justice educator is not a one-time, linear developmental achievement that is 'finalized'. My career is still an open story line. At the age of 63, I am not simply describing representationally how a past naïve self has been

71

transformed into a more mature one. This would not explain the repeated enactments of this pattern in the subsequent contexts and events of my career, both past and present.[9] Every time I face new challenges in my career not only as a teacher, but also in my expanded roles of teacher educator, materials producer and researcher in my educational context, I step into and out of a naïve and insecure position. Every regression is a stepping stone for new development. Emerging inconsistencies/dissonances open up the potential for new positioning with new meaning in the interrelation between the narrated and storytelling self on the one hand, and the storytelling self and the audience, on the other. Herein lies the transformative potential of an autobiographical narrative which a mere representational account of a narrative would miss. The relational functions play a role in capturing the complexities involved in how the self gets constructed in narratives.

An analysis of my autobiographical narrative of my career trajectory as an ESL teacher has illustrated how my self gets created in the interrelations between the voices presupposed in my narrated events and the enacted positioning in the storytelling events where my storytelling self positions myself not only with respect to my past selves, but also with respect to my readers. I am not just representing information, but as a narrator, evaluating it (Labov, 1972, 1982). This results in both distance and parallels between the narrated and storytelling selves. I distance myself, for instance, from my narrated self when I call my past self 'naïve' and I position my present self as more enlightened and therefore better able to understand the situation. Despite this superior status assumed by my narrating self, the distance between the narrator and the narrated selves breaks down at other times to become parallel selves. This parallel is achieved by enacting the story. For instance, I enact my fall from certainty/grace (episode 2) and its pain and shame in the storytelling event in a way that shows that this incident affects me still. By both representing and enacting my development from a novice to a mature teacher, I accomplish that development (Wortham, 2001).

The recurring enactment of my naïve insecure self moving toward more mature positioning in the subsequent storytelling events of my career, continuing into the present, shows that I am recreating characteristic positions that partly constitute my self. It is in these sorts of enactments that my self gets 'established and maintained' (Wortham, 2001) as a certain kind of person.

Conclusion

Exploring the transformative potential of my autobiographical narrative from a dialogic lens convinces me more now than when I began of the explanatory power that lies in a dialogic approach to narrative self-construction. A dialogic approach to autobiographical narrative creates the opportunity to ventriloquate both others and my self. This facility to position myself with respect to my past selves seems to make autobiographical narrative a particularly rich site for creating the self.

A dialogic approach provides a complex understanding of narrative self-construction by foregrounding its ethical, moral, political and transformative aspects as well as its 'social significance'.[10] The inherent qualities of 'addressivity' and 'answerability' foregrounded in a dialogic view of autobiographical narrative bind the narrator and audience in a moral framework, making it socially significant. As both audience and narrator grapple with the recounted story, they are also answerable to the ethical issues raised in it (Rymes & Wortham, 2011). Like me then, others are also engaged in struggles over their own beliefs as they adopt positions with respect to these issues and social groups in the social world. This positioning centred around ethics and morality (Taylor, 1989) helps us to partly create who we are as English language teachers.

Acknowledgement

I would like to thank Cheryl Craig for her valuable review comments.

Notes

[1] 'Event of speaking' and 'narrated event' are terms used by Jakobson (1971) to distinguish the storytelling event from the story told.

[2] Master of Arts.

[3] Refers to Vygotsky's (1978) concept, the zone of proximal development.

[4] The terms, 'upper' and 'lower' with reference to class do not represent my personal values, but rather refer to terms used in the common cultural discourse.

[5] One of the three positions mentioned in Macaro (2001) regarding the use of mother tongue (MT). The virtual position corresponds to the theory of 'maximum exposure', where MT is excluded as having no pedagogical value in second-language learning.

[6] Translated from Kannada, which is the students' vernacular. Culturally, 'doing the lesson' meant reading the English text and explaining it line by line in Kannada.

[7] All the names of the students used here are pseudonyms.

[8] The idea of offering the teacher educators' story as a model for novice teachers to step in and re-enact an analogous story of their own forms the grounding principle of self-study practices. This principle holds rich potential for exploring the interrelation between the represented story and interactional positioning in self-study narrative so as to aid a more robust view of it.

[9] As mentioned earlier, space does not allow a detailed analysis of the subsequent episodes of my career.

[10] Clandinin & Connelly (2000) stress the importance of connecting personal narratives with larger questions of social significance to make the personal more generally relevant.

References

Abraham, S.L. (2014) A Nepantla Pedagogy comparing Anzaldùa's and Bakhtin's Ideas for Pedagogical and Social Change, *Critical Education*, 5(5), 1-19.

Alvermann, D.E. (2000) Narrative Approaches, *Reading Online*, 4(5). http://www.readingonline.org/articles/art_index.asp?HREF=/articles/handbook/alvermann/index.html

Bakhtin, M.M. (1981) *The Dialogic Imagination: four essays*, ed. M. Holquist, trans. C. Emerson & M. Holquist. Austin: University of Texas Press.

Bakhtin, M.M. (1986) *Speech Genres and Other Late Essays*, ed. C. Emerson & M. Holquist, trans. V.W. McGee. Austin: University of Texas Press.

Barone, T.E. (1992) Beyond Theory and Method: a case of critical storytelling, *Theory into Practice*, 31(2), 142-146. http://dx.doi.org/10.1080/00405849209543535

Butler, J. (1990) *Gender Trouble*. New York: Routledge.

Cain, C. (1991) Personal Stories, *Ethos*, 19, 210-253. http://dx.doi.org/10.1525/eth.1991.19.2.02a00040

Carter, K. (1993) The Place of Story in the Study of Teaching and Teacher Education, *Educational Researcher*, 22(1), 5-18. http://dx.doi.org/10.3102/0013189X022001005

Clandinin, D.J. & Connelly, F.M. (2000) *Narrative Inquiry: experience and story in qualitative research*. San Francisco: Jossey-Bass.

Cohen, J. (1996) Rewriting Our Lives, *Journal of Narrative and Life History*, 6, 145-156. http://dx.doi.org/10.1075/jnlh.6.2.03rew

Connelly, F.M. & Clandinin, D.J. (1988) *Teachers as Curriculum Planners: narratives of experience*. New York: Teachers College Press.

Connelly, F.M. & Clandinin, D.J. (Eds) (1999) *Shaping a Professional Identity: stories of educational practice*. New York: Teachers College Press.

Denzin, N.K. (1989) *Interpretive Biography*. Thousand Oaks, CA: SAGE. http://dx.doi.org/10.4135/9781412984584

Elbaz-Luwisch, F. (2011) The Narrative Study of Teaching: ISATT and North American research on teaching, in C. Day & C. Laneve (Eds) *Analysis of Educational Practices: a comparison of research models*, pp. 99-108. Brescia: Editrice La Scuola.

Gee, J. (1985) The Narrativization of Experience in the Oral Style, *Journal of Education*, 167, 9-35.

Gergen, K. & Kaye, J. (1992) Beyond Narrative in the Negotiation of Therapeutic Meaning, in S. McNamee & K. Gergen (Eds) *Therapy as a Social Construction*, pp. 166-185. London: SAGE.

Grumet, M.R. (1987) The Politics of Personal Knowledge, *Curriculum Inquiry*, 17(3), 319-329. http://dx.doi.org/10.1080/03626784.1987.11075295

Grumet, M. (1991) The Politics of Personal Knowledge, in C. Witherell & N. Noddings (Eds) *Stories Lives Tell: narrative and dialogue in education*, pp. 67-77. New York: Teachers College Press.

Gudmundsdottir, S. (1995) The Narrative Nature of Pedagogical Content Knowledge, in H. McEwan & E. Egan (Eds) *Narrative in Teaching, Learning and Research*, pp. 24-38. New York: Teachers College Press.

Hamilton, M.L. & Pinnegar, S. (2014) Intimate Scholarship in Research: an example from self-study of teaching and teacher education practices methodology, *Learning Landscapes*, 8(1), 153-171.

Harding, S. (1992) The Afterlife of Stories, in G. Rosenwald & R. Ochberg (Eds) *Storied Lives*, pp. 60-75. New Haven, CT: Yale University Press.

Hill, J. (1995) The Voices of Don Gabriel, in D. Tedlock & B. Mannheim (Eds) *The Dialogic Emergence of Culture*, pp. 97-147. Urbana: University of Illinois.

Jakobson, R. (1971) Shifters, Verbal Categories, and the Russian Verb, in *Selected Writings*, vol. 2, pp. 130-147. The Hague: Mouton.

Kelchtermans, G. (2014) Setting the Scene: the 'narrative turn' in educational research and teacher education, in L. Orland-Barak & C. Craig (Eds) *International Teacher Education: promising pedagogies (Part A). Advances in Research on Teaching*, vol. 22, pp. 273-291. Bingley: Emerald Group.

LaBoskey, V.K. (2007) The Methodology of Self-study and its Theoretical Underpinnings, in J.J. Loughran, M.L. Hamilton, V.K. LaBoskey & T.L. Russell (Eds) *International Handbook of Self-study of Teaching and Teacher Education Practices*, pp. 817-869. Dordrecht: Springer.

Labov, W. (1972) The Transformation of Experience in Narrative Syntax, in *Language in the Inner City*, pp.354-396. Philadelphia: University of Pennsylvania Press.

Labov, W. (1982) Speech Actions and Reactions in Personal Narrative, in D. Tannen (Ed.) *Analysing Discourse*, pp. 219-247. Washington, DC: Georgetown University Press.

Lassonde, C.A., Galman, S. & Kosnik, C. (2009) *Self-study Research Methodologies for Teacher Educators*. Rotterdam: Sense.

Macaro, E. (2001) Does Intensive Grammar Instruction Make All the Difference?, *Language Teaching Research*, 10(3), 297-327. http://dx.doi.org/10.1191/1362168806lr197oa

O'Loughlin, M. (2007) On Losses that are Not Easily Mourned, in L. Bohm, R. Curtis, & B. Willock (Eds) *Psychoanalysts' Reflections on Deaths and Endings: finality, transformations, new beginnings*, pp.103-120. New York: Routledge.

Olson, M. & Craig, J.C. (2005) Uncovering Cover Stories: tensions and entailments in the development of teacher knowledge, *Curriculum Inquiry*, 35(2), 161-182. http://dx.doi.org/10.1111/j.1467-873X.2005.00323.x

Perry, W.G. (1970) *Forms of Intellectual and Ethical Development in College Years*. New York: Holt, Rinehart & Winston.

Polkinghorne, D.E. (1988) *Narrative Knowing and the Human Sciences*. Albany: State University of New York Press.

Russell, T. & Bullock, S. (1999) Discovering Our Professional Knowledge as Teachers: critical dialogues about learning from experience, in J.J. Loughran, (Ed.) *Researching Teaching*, pp. 132-151. London: Falmer Press.

Rymes, B.R. & Wortham, S. (2011) *Concepts and Methods for Using Narrative in Teacher Education*. http://repository.upenn.edu/gse_pubs/233

Schiffrin, D. (1996) Narrative as Self-portrait, *Language in Society*, 25, 167-203. http://dx.doi.org/10.1017/S0047404500020601

Stetsenko, A. (2009) Personhood: an activist project of historical becoming through collaborative pursuits of social transformation, *New Ideas in Psychology*, 3, 1-10.

Syrjälä, L. & Estola, E. (2013) Narrative Research: from the margins to being heard, in C. Craig, P. Meijer & J. Broeckmans (Eds) *From Teacher Thinking to Teachers and Teaching: the evolution of a research community*, pp. 157-173. Bingley: Emerald Group.

Taylor, C. (1989) *Sources of the Self: the making of the modern identity*. Cambridge, MA: Harvard University Press.

Vygotsky, L.S. (1978) *Mind in Society: the development of higher psychological processes*. Cambridge, MA: Harvard University Press.

Witherell, C. & Noddings, N. (Eds) (1991) *Stories Lives Tell: narrative and dialogue in education*. New York: Teachers College Press.

Wortham, S. (2001) *Narratives in Action: a strategy for research and analysis*. New York: Teachers College Press.

CHAPTER 6

The Influence of Chinese Educational Policy on Teachers of English

LUXIN YANG

SUMMARY This chapter examines the development of Chinese education policy, especially foreign language education policy, over the past 30 years, and its impact on the trajectory of one experienced teacher in teaching English as a Foreign Language (EFL) in a senior high school – a teacher who later became a teacher researcher in her school district. Influenced by the development of theories of and approaches to second-language teaching in the West (e.g. the communicative approach, task-based learning), the objective of teaching EFL in Chinese schools has shifted its focus from language form to language use and intercultural competence. This objective is explicitly stated in the National Curriculum Standards for English as a School Subject. This chapter presents how this experienced teacher entered the English teaching profession and learned to teach English by doing so within the rapidly changing social environment. This teacher's experiences reveal that the Chinese educational policy influences EFL teachers' career trajectory but that teachers' own understanding of Chinese education policy and their consequent actions are even more decisive in their professional development.

Introduction

I belong to the generation that has experienced all the changes in education resulting from the reform and opening-up policy after the Cultural Revolution in China in the late 1970s. I have also experienced dual academic socialization processes from China to Canada as a graduate student and then from Canada to China as a returnee (Yang, 2016). With a master's degree from a Chinese university and having been a full-time English teacher for four years at a university in Beijing, I did my MA studies in the TESL (Teaching English as a Second Language) program at the University of

British Columbia (UBC) from September 1999 to July 2001. I then continued my doctoral studies in a second-language education program at the Ontario Institute for Studies in Education (OISE) at the University of Toronto from September 2001 to March 2006. I immediately returned to China after my doctoral defense and started to work at the National Research Center for Foreign Language Education at Beijing Foreign Studies University. I have experienced many struggles having to do with learning to do research and present my research in both academic English and Chinese. In this process of learning, I have gained deeper understandings of both western and eastern societies. Having spent more time in China, I gradually realized that I needed to expand my 'second language (L2) writing research' (which I focused on in my graduate studies in Canadian universities) in order to establish an 'irreplaceable' position and survive at my research center as a returnee.

The relevant area of my training in L2 writing research was foreign language teaching and learning. Some of my colleagues have conducted a lot of research on foreign language teaching and learning at the tertiary level, implying that it was not wise for me to enter into an already established field. However, I noticed that none of my colleagues studied foreign language teaching and learning at the primary and secondary school levels. Moreover, this domain is especially important to our country, as English is a compulsory school subject in China and it continues to present many teaching and learning problems. Having successfully obtained a national research grant for the project 'Examining the Professional Development of School EFL Teachers in China' in 2010, I started to observe English classes in schools and attend group lesson planning meetings organized by a teacher training school in one school district in Beijing. Over the past five years, through classroom observations and ongoing communication with teachers, I became familiar with the reform in English education in China since 2000 and able to detect problems existing in daily classroom teaching for English teachers in Beijing and other parts of China. In this chapter, I discuss the influence of Chinese educational policy on one experienced teacher of English in Beijing over the past 30 years.

The teacher's name is Huiwen, and she is in her mid-50s. Huiwen was born and grew up in Beijing. After having been a high school English teacher for 22 years, Huiwen became a teaching researcher at a teacher training school in a Beijing district in 2002, supervising English teachers in her district. I came to know Huiwen through my interview with her in the winter of 2008 for a project on English teaching in Beijing. Since then, we have regularly communicated by sharing our ideas on English language teaching and teacher training activities. In 2010, we started to work together on my national research project of exploring the connections between the school district and the university in the professional development of school English teachers. Huiwen's experience as an English teacher and later as an English teaching researcher paralleled the development of English language education in China after the Cultural Revolution.

This chapter is based on multiple sources of data. The primary source is six formal interviews I conducted with Huiwen from 2008 to 2015, with each interview lasting about 90 minutes. I also had a number of informal conversations with Huiwen on the telephone and during my visits to her office over the past 7 years, which I captured as research notes. Over the past 5 years, I regularly attended the group lesson-planning meetings and public lesson study activities organized by Huiwen, which I tape-recorded with the permission of Huiwen and the other participating teachers. With my frequent visits to Huiwen's work sites, the teachers supervised by Huiwen also came to know me better, with some of them becoming my friends. As a result, I was able to have formal interviews with 20 of them about the state of current English education and their concerns about classroom English teaching. All these data served as a supplementary source that helped me to better understand Huiwen's growth as an English teacher and a teaching researcher with the implementation of a series of English education policies in China, which will be presented in the following section.

Brief Review of English Educational Policies in China after 1949

To better comprehend Huiwen's experience, first I briefly review English educational policies in China after 1949. China's interaction with the western world started about two thousand years ago with the Silk Road trade (Fu, 1986). However, the learning of foreign languages as part of a national agenda is much more recent, beginning in the mid-1800s after China lost the First Opium War in 1842. From then on, the learning of foreign languages has been motivated by the desire for China to acquire western modern technology to withstand foreign aggression and to establish itself as a modern nation with economic, scientific and military might (Lam, 2005).

The establishment of the People's Republic of China (PRC) in 1949 brought immense changes in English language education. From 1950 to 1977, the English language curriculum reflected the moods of the socio-political situations in China (Liu, 2015a). Because of the close relationship with the former Soviet Union, Russian gradually became the most popular foreign language in the late 1950s. To meet the increasing demand for Russian-language education, some English teachers were given minimal training and quickly transferred from teaching English to teaching Russian. In the 1960s, with a declining relationship between China and the former Soviet Union, the focus of foreign language education began to shift from Russian to English. Many full-time secondary schools switched to offering English as a foreign language instead of Russian, and, as a result, Russian teachers were transferred to English teaching. However, English-language education came to a halt during the Cultural Revolution. These changes resulted in tremendous problems with teachers' English competence and in poor outcomes of English language education over the next few decades (Liu, 2008).

English began to thrive again in the early 1970s, especially after mainland China re-entered the United Nations and resumed diplomatic relations with the United States (Lam, 2005; Liu, 2008). From 1972 to 1975, foreign languages such as English, Japanese, Russian, French, German and Arabic started to be offered in schools all over China as long as teachers could be found. However, English education during this period was quite disorganized and inconsistent (Liu, 2015a). It was the announcement of the Four Modernizations Policy (to modernize agriculture, industry, science and technology, and national defense) by Deng Xiaoping in 1978, which soon evolved into the Reform and Opening-Up Policy (Dillon, 1998; Lam, 2005), that made the State quickly realize the crucial importance of foreign language education. English and other foreign languages were considered as important tools to learn from the West and to ensure the integration of China into the international scene while protecting the Chinese nation from possibly threatening cultural influences from the West (Li, 2004). As a consequence, foreign languages, especially English, brought more educational, occupational and economic advantages to individuals.

In 1978 and 1982, the State Education Commission (SEC), which was later called the Ministry of Education (MOE), organized two national conferences on foreign language education in schools, and afterwards issued reports calling for a greater focus on foreign language education. The reports reiterated the importance of foreign languages to China's development. The reports also stated that foreign language should be regarded as a compulsory subject in schools. They also addressed several principles for teacher training, compilation of materials, and experimenting with teaching methods. These conferences were crucial. They increased the confidence of teachers and researchers in overcoming difficulties they encountered in the process of promoting foreign language education (Liu, 2015a). English then became a compulsory course in many secondary schools, as long as the schools could find teachers.

With the growing popularity of English, the SEC then introduced key educational policies and actions to guide English language teaching (ELT) (CTMRI, 2001). Among them, two actions have been particularly important in China's foreign language education history: (1) the implementation of English syllabi from the late 1970s to the 1990s; and (2) the implementation of English Curriculum Standards (ECS) in the 2000s (Cheng & Xie, 2015). The SEC recognized that there were problems in the quality and quantity of existing secondary school English teachers. The primary goal was to improve the quality of teachers, at least in the key secondary schools.[1] Then, the national English syllabus was drafted in 1978 and underwent several revisions from then until the late 1990s to meet students' needs and abilities. In particular, in 1988, the *English Syllabus for Full-time Junior High Schools in the Nine-Year Compulsory Education* (initially approved edition) was designed, and in 1993 the *English Syllabus for Full-time Senior High Schools* (initially approved edition) was written to connect with the junior high school syllabus. The English syllabus included new concepts: (1) the communicative approach highlighting English for communication; and (2) the introduction of a list of 'Functional and Notional Items', later entitled 'Daily Expressions for Communication'. These syllabi brought great changes to English language teaching in China; they underwent more than one revision and continued to be used until 2000 (Liu, 2015a). All the syllabi stated that foreign languages were an important tool for acquiring and assimilating information from all parts of the world, as well as for communicating with foreign countries. With the implementation of the syllabi, the role of the English language in school education was identified and clarified.

From the early 1980s to the 1990s, an emphasis was gradually placed on the practical use of English. The curriculum designers put forward several key principles to guide teachers, encouraging them to give students adequate practice so that they were able to use English instead of simply memorizing language rules. For example, teachers were directed to:

> explain the basic language knowledge concisely and train the
> students' ability to communicate with people; train the four skills
> comprehensively with particular emphasis on one or two (namely,
> emphasis on listening and speaking at the beginning, and on
> reading comprehension at a later stage); use English if possible,
> and use Chinese when necessary [when conducting the class].
> (CTMRI, 2001, pp. 210-211)

However, the quality of English language teaching was hampered by the influence of the long-prevalent grammar-oriented and behaviorist audiolingual teaching methods, a shortage of qualified teachers and teaching resources, and written examinations that focused on grammatical knowledge. The problems of teaching quality in English and other subjects brought a comprehensive campaign for reform in basic education near the end of the twentieth century, which was initiated by the MOE. The goal was to improve the character of Chinese citizens and promote their physical and mental development, with an emphasis on fostering creativity, the ability to apply learning in real-life situations, and the capacity for lifelong learning.

The term 'syllabus' was replaced by 'curriculum standards', indicating that the students were expected not merely to reach academic requirements in each subject but also to acquire proper attitudes and values, along with knowledge and skills (Chen et al, 2002). The English Curriculum Standards (ECS) for Full-time Compulsory Education and for Senior High Schools were released in 2001. In 2011, the revised version of the English Curriculum Standards for Compulsory Education was published after a long process of gathering opinions and suggestions. Currently, the English Curriculum Standards for Senior High Schools is in a process of revision.

English became a compulsory subject in urban primary schools from grade three (age 8) onwards, though in some larger cities it was offered as early as grade one (age 6) (Cheng, 2011). The objectives of the ECS were not limited to developing language knowledge and skills but also included learning strategies, cross-cultural awareness, and effective attitudes. The five objectives work together to cultivate students' comprehensive language competence. The application of the five objectives was realized through nine levels: five in the ECS for compulsory education, and four for senior secondary education. Schools were also encouraged to offer elective courses for students at the eighth and ninth levels, if students wished to continue their English studies after they reach the seventh level. These actions initiated by the MOE triggered enormous changes in teaching materials, methods, assessment and management over this past decade (Liu, 2015a).

In sum, curriculum innovations related to English language teaching in China have reflected wider political and economic policies for China's modernization (Hu, 2005; Feng, 2007; Wang, 2007; Perez-Milans, 2013). The Chinese have gradually shifted their view of English from being a necessary tool for knowledge acquisition in the late 1970s and 1980s, to being a resource for international communication in the 1990s and a means of gaining intercultural competence in the 2000s. Consistent with the changing view of English language teaching, the pedagogical approach to English learning also transferred from audiolingual and grammar translation methods (Wang, 2007) to communicative language teaching methods (Ministry of Education, 1993) to the cultural adaptation of international teaching methodologies to the Chinese educational context (Ministry of Education, 2000, 2001). The actual impact of English curriculum innovations on teachers of English will be further examined in the context of Huiwen's career trajectory.

Huiwen's Development as an English Teacher and Teaching Researcher

Huiwen's growth as an English teacher and later as a teaching researcher reflected the changes in English educational policies in China after the late 1970s. Interestingly, close examination of the interview and observation data indicates that Huiwen was primarily influenced by her personal goals of pursuing a high academic credential and making her English classes effective rather than by educational policies. In fact, she rarely read any of the English educational policies, including the English Syllabus and the English Curriculum Standards, before she became a teaching researcher. Her knowledge of those English educational policies mainly came from what she heard from her colleagues during class breaks and group lesson planning meetings. In Huiwen's view, teachers tend to have their own understanding of what and how to teach based on the examinations that their students must take. In this sense, English educational policies may create social pressure or influence teachers' beliefs and practices in English teaching, but they may not have a decisive role regarding teaching quality in actual classroom teaching. This section presents Huiwen's development first as a preservice English teacher, then as an English teacher, and finally as a teaching researcher, situated in the broader social milieu of English curriculum innovations in China.

Becoming a Preservice Teacher of English

Huiwen attended a foreign language school immediately upon her graduation from junior high school in January 1977 on the condition that she would become an English teacher in a school after her three years of study. She worried that she would have to go to the countryside to do farm work after senior high school as universities were closed to the public at that time. This was early 1977 when everything was still chaotic as it was the latter part of the Cultural Revolution. As discussed earlier, China was gradually opening its doors to the world at that time but there was an extreme shortage of teachers of foreign languages. To meet the needs of the Open Door Policy, the foreign language school administered by the Beijing municipal government recruited top students from junior high schools as preservice teachers. Huiwen became one of those preservice teachers and, hence, avoided the fate of going to the countryside during the Cultural Revolution.

However, a half year later, in the summer of 1977, the university matriculation examination in mainland China was resumed after being interrupted for a decade by the Cultural Revolution. Huiwen and her classmates at this foreign language school fought hard for the right to take the university matriculation examination in three years' time. Their efforts failed because they had signed the agreement when they were accepted by the foreign language school. The main reason for their unsuccessful appeal was that Beijing was extremely short of English language teachers at that time. After three years of study at the foreign language school, in 1980 Huiwen became an English teacher at a key high school in Beijing offering a high school diploma.

Because of the shortage of English teachers in 1980s, Huiwen missed all the opportunities to continue her university studies. She could not find any replacement teacher as required by her principal. However, Huiwen did not give up her desire to achieve her academic credential. She registered in a self-study program and managed to pass all the required examinations within three years. In 1985, she obtained her two-year college diploma. As a large number of teachers did not have academic credentials in the 1980s, continuing education programs were encouraged from the late 1980s onward to help improve the qualification of teachers. Huiwen then acquired her bachelor's degree in 1995 after her three years of studies at a continuing education program for in-service teachers offered by Beijing Education

Institute. Through this long and complex journey of pursuing her university education, Huiwen eventually fulfilled her goal of having a bachelor's degree.

Becoming a Teacher of English

Huiwen experienced tremendous difficulties in her first year of teaching. She had no idea how to teach English to high school students, as she had not received any pedagogical training regarding language teaching at the foreign language school. Although she was accepted as a preservice teacher of English, the faculty in the foreign language school had excellent English literacy abilities but little experience with preservice teacher education, because the school trained Chinese diplomats before the Cultural Revolution. The courses she took were all about improving her English competence. At that time, the audiolingual method was popular. In class, she had a lot of opportunities to practice English, especially in the domains of speaking and listening. She was also exposed to a remarkable amount of reading and listening inside and outside of class. However, she did not take any courses relating to teaching methodology and pedagogy, or student psychology. She also did not have a teaching practicum experience prior to becoming a teacher. In other words, she was an English major, not a teacher of English. Her ability to hold students' attention in class came from her English competence. With the systematic English learning at the foreign language school, Huiwen learned to speak English fluently and accurately with a standard British accent, which helped her gain students' respect and trust. In other words, Huiwen had sound subject-matter knowledge, an important criterion to be a qualified English teacher.

As a teacher of English with little training in teaching methodology, Huiwen basically followed her intuition drawn from her own language learning experience. At that time, traditional methodologies such as the audiolingual and grammar translation methods were dominant in English language teaching (Wang, 2007). Listening and speaking were the primary focus in language teaching, supported by the teaching of reading and writing. Huiwen and her colleagues believed that language was acquired through a process of habit formation and repetitive pattern drilling. In her classroom teaching, Huiwen exposed her students to pattern drilling practice in order to help them memorize structural patterns. In the interview, Huiwen said, '[E]ven now I still think pattern drills are useful in language learning. Patterns drills will make students get familiar with vocabularies and structures. This familiarity is the foundation of acquiring a language.' Although she did not know any theories such as situational language learning, she noticed that students tended to lose interest in mechanical pattern drilling after a period of time. To engage students, Huiwen tried her best to relate pattern drills to students' lives. As she said, '[U]sing current popular terms, I tried to create a context for my students to practice pattern drills at that time.'

Gradually, Huiwen found that it was not enough to only do pattern drills. Although she spoke English well, she hardly knew how to explain the grammar rules concerning those language patterns, because she had not learned grammar in her studies at the foreign language school. Her brain went blank whenever her students asked her about grammar rules. After a couple of incidents of being unable to respond to students' questions on grammar, Huiwen started to feel she was in a state of crisis. She realized that her students would doubt her credentials as an English teacher if she did not know how to explain grammar. Therefore, Huiwen turned to one of her experienced colleagues, John (a pseudonym), for help. John, in his mid-40s at that time, had graduated from a normal college and was well trained in teaching methodology. He was especially good at explaining grammar and was popular among the students, though his English pronunciation was full of his dialect accent. Students usually had more questions to ask when they were in the third year (final year) of senior high school. Thus she observed John's teaching in the third year of senior high school for a whole academic year. By observing John's teaching, Huiwen gradually learned how to teach grammar. While observing John's teaching, she often asked herself how she could make John's methods part of her approach and create her own style of teaching grammar. She kept searching and practicing various methods of teaching grammar, stimulated by John's teaching methods. Whenever she encountered problems in her teaching, Huiwen would seek John's advice. After about a year of practice, Huiwen gained expertise in teaching grammar.

With the introduction of a series of English Syllabus for High Schools in the 1980s and 1990s, Huiwen became exposed to a number of new concepts regarding English language teaching, such as the communicative approach, task-based language teaching, and notional-functional syllabus, through talking to her colleagues and attending group lesson planning sessions organized by the school district. Huiwen noticed the changes in English textbooks she was required to use for English teaching. In general, along with English curriculum innovations, English textbooks were undergoing a series of revisions and rewriting. English textbooks in the 1980s were designed according to the structural approach, the audiolingual method and the grammar-translation method. However, English textbooks in the 1990s were designed according to the structural-functional approach and the eclectic approach; and English textbooks from 2001 to the present were designed according to the structural-functional approach, task-based language teaching principles and the eclectic approach (Liu, 2015b). To Huiwen, the obvious change in the revised textbooks was that dialogues replaced pattern drills at the beginning of each unit, followed by listening and speaking activities and then reading passages. With the use of revised textbooks and various kinds of training given by the school district, Huiwen and her colleagues became gradually exposed to communicative language teaching methods, which focused on authentic language and communication opportunities. Huiwen, in turn, paid more attention to students and tried to create authentic or simulated contexts for students to practice English instead of drilling and memorizing decontextualized vocabulary and structure.

Huiwen said that she made gradual changes to her teaching methods through her teaching practice and by observing her colleagues' teaching rather than by studying the English syllabus. These changes mainly happened subconsciously and incidentally, depending on her intuitive understanding of effective language teaching. For example, where grammar teaching was concerned, she used to lecture grammar rules first and then let students practice these grammar rules through drilling exercises, usually ignoring the situational context for the use of grammar rules. With her increasing understanding of communicative language teaching methods, Huiwen realized the importance of providing situational contexts in grammar teaching and the need to allow students to explore the language phenomenon and figure out the grammar rules. Once students understood the grammar rules, Huiwen prepared three types of exercise: first controlled exercise; then semi-controlled exercise, and finally open exercise. She decreased her guidance and support according to students' grasp of the grammar rules demonstrated in the exercises. Recalling her methods of teaching grammar, Huiwen said:

> I gradually paid more attention to the needs of students and tried my best to activate students' prior knowledge and cognition, giving students opportunities to observe and experience the use of vocabularies and structures and then learn to use them through controlled, semi-controlled and fully open situational contexts.

In short, Huiwen was committed to improving the quality of her teaching. She created careful lesson plans and always reflected on the strengths and weaknesses of each of her lessons in order to figure out more effective ways to help students learn English well. Through her efforts, her students performed well in all kinds of examinations. As a result, she became a leading teacher in her school after 14 years of teaching. After that, she was awarded the title of outstanding teacher by the Beijing Municipal Education Committee after 22 years of teaching. Yet, Huiwen was never satisfied with her achievement and continued to seek challenges in her career. Consequently, she became a teaching researcher in her local school district.

Becoming a Teaching Researcher

After 22 years of teaching in the same school, Huiwen desired a change in her professional life. She was given the opportunity to become a teaching researcher at her district's teacher training school in 2002. As a teaching researcher, her main responsibility was to support the development of English teachers in her school district. Her focus then shifted from enhancing her own teaching quality to developing the quality of English language teachers in the whole school district. Each semester Huiwen needed to observe 40-50 lessons taught by the teachers of English in her school district.

She also needed to organize group lesson planning meetings every two weeks and to attend at least two public lesson study events. Finally, she was required to design monthly quizzes, mid-term tests and term examinations.

As a teaching researcher, Huiwen started to carefully study English educational policies, especially the English Curriculum Standards issued in the 2000s. She needed to rely on these documents to verbalize her previous unconscious or subconscious understanding of effective language teaching explicitly when commenting on classroom teaching activities of the English teachers in her school district. From her own experience, Huiwen knew that few teachers indeed read through English curriculum documents, let alone use them as guiding principles for their daily classroom teaching. This is because many teachers organize their teaching foci according to examination syllabi or their understanding of major knowledge areas covered in the university matriculation examination. It was one of Huiwen's responsibilities to disseminate the principles promoted in the English curriculum documents through the activities she organized for the teachers.

As she regularly visited classrooms as a teaching researcher, Huiwen learned more about the realities of teacher qualifications and the teaching quality of the English teachers in her school district. She noticed the negative consequences resulting from the hasty enforcement [2] of the ECS in Beijing. In fact, many teachers were not ready to implement the principles promoted by the ECS in their classroom teaching, though many teachers were familiar with a number of transformational concepts through intensive training. For example, teachers could talk about the concepts of a whole-to-part style of class presentation and the importance of arousing students' interest. That is, teachers clearly knew they were expected to draw students' attention to the comprehension of a text first and encourage students to guess the meaning of unknown words from the context if possible before getting into the study of structures and vocabulary in detail. The teachers were also aware that they should engage students in classroom teaching by adopting more pair and group activities, relating new knowledge to students' prior knowledge and encouraging them to raise questions. These English teachers understood that English teaching should enable students to eventually develop comprehensive language competence and overall development rather than simply getting high scores in examinations, as stated in the ECS. To achieve these objectives, teachers were encouraged to employ the principles of experiential learning, discovery learning and task-based language teaching (TBLT) in teaching while taking part in various teacher training sessions on understanding and implementing the ECS.

However, based on Huiwen's and my observations, many teachers experienced difficulties in implementing these new ideas and methods in their classroom teaching. The first obstacle was the large class size (at least 40 students each class), which impeded teachers from carrying out more interactive activities such as pair and group work and/or giving students more opportunities to raise questions in class. Second, the innovative teaching principles such as TBLT placed higher demands on teachers in both teaching and professional development (Hu, 2002). However, teachers often faced the dilemma of choosing between spending more time having students work out a grammar rule and asking students to do more exercises related to the university matriculation examination with more explicit explanations of grammar rules. In other words, the existing examination system still focuses more on assessing students' mastery of language knowledge rather than on language use, which constrains many teachers to varying degrees from following innovative teaching principles (e.g. experiential learning and TBLT) and from going beyond preparing students for the university matriculation examinations. Additionally, influenced by the examination system, many students became practical about their English learning as well, expecting their teachers mainly to prepare them for examinations. Third, teachers differ greatly in their English language competence and their understanding of the essence of the ECS. For example, in terms of teaching reading, the English Curriculum Standards encourage teachers to shift their focus from language studies to nurturing students' reading ability, such as retrieving and abstracting information and reading critically. However, in the classes I observed with Huiwen, the teachers approached teaching formulaically by engaging in pre-reading, while-reading and post-reading activities. In the pre-reading stage, teachers usually used some pictures, songs or questions to arouse students' interest in the topic for reading. In the while-reading stage, teachers asked students to do fast reading first to apprehend the main ideas of the text within 2 to 4 minutes, and then to read the text a second time to provide the missing information in the table designed by the teachers, and finally checked their answers with the class. In the post-reading stage, teachers felt that students were ready to have 'output' through previous 'input' activities. Thus, they tended to design some writing or speaking tasks and give students about 5 to 10 minutes to prepare. All the activities were quick. These appeared to be 'performance' or 'show' classes as the students did not have sufficient time to digest the reading text and had little opportunity to study the language use in context. Huiwen and I agreed that the ECS enforcement movement had made some teachers develop this routinized teaching style because they did not grasp the core ideas of the ECS. As a teaching researcher, Huiwen tried her best to help teachers teach English following the methods of language learning and the principles of the ECS through public lesson studies. However, Huiwen pointed out that some teachers could make great progress in the improvement of teaching quality through preparing and giving public lessons, but other teachers made little improvement in teaching after giving public lessons. Huiwen attributed this difference to the teacher's own English language competence and education background. Having spent more than 13 years as a teaching researcher, Huiwen found it difficult to change a teacher's belief and practice in language teaching unless the teacher was an excellent language learner and had advanced English language competence. Recalling her own experience of learning to teach English, Huiwen said, 'I benefited a lot from my experience of learning English at the foreign language school because I gained a solid foundation of English language and could draw on my language learning experience in my teaching.'

Conclusion

This chapter has reviewed the development of Chinese education policy, especially English curriculum innovations, over the past 30 years, and its impact on the trajectory of one experienced teacher, Huiwen, who taught English as a foreign language in a senior high school, and who later became a teaching researcher in her school district. Huiwen's experience illustrates that political and social changes have great impact on an individual's choice of career and professional development at the macro level. In the late Cultural Revolution, Huiwen attended a foreign language school, lost the opportunity to go to university, and had to become a teacher of English in a high school. Given the shortage of English language teachers, Huiwen could not leave her teaching position to study as a full-time university student. To pursue her academic credential, Huiwen became involved in a continuing education program that was available to her in the 1980s and 1990s. Along with learning about English curriculum innovations since 1978, Huiwen learned to teach English well and later became an outstanding teacher through self-reflection, observing her colleague's teaching practice, and following up the new ideas promoted in English curriculum innovations. Unsatisfied with only being an excellent English teacher, Huiwen took up the challenging position of being a teaching researcher, shouldering the responsibility of supervising the quality of English teaching and supporting the professional development of other English teachers in her school district. Huiwen's story indicates that social and political contexts do affect the development of English curriculum innovations, but that teachers themselves play a more pivotal role in the implementation of English curriculum innovations in their language teaching as well as in their own professional development.

The negative consequence of hasty enforcement of the ECS suggests that implementation of any educational policies needs to give teachers sufficient time to digest the essence of the policies. Due to the variability in English language competence and educational background among the teachers, it is better to develop training activities according to the needs of the teachers. For example, some sessions could be more theoretical, emphasizing the rationale behind educational policies, and some could be more practical, focusing on how to implement educational policies in classroom teaching through a variety of hands-on activities.

The good intentions of English curriculum innovations cannot be realized unless there are English teachers who can understand and apply the essence of curriculum innovations in their daily classroom teaching. Ultimately, it is teachers who make all the decisions about the topics to be covered, the forms of interaction, activities and other teaching routines. To decipher the influence of any educational policy, we need to approach teachers and to study what is happening in their classrooms where English language learning is concerned.

Acknowledgements

Support for this research is gratefully acknowledged from the Humanities and Social Science Research Base Project 'Examining the Status Quo of School EFL Teacher Researchers in China' (13JJD740006) sponsored by the Ministry of Education of China, and Program for New Century Excellent Talents in University (NCET-12-0792) sponsored by the Ministry of Education of China to the author.

Notes

[1] In the early 1980s, the concept of 'key schools' came into being. In keeping with Deng Xiaoping's idea to 'let a number of people become [economically] well off first', the government decided to turn better-equipped schools into 'key schools' with the intention of using them as educational models for others to follow (Liu, 2015a).

[2] Beijing spent two years (2007 and 2008) giving English teachers of senior high school intensive training on applying the ECS in classroom teaching during the summer holidays and winter vacations.

References

Chen, L., Wang, Q. & Cheng, X. (Eds.) (2002) Interpretation of the English Curriculum Standards for Nine-year Compulsory Education and Senior High Schools. Experimental draft, in Chinese. Beijing: Beijing Normal University.

Cheng, X. (2011) The 'English Curriculum Standards' in China: rationales and issues, in A.W. Feng (Ed.) *English Language Education across Greater China*, pp. 133-150. Bristol: Multilingual Matters.

Cheng, X. & Xie, M. (2015) Research on English Language Teaching in China, in D. Liu & W. Zhao (Eds) *English Language Education in China: past and present*, pp. 315-334. Beijing: People's Education Press.

Curriculum and Teaching Materials Research Institute (CTMRI) (Ed.) (2001) *A Collection of Primary and Secondary School Syllabi and Curriculum Standards in China in the Twentieth Century: foreign language session (English)*. In Chinese. Beijing: People's Education Press.

Dillon, M. (Ed.) (1998) *China: a cultural and historical dictionary*. Richmond: Curzon Press.

Feng, A. (2007) *Bilingual Education in China: practices, policies and concepts*. Clevedon: Multilingual Matters.

Fu, K. (1986) *A History of Foreign Language Teaching in China*. In Chinese. Shanghai: Shanghai Foreign Language Education Press.

Hu, G. (2002) Recent Important Developments in Secondary English-language Teaching in the People's Republic of China, *Language, Culture and Curriculum*, 15(1), 30-49. http://dx.doi.org/10.1080/07908310208666631

Hu, G. (2005) English Language Education in China: policies, progress and problems, *Language Policy*, 4, 5-24. http://dx.doi.org/10.1007/s10993-004-6561-7

Lam, A.S.L. (2005) *Language Education in China: policy and experience from 1949*. Hong Kong: Hong Kong University Press. http://dx.doi.org/10.5790/hongkong/9789622097506.001.0001

Li, L. (2004) *Education for 1.3 Billion: former Chinese vice-premier Li Lanqing on 10 years of education reform and development*. Beijing: Foreign Education and Research Press, Pearson Education.

Liu, D. (Ed.) (2008) Report on the Development of Basic Foreign Language Education (1978-2008). In Chinese. Shanghai: Shanghai Foreign Language Education Press.

Liu, D. (2015a) English Curriculum Development for Schools in China: tradition, reform, and innovation, in D. Liu & W. Zhao (Eds) *English Language Education in China: Past and present*, pp. 62-116. Beijing: People's Education Press.

Liu, D. (2015b) Development of English Teaching Materials and Other Resources: adaptation, integration, and innovation, in D. Liu & W. Zhao (Eds) *English Language Education in China: past and present*, pp. 117-176. Beijing: People's Education Press.

Ministry of Education (1993) *English Syllabus for Full-time Senior High Schools*, initially approved edn. Beijing: People's Education Press.

Ministry of Education (2000) *English Syllabus for Full-time Senior High Schools*, trial edn rev. Beijing: People's Education Press.

Ministry of Education (2001) Action Plan for Vitalizing Education in the Twenty-first Century, *Chinese Education and Society*, 34(49), 18-28.

Perez-Milans, M. (2013) *Urban Schools and English Language Education in Late Modern China: a critical sociolinguistic ethnography*. New York: Routledge.

Wang, Q. (2007) The National Curriculum Changes and their Effects on English Language Teaching in the People's Republic of China, in J. Cummins & C. Davison (Eds) *International Handbook on English Language Teaching*, pp. 87-105. New York: Springer.

Yang, L. (2016) Doctoring Myself: observation, interaction, and action, in K. McIntosh, C. Pelaez-Morales & T. Silva (Eds) *Graduate Studies in Second Language Writing*, pp. 71-92. Anderson, SC: Parlor Press.

CHAPTER 7

In Times of a Changing Linguistic Context: the career trajectory of an EFL teacher in Iceland

HAFDÍS INGVARSDÓTTIR

SUMMARY English has been taught as a foreign language in Iceland for over a century, along with Danish, French and German. Paradoxically, in the 2011 National Curriculum, English is still defined as a foreign language, but it is also given the status as one of the three core subjects, along with Icelandic and mathematics. Recent research, however, has found growing evidence that a new linguistic context is developing in Iceland where English seems to be neither a first nor a second language but seems to exist on a continuum between the two, a phenomenon that may be due to high English-language exposure through media and pop culture. Simultaneously, the role of English in the workforce and not least in higher education has increased at an unprecedented speed The question therefore arises: How do English teachers experience this change? How do they feel that their role has changed over time and in what way? How has their education prepared them for this development? In this chapter the author follows the career trajectory of an experienced secondary school teacher of English through her pedagogical narratives, from the grammar translation approach in a foreign language situation, to the present-day situation in which she is expected to ensure that her students reach the advanced near-native proficiency level of an educated user in all areas of the language.

This chapter is divided into five sections. The first gives a short overview of the Icelandic upper-secondary school. The second reports a paradigm shift in the theoretical discourse on the teaching of English along with recent studies on the teaching of English in upper-secondary schools in Iceland. The third describes the methodology used to elicit the stories on which this study is based. Section four portrays the stories, and the final section presents the conclusion and discusses what the stories reveal, followed by some concluding words.

The Icelandic Secondary School

The Icelandic upper-secondary school has been defined as a four-year school and ends with a matriculation examination which serves as an entrance qualification to university. The students enter at sixteen years of age after ten years in elementary school, *grunnskóli* (the last three years being the equivalent of lower secondary). Although the school has been organised as a four-year school, it is possible, within a modular system, to finish earlier or later. Secondary schools differ in their structure and objectives. Each school is independent to some extent and can offer different emphases and programmes, although all are bound by the *Aðalnámskrá* (National Curriculum Guide). Although one school might emphasise arts, another health studies and the third business studies, or simply academic subjects, all have a minimum common core in three academic subjects: Icelandic, English and mathematics. There are no standardised tests, and there never have been.

New radical curriculum guidelines were published in 2011. Upper-secondary schools were given three years to adapt to the new curriculum and are from now defined as three-year schools. They are thus in a transition from adhering to a rather conventional top-down curriculum to a new curriculum characterised by major changes in work procedure as well as ideology, changes which affect all subjects. Six fundamental pillars are presented in the 2011 Curriculum Guidelines, which form the essence of the educational policy: literacy, sustainability, health and welfare, democracy and human rights, equality, and creativity (National Curriculum Guide, 2011). Schools are given the freedom and power to design their own individual curriculum based on these guidelines. This new curriculum gives teachers an unusual freedom to choose curriculum material, evaluation methods and teaching practices.

New Challenges for EFL Teachers in Secondary Schools

Multifaceted research on language acquisition in the latter half of the twentieth century called for a paradigm shift in language pedagogy. This shift, which is from a teacher-focused to a student-focused approach, has made new demands on both teachers and learners as both have to take on new roles. Instead of being a provider of knowledge, the teacher becomes a facilitator of learning. These ideas call for radical changes in teaching approaches and a move away from the traditional teacher-centred classroom, with its emphasis on grammar rules, translations and demonstrative knowledge about the language, to approaches introducing learner autonomy and a more holistic view of language (Hinkel, 2005; Ingvarsdóttir, 2005,

2011; Little, 2007). One could say that the shift is from product-oriented teaching to process-oriented learning, and to connecting the learner to the real world beyond the classroom (Little, 2007).

Research on the teaching of English in upper-secondary schools in Iceland indicates that this changed emphasis in instruction and in the choice of the curriculum has not yet reached the classroom to any extent (Ingvarsdóttir, 2011). The emphasis is still mainly on the receptive skills, primarily reading and vocabulary (Ingvarsdóttir, 2011). The findings suggest that there is a heavy dependence on textbooks written for a market where English is clearly a foreign language (i.e. EFL), which may not suit the needs of Icelandic students. The tradition has been that, as upper-secondary school students reach higher-level English courses, the generic textbook is abandoned and replaced by literary texts (i.e. novels, short stories or plays), and literary assignments become the basis of evaluation.

Studies in Iceland and other Nordic countries have found that students overestimate their reading proficiency in English with respect to what is required of them in higher education (Hellekjær, 2010; Pilkinton-Pihko, 2010; Jeeves, 2014). Furthermore, the required hours for English taught in upper-secondary schools have been reduced greatly in the *Aðalnámskrá* (National Curriculum Guide) of 2011. The reduction is justified by changes in the National Curriculum for compulsory schools, where English now starts in grade four instead of grade six. Here there seems to be a disregard of the fact that the language skills required for university studies cannot be acquired simply by starting earlier. For students to be ready to read and work with language at tertiary level they need to have reached sufficient cognitive maturity to process to a high level of literacy texts needed for that level (Arnbjörnsdóttir & Ingvarsdóttir, 2014). However, it seems to be taken for granted that the Icelandic *stúdentspróf* (matriculation exam), with only three semesters of English at upper-secondary level and an emphasis on reading mainly literary texts, is sufficient to provide Icelandic students with reading proficiency which enables them to understand academic texts in any field. This is one of the challenges that English teachers face in Iceland today.

In this section the context in which the stories took place has been presented. In the next section we shall learn how the stories were elicited.

Rivers of Life

Diamond (1992), drawing on Kelly (1969), talked about using career trajectories to sketch teachers' own professional progress. He suggested that teachers could explore the changing meaning of their individual life courses by dividing their time-lines chronologically from birth to the present into what they consider meaningful periods or stages in their life. Yaxley (1991) argued that teachers were constructing their own life story from what to them were the most influential incidents or events. Teachers could be asked to attend to what they saw as the nuclei that opened up or closed off possibilities, and even the basic or recurring themes of their sequence of transitions. When did they first decide to become teachers? What lies ahead? What are crucial events or life-turning points? Is the transformation abrupt or gradual? These crucial events have also been called critical incidents – that is, key events in individuals' lives, around which pivotal decisions revolve (Kelchtermans, 1993). Kelly also referred to those significant moments: 'The constructions of many experiences in an autobiographical account give such incidents their semiotic place in the chain of events or life contours that follow' (Kelly, 1969, p. 165). In accordance with this school of thought, I chose to use the 'river technique', also referred to as career rivers or rivers of life (or even snakes), when collecting career stories from teachers. This technique, in the constructivist tradition, was developed by Pope and Denicolo (2001). The river technique is a drawing technique to explore the influence of the past on the present.

> The essence of the rationale for these drew on our recognition that constructs evolve over time and are particularly influenced, consciously or unconsciously, by formative experiences. Only by understanding these constructs by reflecting on their origins can the opportunity be provided for contemplating alternatives and breaking free from biography. (Pope & Denicolo, 2001, p. 112)

When using the river technique, the teachers are asked to think back on their life experience and elicit particular incidents and experiences which might have influenced their career path. Participants are given time to reflect in private, where they draw up their lives as a bending river in which each bend represents a change in direction of, or intention for, their career (Ingvarsdóttir, 2005, 2014). For each twist, they are then asked to write brief annotations about the incident which led to the change. The rivers are then analysed for themes and followed up with in-depth interviews about the significance of those themes as formative experiences, as well as about the storyteller's personal style as practitioner. One of the benefits of using the river technique is that the subsequent interview/story becomes more of a personal interrogation; a storied account, by the teacher. During the interview the teacher gives reasons for choosing these particular incidents and the consequences they had for her career; this thus requires the bare minimum of intervention on behalf of the researcher (Ingvarsdóttir, 2014).

My reason for choosing this particular approach was to provide a way of capturing the teacher's voice almost without interference. I was thus adhering to the inside-out approach (Hunt, 1987), emphasising Kelly's idea that the teacher was the expert who was telling her stories as she chose to tell them (Kelly, 1969). The river technique automatically allows for the distribution of roles, giving the teacher the roles of playwright, actor and instructor, whereas the researcher takes the part of the attentive audience and interpreter, the significant other. The teacher selects and draws up the highlights of her story in private, and is then given the opportunity to elaborate on it without being interrupted or, even more importantly, guided into talking about issues which might be of interest to the researcher but might not be relevant in the particular story being told. Through this technique the storyteller is given, as Elbaz (1990) put it, 'power to define her own reality'.

The career trajectories which are presented here are based on two sets of data. The first set was collected when the teacher, Birna (pseudonym), had been teaching for twelve years, and the second set of data was collected fifteen years later, where she discusses the changes which have been happening in the time which has elapsed since the first story. After drawing up the river of life for the first interview, the rivers were analysed, resulting in six themes on which the subsequent story was based. Prior to the latter interview Birna was invited to take a look at her river again to explore if there were not occurrences she would like to add.

Birna's Stories

We will now follow Birna's career trajectory as she conveys her teaching stories. The story section is divided into two parts: the former narrates the story of the development of the younger teacher, and the latter tells the story of the mature teacher who reflects on her teaching over the years and on her experience of the changes in the linguistic context in Iceland and the recent curriculum developments.

Discovering the teacher is the first part of Birna's story. As we will hear from her story, Birna never imagined becoming a teacher when she was a child or adolescent. After finishing a BA degree in English language and literature, she started out as a teacher in a lower-secondary school (13-16) but has for many years been teaching in an upper-secondary school in the capital, Reykjavík. This school is considered progressive and attracts good students. In our first meeting I explained the idea behind the river, gave her the instructions and asked her to draw her own river. After a couple of days she sent me the river. Analysing her river resulted in the following themes:

- Carefree youth
- Outsider
- Transformation
- Becoming a professional
- A new challenge
- Contentment

Birna was now ready to begin her story. She was born in the capital and has always lived in that area. She has only one younger brother. As a child she was doted upon, received a lot of attention, and was used to having her own way: she had a very *carefree youth*. When one of her classmates from school decides to go to teachers' college after tenth grade, Birna remembers thinking she would definitely never become a teacher. Instead, she goes to grammar school where she finds out that she loves languages but hates mathematics.

French is her favourite subject but she also likes English, at which she excels. After graduating from upper-secondary school she considers becoming an English teacher in a primary school. All her family as well as her boyfriend advise her not to do so, saying that she was not teacher material, too impatient and too hot-tempered. An elderly aunt says that she would kill the poor children with her temper. Before deciding what to do, she discovers that she is expecting a child and gives up any idea of going to university. She is terribly unhappy about this. 'Women's lib was at its height, this was 1975 [1] so you can just imagine how I felt.' She works part time in an office but after having her second child she becomes a full-time housewife. Throughout this time she feels frustrated about not going to university like her friends and as the 1980s approach this grows worse – she feels like *an outsider*.

> We [young women] were all supposed to be so strong and big,
> educated and good mothers and everything. This was about the
> time when Vigdís [2] was elected as president ... I felt such a loser.

When the younger of her two children start kindergarten she finally decides to take up university studies and enrols in English: 'because I wanted to be sure that I chose something I could handle because I have always been so afraid of not being able to cope'. She immediately likes the course very much and says: 'by going to university my life was completely transformed'. This is the *transformation* bend in her river. She feels that her self-identity takes on another form, meeting a challenge like this. One of the lecturers predicts that all his students are going to become teachers, but she remembers thinking that she would definitely not do so.

After completing a BA degree she begins working in the family business but does not like it and tries, unsuccessfully, to get work as translator. A friend suggests that she should take a teaching diploma and after thinking hard and long she thinks that perhaps this is something for her after all. She has nothing to lose; although she is unemployed, she is financially secure. 'So I just started and it was such fun. It was in a way another transformation.' She learns a variety of methods and a whole new way of teaching languages, which she instantly likes. She much prefers the ideas of the communicative approach to the grammar translation methods she knew from her schooldays. She thinks the course on language teaching methodology completely changed her way of thinking about language teaching.

By the time she finishes her teacher education course at the age of thirty-six there is no doubt that she wants to teach. However, the teaching practicum in an upper-secondary school had been a stressful time. Once again she feels that she is not good enough and would not be able to cope. The idea of teaching in an upper-secondary school makes her anxious that she would make mistakes and suddenly she feels her English is not good enough since she has never lived in an English-speaking country. 'I was not mature enough to understand that everyone makes mistakes.' However, she is clear about wanting to teach and obtains a position in the neighbouring lower-secondary school (11-16), where she teaches for nine happy years. She has finally become a *professional*. Teaching is fun: 'I have always thought teaching was fun ever since I began teaching' – which is surprising considering how reluctant she had been to become a teacher. The school is in an affluent community and she can buy books and equipment and soon becomes head of the small English department and can do things her own way (i.e. adopt ideas from university): 'I am still using activities from that time,' she says.

Eventually, despite the positive feedback from pupils and parents alike, Birna becomes 'tired of mothering', which primary school teachers cannot escape, and she also wants a more intellectual challenge: 'I think it is in people's nature to want to take on something new.' So she decides to change school level and teach at upper-secondary school. She does not regret the change, although in some ways it was like beginning anew. This is a much bigger school with many teachers of English and the material is new to her and more challenging in some ways. This is indeed a *new challenge* in many ways. When she starts, her new colleagues have planned everything. In many instances their ideas on teaching are not in accordance with hers and the grammar translation method is still lingering. She gradually starts working on changing the syllabus. After a couple of years she begins to feel that her colleagues trust her and listen to her. 'And you are of course always in charge in your own classroom' – meaning that she can use the teaching approaches she prefers although she is bound by using the same textbooks as the other English teachers.

Due to her seemingly deep-rooted insecurity, Birna asks in the beginning only to teach the first two levels out of the four, but has now acknowledged that she is a competent and skilled teacher and can teach at all levels. 'I know I am just as good a teacher as many who have a master's degree.' She would, however, like to do an MA one day, not necessarily in English, but rather in teaching English as a Foreign Language (TEFL).

Birna has always spent a lot of time on preparation. 'I haven't watched TV since I began teaching. I know this is crazy but this is the way I am.' She feels she has to take home a lot of papers to check because the students need this check, claiming that they need to get feedback to know where they stand, although it does not always have to be a grade. She claims that she also needs feedback from students. She needs to be acknowledged by them. 'I want to reach out to them as individuals and I want them to acknowledge me as a person.' She learned a great deal from her mentor in the teaching practicum in the upper-secondary schools, her demeanour toward the students and how to give students feedback. Birna is happy in this school. One of the advantages is that she recently got a young colleague who shares her ideas and they can divide the work between them, which she claims is crucial in developing new ideas. Here we have the theme *contentment* from her river. She says she has not changed her ideas about teaching since university but has been to many seminars and courses where she has learned new activities for teaching. 'It is such great fun when you try out something new and it works.' She gives a couple of examples of things she has been trying out. She also says that some of her colleagues are afraid of trying anything new and hide behind the old phrase of lowering standards. 'This low-level talk is just crap, making a video is not a lower level than writing translations. They are just afraid.' She often hears teachers complain that they do not have time to try out new things. 'They should just make the syllabus more flexible. You can be doing something worthwhile and interesting with your students without going through these uninspiring textbooks.' And then she starts talking about a recent poetry lesson the researcher had observed where the students were reciting a poem and justifying their choice of their poem. 'Did you see how engaged they were?' She thinks it motivates students to bring a poem of their own choice:

> The most important thing for me as a teacher is that they feel
> what we are doing applies to them and that they are willing to put
> in some effort, or, to put it another way, that they are willing to do
> what I suggest so they will accomplish what we set out to do.

From those words it can still been detected that although she is loosening up a little she is still far from the idea of learner autonomy.

Teacher Growth

In the autumn of 2014 I visited Birna again and asked if she would be willing to look at her river again to see if there might be any new bends. Was there anything she would like to add in the light of all the years that had passed since she designed her river? After a good deal of reflection on how she has developed, she added three more bends. The new themes from those bends turn out to be: confidence, new horizons and gratification.

Below is the final version of the themes from her river:

- Carefree youth
- Outsider
- Transformation
- Becoming a professional
- A new challenge
- Contentment
- Confidence
- New horizons
- Gratification

I then ask her to elaborate on those new themes, to which she responds: 'I feel greater satisfaction which comes with greater *confidence*. I recognise the inferiority complex I used to have because I had not studied in an English-speaking country but I don't feel that any more.' She explains that she has attended many TPD (Teachers' Professional Development) courses in

England and the USA as well as Iceland which she thinks more than compensate for this lack of a second degree which she never completed. She says that due to the great changes in the status of English in Icelandic society the students are much more proficient than they were when she started teaching. This, however, does not intimidate her in any way as it might have done earlier. We recall that she was hesitant to take on the upper levels but now she is teaching courses for students in their last year where the curriculum material consists of journals like the *Economist* and some medical journals and students choose articles according to their interest area. The new curriculum has had an immense influence on study material and accelerated a development which had already begun. This makes much greater demands on the teacher.

> You don't stand any longer in front of the blackboard with a book in hand. The demands are enormous, enormous. I am collaborating now with a history teacher and a social science teacher. We are teaching a module for the third time which we call 'The Scottish Module' and then one teaches about history and one about society, you know, from the beginning how it has developed over time and I teach them Scottish [here she gives a big smile]. That is I tell them about the language and how it developed. They listen to tapes in a Scottish accent and tomorrow they are going to make a website on Burns' Supper. I think this is great fun but very demanding.

She, however, admits that now that they are adhering to the new curriculum and teaching fewer modules of English she misses having older students who are more mature and can be engaged in more meaningful discussions. The new curriculum which gives teachers all this freedom has meant that the teachers have had to do a lot of extra work.

> We had to change, make big changes and we did. We don't have as much time as we used to but students know much more English than they did before. We decided not to teach grammar explicitly any longer. The kids are so used to hearing English that they have a much better feel for the language.

They could also finally abandon the traditional English textbooks. There were other things in the new curriculum she did not like too much, though, such as the six pillars.

> In our department we thought this was just a lot of nuisance, something from the Ministry but when we started working on it we realised we were doing a lot of this already.

They had already been choosing texts and working on matters like equality and human rights. She feels that it is mainly the 'sustainability' pillar they had to look closer at.

In the last decade or so there have been many more opportunities to do interesting things due to Nordic and European funds and projects. She has had the opportunity to work with other countries – for example, with the Nordic countries – and recently she went with a group of students and the geology teacher to Sicily for two weeks through a huge Comenius project. There are in so many ways *new horizons* within the school and outside the school. Birna has come a long way from the teacher who, she says in retrospect, 'spent a lot of time on covering the textbook which did not allow time to do alternative things the students would benefit just as much from'. 'And now I am contemplating on doing something on Britain which will be, you know, just mine.' She explains that she would like to use the freedom she now has to design a new project from scratch.

The final bend in Birna's river reflects *gratification* for having had the opportunity to work as a teacher, which she thinks is such a rewarding career, and for so many years, and in this school she is so fond of. Towards the end of our conversation, Birna concludes her story by talking about the fact that she has now turned sixty and could retire:

> I enjoy teaching so much that I'm not ready to retire, I would miss my fellow teachers, and the atmosphere here is so good. I enjoy going to work every day. The students are on the whole wonderful people, there are of course one or two rotten apples but that does not spoil things, there are usually some reasons for this. I just enjoy the new challenges and find teaching more and more enjoyable.

Conclusions

From her stories we see that Birna's career trajectory can be divided into three main phases: her beginning years in lower-secondary school, her earlier years in upper-secondary school, and lastly, her later years at upper-secondary school. In the first two periods she was teaching English as a foreign language, while in the third, present phase she is preparing her students to use English almost like a native speaker would do at university and at work. The first phase would be her indirect path into teaching and her initial teaching period. Birna struggles not to become a teacher but finally enters a teacher education programme which seems to have had a strong impact on her attitudes to teaching and how to teach languages.

Birna's second career phase starts when she begins to teach in upper-secondary school. There she meets experienced teachers who are teaching the way she has rejected. Little by little, as new colleagues enter who share her thinking, she takes up cooperation with them to try out new ideas. English is, however, still taught as a foreign language and the role of the teacher is to be knowledgeable and hold all the reins.

The third phase narrates the present when the proficiency of her students has been building up over the years through increasing exposure from TV, film and other media (Arnbjörnsdóttir & Ingvarsdóttir, 2014). At the same time there has been a change in the ecological context in Iceland where English no longer fits the definition of a foreign language. Birna and her colleagues now have both the agency and the freedom to rethink their teaching. This has finally changed her role and she is moving from the traditional teacher-centred classroom where she began with its emphasis on teaching *about* the language and emphasising grammar rules to approaches offering a more holistic view of language, connecting it to the real world (Little, 2007). Birna has moved from being a provider of knowledge towards becoming a facilitator of learning.

Birna's narrative can be seen as a success story about the development of a teacher through her career. Therefore it needs to be emphasised that this has been a long and winding process covering nearly three decades. It also needs to be pointed out that the progress has not been linear – for example, when Birna starts teaching at upper-secondary level and has to some extent to go back to the traditional methods. There have been both triumphs and defeats. From Birna's narrative, based on her river, we can detect the important elements in her success story that we may all learn from: the delight she takes in teaching, the trust she shows colleagues she cooperates with, unusual teacher autonomy, the changes in the role of her subject in Icelandic society leading to much greater requirements and, last but not least, her own ambition and search for excellence.

Notes

[1] In October 1975 women in Iceland went on a one-day strike to show the importance of women's contribution to the workforce.

[2] Birna is referring to Vigdís Finnbogadóttir, who was the world's first democratically elected female president.

References

Aðalnámskráframhaldsskóla (2011) Almennur hluti 2011. Greinasvið 2013. Mennta- og menningarmálaráðuneytið [National Curriculum Guide for upper-secondary schools, general section 2011]. http://www.menntamalaraduneyti.is/utgefid-efni/namskrar/adalnamskra-framhaldsskola/ (accessed 14 April 2015).

Arnbjörnsdóttir, B. & Ingvarsdóttir, H. (2014) English at the University of Iceland: ideology and reality, in A.K. Hultgren, J. Thøgersen & F. Gregersen (Eds) *English at Nordic Universities: ideologies and practices*, pp. 179-192. Amsterdam: Benjamins.

Diamond, C.T.P. (1992) Autoethnographic Approaches to Teachers' Voice and Vision, *Curriculum Inquiry*, 22(1), 67-81. http://dx.doi.org/10.1080/03626784.1992.11075394

Elbaz, F. (1990) Knowledge and Discourse: the evolution of research on teacher thinking, in C. Day, M. Pope & P. Denicolo (Eds) *Insight into Teachers' Thinking and Practice*, pp. 15-42. London: Falmer Press.

Hellekjær, G.O. (2010) Lecture Comprehension in English-Medium Higher Education, *Hermes – Journal of Language and Communication Studies*, 45.

Hinkel, E. (Ed.) (2005) *Handbook of Research in Second Language Teaching and Learning*. Mahwah, NJ: Lawrence Erlbaum Associates.

Hunt, D.E. (1987) *Beginning with Ourselves*. Cambridge, MA: Brooklyn Books.

Ingvarsdóttir, H. (2005) You Cannot Put Academic Learning in the Freezer for Nine Years': a case study of a woman's life history, in Ú. Hauksson (Ed.) *Rannsóknir í félagsvísindum* VI, pp. 683-694. Reykjavík: University of Iceland Press.

Ingvarsdóttir, H. (2011) Teaching English in a New Age: challenges and opportunities, in B. Hudson & M. Meinert (Eds) *Beyond Fragmentation: didactics, learning and teaching in Europe*, pp. 93-106. Opladen: Budrich.

Ingvarsdóttir, H. (2014) Reflection and Work Context in Teacher Learning: two case studies from Iceland, in C.J. Craig & L. Orland-Barak (Ed.) *International Teacher Education: promising pedagogies, Part A. Advances in Research on Teaching*, vol. 22. Bingley: Emerald Group. http://dx.doi.org/10.1108/s1479-368720140000022008

Jeeves, A. (2014) The Relevance of English Language Learning in a Changing Linguistic Environment in Iceland: the L2 self of young Icelanders, *Multilingua*, 33(3-4), 267-290. http://dx.doi.org/10.1515/multi-2014-0013

Kelchtermans, G. (1993) Getting the Story, Understanding the Lives: from career stories to teachers' professional development, *Teaching and Teacher Education*, 9, 443-456. http://dx.doi.org/10.1016/0742-051X(93)90029-G

Kelly, G.A. (1969) Clinical Psychology and Personality, in B. Maher (Ed.) *The Selected Papers of George A. Kelly*. New York: Wiley.

Little, D. (2007) Language Learner Autonomy: some fundamental considerations revisited, *Innovation in Language Learning and Teaching*, 1(1), 14-29. http://dx.doi.org/10.2167/illt040.0

Pilkinton-Pihko, D. (2010) English as Lingua Franca: lecturers' self-perceptions of their language use, *Helsinki English Studies*, 6, 58-74.

Pope, M. & Denicolo, P. (2001) *Transformative Education: personal construct approaches to education and research*. London: Whurr.

Yaxley, B.G. (1991) *Developing Teachers' Theories of Teaching: a touchstone approach*. London: Falmer Press.

CHAPTER 8

A Long Way from Home: English as an Additional Language teaching in remote community schools in Australia

JILL BROWN

SUMMARY Sarah and Wendy are both experienced and well-qualified teachers of English as an Additional Language (EAL). Both chose to leave the big city and travel thousands of miles to work with Aboriginal children in small remote community schools in Australia. Sarah returned to mainstream teaching in less than a year. Wendy is still there today. What motivated these two teachers to try a very different type of teaching? What enabled Wendy to stay and thrive while Sarah gave up in despair? There are very few teachers like Wendy. Teacher retention rates in such rural schools are appallingly low, with one study indicating the average length of stay is eight months. The impact of this constant turnover in teaching staff is clear. Aboriginal students in Australia are severely disadvantaged in terms of education and students in remote community schools are even more disadvantaged than their peers in regional and city centres. Studies suggest that between 70 and 80% of children in these schools are below national standards in literacy and numeracy. Teachers are the key to quality schooling, and continuity of teaching staff is essential in addressing issues of educational disadvantage; yet, many teachers in remote schools are like Sarah and find themselves unable to stay the distance. Data for this chapter are taken from a study of the experiences of non-Indigenous teachers working with Aboriginal students and focus on the motivation, experiences and identity construction of the teacher participants.

Introduction

I have been involved in teaching English as an Additional Language (EAL) for many years. There have been several versions of this role: I have worked in government secondary schools in low socio-economic areas, I have worked with refugees in on-arrival language centres, and for the past fifteen years I have been an academic in the Faculty of Education at Monash University. During this time I have taught in the pre-service program preparing beginning EAL teachers for their work. I have worked with postgraduate research students, many of them experienced EAL teachers, most of them international students. I have also had the enormous privilege of being able to pursue my interest in EAL teacher work as a means of achieving social justice and equity, an interest that has been the basis of my teaching career. This has led to several research studies focusing on the ways in which Indigenous peoples around the world are either included or marginalised by mainstream education systems.

There are an estimated 517,000 Aboriginal and Torres Strait Islander people in Australia, 2.5% of the total Australian population. Children and young people represent more than half of the total population. The average age of 21 years is much lower than that of non-Indigenous people (37 years). This relatively young age is due mainly to higher fertility and mortality rates. The population is largely urbanised, with 32% of Aboriginal and Torres Strait Islander children and young people living in major cities, 44% in regional areas and 24% in remote parts of Australia. The uneven distribution of population in Australia, with the majority of the population living in large cities on the eastern seaboard and relatively small numbers of people in remote and very remote areas, means that although a larger proportion of the Aboriginal population lives in major cities, Aboriginal people represent only 1% of the population in these areas. In very remote communities they are 50% or more of the total population (ABS, 2011). There are decreasing but still very significant differences between the educational achievements of mainstream and Aboriginal Australian children. The latter 'remain the most educationally disadvantaged in the country with educational outcomes, school retention rates and the completion of tertiary education well below those of non-Indigenous peers' (Santoro & Reid, 2006, p. 289). Indigenous students in remote community schools are even more disadvantaged than their peers in regional and city centres. According to nationwide tests of literacy and numeracy, more than 50% of Indigenous students in remote Indigenous schools fail to reach minimum standards in writing, spelling, grammar, punctuation and numeracy in years 3, 5, 7 and 9 (Hughes & Hughes, 2010a). Other studies suggest that between 70% and 80% of children in these schools are below national standards (Hughes & Hughes, 2010b). At the same time as results attest to continuing disadvantage, it is recognised that education can be an equalizer, a tool for achieving social equity, and that teachers have a central position in this process in that they turn political decisions into practice (Vinzant & Crothers, 1998). The pressure on schools and teachers to 'fix' the many problems confronting Indigenous communities is typified in the following quote taken from a leading national newspaper: 'Aboriginal disadvantage in employment, housing and, ultimately, life expectancy can be removed only if education is fixed up' (Pearson, 2009). It is beyond question that quality teaching is fundamental to improved student outcomes. In remote community schools many children start school with few or no English language skills, meaning that the quality teaching needed is quality EAL teaching.

In a number of ways, the conditions for teaching in remote settings in Australia are attractive. Good pay rates and conditions of service that include high rental subsidies, additional annual leave, tax and travel incentives, and good promotion and transfer arrangements are examples of government attempts to attract and retain staff (Harrison, 2008). However, there are huge problems in creating teacher continuity in remote Indigenous schools in Australia. One study indicates that the current average length of time for teachers to remain in remote Indigenous schools is eight months (Garrett, 2011). It should also be noted that although most remote community schools have assistant teachers who are community members, the vast majority of teachers working in such schools are non-Indigenous. Despite the impact of poor teacher retention rates on the educational achievements of Indigenous children, there has been little research to date on non-Indigenous teachers working in Indigenous work contexts (Brown & Cadman, 2011; Parding, 2013).

This chapter draws on data from a small-scale qualitative study and is based on semi-structured interviews with a number of teachers, the majority of whom are no longer teaching in remote community schools. The interviews were tape-recorded and addressed how the teachers experienced their work situation. The focus points for discussion were qualifications, initial motivation, daily routine, challenges and rewards, goals for students and advice for teachers thinking of working in a similar context. The pseudonyms Wendy and Sarah have been used for the two teachers whose stories are told in this chapter. They are similar in a number of ways. They are both highly qualified EAL teachers, they are both motivated to improve equity and access through their work, they are both confident and resilient and they both decided to leave the big city and work many thousands of miles away from home in remote community schools. There is, however, a fundamental difference. After less than a year Sarah left the community in which she was working and came back to the city. Wendy is still there today and has no plans to leave. What motivated these two teachers to try a very different type of teaching? What enabled Wendy to stay and thrive while Sarah gave up in despair?

Initial Motivation

Their reasons for choosing to work in remote outback communities go some way to explaining the different experiences and outcomes for Sarah and Wendy. Sarah 'just wanted to get out of Sydney'. At the time she was working in an intensive language centre with 'wonderful, highly motivated students ... a lovely, lovely job'. The teaching in this context was so enjoyable that Sarah felt she could 'stay doing this forever and never move and never do anything else'. Her decision to leave this perfect job was the result of two factors, one the desire for change and adventure – 'I want to see other places and I'd always wanted to go to Broome and the Pilbera and Western Australia.' The other reason was less positive – 'I had recently left a long term relationship ... he was going back to America and I was going to the desert.'

Wendy came to remote teaching with a very different motivation. She had not initially planned to be a teacher. On completion of her undergraduate degree Wendy was heading north, off for a backpacker year in Asia. At the time her sister was working as a nurse in a remote community:

> I stopped with her on my way to Asia, got a job in the school
> canteen and stayed for six months. I saw some really terrible
> teachers with no understanding. These kids were coming to school
> and doing all this learning in a second language and managing to
> stay at school all day and learn in that environment in English all
> day every day, even little kids. I just thought there were so many
> things to be celebrated and rewarded but they gave awards for
> being clean – you know become like us and have a shower every
> day. ... the only thing I could do [in response] was to become a
> teacher so that's what I did.

Wendy went back to the city and enrolled in a teacher education program that would give her the skills she needed to work as an EAL teacher and that would also allow her to complete a teaching practicum in a remote community school. Her first appointment was to the school in the remote community in which her sister worked. Her second appointment was to the school in which she is currently employed and where she has been for the past eight years.

Context of Work

Sarah was sent to an outstation school in the outback of Western Australia, a school owned and run by the local community. Outstation schools cater for small groups of people who live 'in-country' on their traditional homelands, rather than as part of a larger community. The school in which Sarah worked had a small but constantly changing student population – 'about fifteen kids but if there's something happening kids don't come and if there's another mob in the community they'll come to school as well and you've never seen them before so there's swapping and changing all the time'. Sarah was the only teacher and the only non-Indigenous person living in the community. The school building was basic, a single room with teacher accommodation attached to the classroom – 'They put a transportable building there for me so I lived in two-thirds of it and the school was the other third. They put a dividing wall so I'd walk out one door and into the next.' Sarah did as many conscientious new teachers do: she 'went to the community five days early to get ready for school and there was totally no-one there'.

The school in which Wendy works is in a remote area of northern Australia, many hundreds of kilometres from the nearest city. Travel to the community is by light aircraft to a small rural airport and then a long drive on an unmade road that is only accessible in the dry season. Cyclones and monsoonal rains affect the region during the wet season between November and April, when the community can be cut off from the outside world for weeks at a time. There is a large mine operating on part of the community land and royalties from this help to pay for the school, which is at the centre of the community. The buildings are comparatively new and well equipped. The school has a total enrolment of two hundred students and, as the school's English as a Second Language (ESL) teacher, Wendy works across all the classes. There is a strong first-language program that aims to see children acquire literacy in both first language and English. Classes run from pre-school to year 12, the final year of secondary schooling. The teachers are mainly non-Indigenous, but Indigenous teaching assistants are employed to work in every class. Houses are provided for the teachers; these are basic but comfortable.

Rewards

Both Sarah and Wendy found aspects of their work rewarding in the extreme. Sarah was impressed by the clarity of the aims for education that were held by the 'old men', the elders of the community. Similar to the community in which Wendy worked, there was a determination to maintain language and for children to be literate in both English and first language. They also wanted a mainstream education that would give the community the skills needed to negotiate with government departments – 'we want our kids to be able to deal with government fellows, to be literate, to be able to read the agreements and deal with government people'. There were individual students whose determination to learn was remarkable. Sarah spoke of one boy who left school at fourteen to 'go through the law'. After this the boys are considered to be men and most no longer attend school – 'I did have one boy who came back because he really did want to learn'. An elderly man also attended Sarah's classes – 'he was really old, he could scarcely see. He came to school every day and if I wrote on the whiteboard he would copy everything trying to learn himself.' Sarah also describes the magical moments of being part of a culture that was very different to anything she had ever experienced before:

> This [life in the community] is all about spirits and medicine men. I mean you go out with the girls after school to go swimming and driving back you go past one particular tree and everyone is on the floor of the car hiding because it's a sacred tree. It's two different worlds. I had quite a few different experiences which made me

just think how can this difference be bridged because it's huge. You go out hunting and you get a kangaroo and you're sitting around and the old men are singing the clouds away so it rains on some one else and they're singing the clouds back so it's like a war of singing going on and you can actually see the clouds move.

Sarah was made part of the community and given a 'skin group'. This is not done for all teachers in remote community schools; the community decides which teachers they want to make part of the community. Sarah's skin group identified her relationship to other community members and clarified the ways in which they were able to relate to each other – 'I had kids in my class from different skin groups so they had to give me a skin group so we'd know how to relate to each other. One girl was like my mother and other girls were my sisters so I had to show that level of respect to them – so that was how they placed me in the community.' The strength and complexity of these relationships, combined with the willingness to include her, made a lasting impression on Sarah.

Wendy has also been given a skin group and is actively involved in 'women's business' in the community. She is fluent in the shared language and this, combined with her detailed understanding of the ways in which her students are related to other members of the community, means that she is respected by the children she teaches and that her classes are marked by the productive on-task learning which takes place. Her local knowledge also means that she is able to use content that is both valued and relevant – 'right now we're working on documenting bush foods, drawing pictures and describing how they can be used. This is part of the whole bush food garden that we've planted and that's used in the school canteen.' Wendy works closely with the first-language teachers so skills in first language and English are developed simultaneously. I was part of a lesson where the children sat on the beach and recorded shifts in the tide line, listing and drawing the materials left by the outgoing tide, before describing what was happening in both languages. The work produced indicated both impressive understanding of the natural world and the ability to shift between languages with relative ease. Wendy shares my admiration for the achievements of her students – 'every day I am inspired and I learn something ... the kids amaze me, learning to read and write in two languages. If you really look at what they can do, they are just amazing. It's hard work but it's rewarding. The kids just make it.'

Challenges

If there are rewards to be found in EAL teaching in remote community schools, there are also challenges, especially so for Sarah. Her first few weeks were especially difficult. After arriving to find the community deserted, she drove back to the nearest town, a journey of several hundred kilometres, returning on the day that school started. She describes her feelings as those of 'really intense culture shock'.

> Every night there was yelling and fighting and screaming and everything in Aboriginal language. When you hear a different language you don't know if people are angry or not because it's a different tone so after about Wednesday of that week I just started crying and I couldn't stop crying ... what happens in Aboriginal communities is if someone steps out of line there's a big community meeting. So there's a huge group of people surrounding some one who's the perpetrator and people walking up and yelling at them and brandishing sticks and sometimes hitting them – it just felt incredibly aggressive and incredibly violent and it was all around me all the time. It really shocked me. I didn't have any strategies to cope with it.

As the only non-Indigenous member of the community, Sarah found comfort and support in radio contact with other teachers who were also newcomers to remote teaching – 'you just get in touch and say I really need to talk and they're hundreds of kilometres away but it helps'.

Sarah also struggled to find a teaching approach which worked for her students. She was an experienced EAL teacher, responsible for curriculum development in her previous school and highly regarded by her colleagues. She had taught at many different levels, had taught many different student groups and cultures, and had been able to move between levels, groups and cultures with little difficulty. Now she was in a situation where 'absolutely nothing worked'. Her previous teaching had been based on shared values; hard work results in achievement, achievement results in a good job, which in turn results in a good life. This was not a vision of the future shared by her students or by the community. Any praise which singled out an individual student was rejected; the class moved at the pace of the slowest and the learning that did take place was essentially a group activity.

> They want to move together as a group so the slowest kid, that's the pace you go at because they don't want that kid to be left behind. It's all about unity, the unity of the group. They don't want to be pointed out and made special by the fact that they've done really well.

Sarah found the pace of learning and the apparent lack of ability to transfer knowledge incomprehensible. After successfully, or so she thought, teaching some basic maths concepts, the children seemed unable to shift the concepts to real-life application – 'they could add and divide and multiply and all that sorts of stuff but if I said well you're going to drive 100 kilometres and you go at 25 kilometres per hour how long will it take you they would look at me and say "add, multiply"?' That the elders wanted the children to stay on traditional land as part of the community meant that there was no future goal to be achieved, no way to construct a future in any way different to the present. The notion that education leads to a better life, a concept basic to Sarah's sense of self as teacher, had no place and it was perhaps this that made it impossible for Sarah to stay:

> I felt like I was trying to change something that was beyond me
> and I didn't even know what it was and I think that's how a lot of
> teachers in communities feel. You try and try and try ... in many
> ways it's unfulfilling as a teacher because you don't see much
> change. In teaching you put all the effort in to change and any
> change was so slow and so small.

Wendy also acknowledges the difficulties involved in teaching children who are not motivated by the normal system of reward for effort. Her advice for teaching intending to work in remote schools – 'forget everything you know because it won't work'. The challenges that Wendy faces are not, in the main, connected with her students. As the only EAL teacher in the school she feels responsible for ensuring that all teachers understand the needs of children who are learning in a second language.

> There's a lot to do. Coping with different teaching styles and skills
> levels and different personalities. A lot of teachers come in
> knowing nothing about ESL appropriate teaching so it's like
> professional development work helping them understand what to
> do.

Wendy works closely with the first-language teaching team in the development of materials, trying to ensure that similar content is covered in both first language and English. This is in addition to her normal teaching load and the work with class teachers described above. In Wendy's words, 'it's not easy getting that organised'. Wendy also feels isolated from the EAL profession but copes with this by involving herself in further education. She is currently completing further qualifications in TESOL in Indigenous contexts by distance and regularly travels hundreds of kilometres to take part in professional development programs. Another and more serious challenge was the appointment of a principal who did not support language teaching. His approach was to mandate an English-only approach without any attempt to ensure the children had the language skills to make this possible. For some months it seemed that Wendy would not be re-appointed for the following year and that the first-language program would not continue. Community reaction resulted in the principal being moved and the language program continuing. It is, however, disturbing to think that a change in leadership can have such a negative impact. It also suggests that EAL teaching is not regarded as being a fundamental part of education in remote community schools – this despite it being one of the key essentials that Wendy believes all teachers need to work in such schools – 'enthusiasm, flexibility, ESL skills and high expectations'.

Conclusion

So what is there to be learned from the stories of Sarah and Wendy? What can be taken from their experiences which can help to frame an appropriate response to the ongoing challenge to teachers to 'fix up' Indigenous education? While there were personal issues which impacted on Sarah's reaction to the demands of remote teaching, there were other factors which clearly indicate the need for much greater support for teachers working in such extreme situations. Although Sarah was a well-qualified and experienced EAL teacher, she had never worked with Indigenous students and had no experience of life in the outback. There was one week between her appointment after a phone interview and the time she left for the community. She had very limited information about the school and there was no orientation program offered to assist her in understanding what was required of her. Nor was there any ongoing support. In contrast, after time spent in a remote community, Wendy made a conscious decision that teaching in remote community schools was what she wanted to do. She sought out an appropriate teacher education program and completed her teaching practicum in a remote setting. She has found a place in the community and created a professional support network for herself. She is both happy and productive, but it should be noted that this is the result of her own efforts. There are no systematic requirements that all teachers in remote schools have appropriate qualifications and experience prior to their appointment. Nor is there a formal system of support. It seems obvious that until this is done, the teacher retention rate in remote schools will remain low, educational outcomes will be lower than those in the mainstream and children will continue to compare teachers to seagulls who 'fly in and fly out' with as little impact on their lives as birds who feed on food scraps on land, then quickly return to sea.

References

Australian Bureau of Statistics (ABS) (2011) 4725.0 – *Aboriginal and Torres Strait Islander Wellbeing: a focus on children and youth.* www.abs.gov.au

Brown, J. & Cadman, K. (2011) TESOL and TESD in Remote Aboriginal Australia: the 'true' story?, *TESOL Quarterly*, 45(3), 440-462. http://dx.doi.org/10.5054/tq.2011.256794

Garrett, P. (2011) New $5m Scheme for Teachers in Remote Communities. *Ministers' Media Centre: Education, Employment and Workplace Relations*, 20 June 2011. http://ministers.deewr.gov.au/garrett/new-5m-scheme-teachers-remote-communities (accessed 16 December 2011).

Harrison, N. (2008) *Teaching and Learning in Indigenous Education.* Melbourne: Oxford University Press.

Hughes, H. & Hughes, M. (2010a) *Policy Monographs: indigenous education.* Policy Monograph 110, Centre for Independent Studies. www.cis.org.au/publications

Hughes, H. & Hughes, M. (2010b) Education Fails Indigenous Kids, *The Australian*, 29 April.

Parding, K. (2013) The Need for Learning Arenas: non-Indigenous teachers working in Indigenous school contexts, *Education, Citizenship and Social Justice*, 8(3), 242-253.

Pearson, N. (2009) A People's Survival, *The Australian*, 3 October.

Santoro, N. & Reid, J.-A. (2006) 'All Things to All People': Indigenous teachers in the Australian teaching profession, *European Journal of Teacher Education*, 29(3), 287-303.

Vinzant, J. & Crothers, L. (1998) *Street-level Leadership: discretion and legitimacy in front-line public service*. Washington, DC: Georgetown University Press.

CHAPTER 9

Self-reflexive Inquiry in Teacher Education for Diversity: tapping and leveraging resources for language teachers' career trajectories

STEVEN Z. ATHANASES, JOANNA W. WONG & LESLIE C. BANES

SUMMARY This chapter draws upon a program of research focused on how self-reflexive inquiry into language and culture may support learning and teaching in multicultural teacher education. Such inquiry can foster metalinguistic awareness as prospective teachers reflect on their language development histories, inventory the linguistic repertoires they tap into for multiple uses, and reflect on the varied ways in which contexts and audiences shape their language choices. Through such inquiry, future teachers also articulate their conceptions of language and ways their language ideologies shape their ideas and practices for teaching. This articulation of experiential knowledge, enabled by reflection and supported by human and material resources, can help to leverage the special perspectives and understandings that bilingual preservice teachers of color bring to their work of teaching English to linguistically diverse learners.

Introduction

Despite the increasing cultural and linguistic diversity of students in US schools, teacher education in the USA has been slow to address linguistic diversity in preparing teachers for the diverse students they will serve, possibly throughout their careers (Lucas & Grinberg, 2008; Zeichner, 2009). Greater attention is needed to deepen teachers' knowledge of language diversity as their careers unfold. Doing so will help teachers keep pace with what we need to know about students and their language uses. Language, in our view, is a resource that students can tap into and develop in both academic learning and contexts beyond school. Teachers who begin their careers with an understanding that language is situated within a socio-political context, and who are reflective about their own experiences with and beliefs about language, may be better equipped for a full career ahead of designing linguistically responsive curriculum and dynamic spaces of language learning for students.

US and California Contexts for Language Teaching

As each state within the United States has autonomy to establish teacher-credentialing policies, there are inconsistencies in teacher preparation from state to state, particularly related to addressing the education of linguistically diverse students. In addition, teacher education frequently provides language coursework only to those earning specialty certificates to teach linguistically diverse students and/or bilingual education, rather than providing coursework program-wide to all teacher candidates who will certainly need it along their unfolding career trajectories.

California, the site on which we report in this chapter, has one of the most linguistically diverse K-12 populations in the United States, with almost a quarter of students identified as English Learners (ELs).[1] The largest group of EL students in California is identified as Latina/o. They speak Spanish as a primary language and account for over 83% of ELs (California Department of Education, 2015). The next most commonly spoken languages by California students are Filipino/Tagalog, Mandarin, Cantonese and Arabic. Although preservice teachers in California are required to take courses that prepare them to serve culturally and linguistically diverse students, expectations for teacher preparation are not clearly articulated in state education policies, and actual preparation is often inadequate. Consequently, linguistically diverse students often continue to be underserved as they negotiate tensions of maintaining a home language while acquiring English as an academic language within the English-dominant context of the United States.

Socio-political Issues

The majority of the teacher population in the United States is White, accounting recently for 92% of credentialed teachers (Zumwalt & Craig, 2005). This teaching majority does not reflect the diversity of students in US schools. In addition, these teachers tend to be monolingual. We propose that more needs to be done to attract bilingual teachers of color and to retain them for successful careers in teaching. These teachers more likely possess personal experiences and awareness as English language learners that may be leveraged as resources to assist their own students in navigating the socio-political contexts of language and learning.

In the United States, new attention to language and literacy education is evident in the national articulation of the Common Core State Standards (CCSS) currently adopted by 43 of 50 states. California also has aligned English Language Development (ELD) standards with the CCSS. These ELD standards reflect a dramatic shift from a structural approach to L2 instruction, to one premised on sociocultural understandings of language development. In this vein, California's new ELD standards reflect greater attention to developing students' metalinguistic awareness with the goal of leveraging students' home-language knowledge and culture as resources for academic learning. We argue that all teachers must also be equipped with metalinguistic awareness to be able to analyze and understand the dynamic nature of language use, and to be able to value ways their diverse students use languages and literacies to think and learn. This is awareness and knowledge teachers will use across the span of a career.

Teacher Education and Linguistic Diversity

In California, teacher education occurs post-Baccalaureate. However, in our project, an undergraduate course on cultural diversity and education is intended to launch potential teachers (approximately two-thirds of enrolled students) on a trajectory of engaging issues of diversity, leveraging their experiences, and developing knowledge for use in teaching. Of those who become teachers, many will be tasked with teaching academic content (e.g. history, science, mathematics) through the English language. We argue that awareness and understanding of language is equally crucial for teachers who teach content through language as it is for those who will teach English as a separate content area. A feature of our work is self-reflexive learning about language and culture, which may support learning and teaching in multicultural teacher education (Asher, 2007). Such inquiry can foster metalinguistic awareness as prospective teachers reflect on their language development histories, inventory linguistic repertoires they tap for multiple uses, and reflect on varied ways contexts and audiences shape their language choices. Through such inquiries, future teachers also articulate conceptions of language and how their language ideologies shape their ideas and practices for teaching.

This self-reflexive feature implicates the self as a cultural, linguistic, gendered and classed being whose perspective is shaped by both autobiography and socio-political contexts. The course links self-inquiry and socio-political knowledge for current and future use. For linguistic diversity, students read about studies and laws regarding linguistic rights, read and discuss linguicism, and participate in a workshop where a math lesson in Portuguese gets taught twice, once using no supports for language learners and a second time with many language learning supports (de Oliveira, 2011). The workshop places all students in the role of being language learners and highlights pedagogical tools. Course assignments invite self-reflexive inquiry into language, including a Personal Language Inventory prompted by Amy Tan's (1999) 'Mother Tongue'. Tan describes a lecture she gave with her overseas-born Chinese mother in the audience, reflecting on her own and her mother's English language use and their experiences of linguicism, or discrimination based solely on their use of language (Skutnabb-Kangas & Cummins, 1988). In response to this essay, students document, reflect on and analyze their language use during a single week. They engage in other essay writing about language diversity and education. In many discussions, students explore issues of language diversity and socio-political factors shaping individuals' lived experiences of language variation. Articulation of experiential knowledge, enabled by reflection and supported by human and material resources, can help leverage special perspectives and understandings bilingual preservice teachers of color bring to their work as they begin their careers and at any given point on their career trajectories.

Context for Our Work: data-gathering approach and tools

The research informing this chapter was conducted in an education course designed for prospective teachers, education minors and others at a large California university. In racial/ethnic self-identifications, approximately two-thirds of students across years identified as students of color or mixed, with the largest group being Asian/Asian Americans of a wide range of ethnicity including Chinese, Japanese, Korean, Vietnamese, Hmong and Filipino, and a fairly large number of students identifying as Latina/o, mostly of Mexican descent but also Guatemalan, Salvadoran, Nicaraguan, Peruvian and Colombian. Several students per year identify as African/African American/mixed, several of Middle Eastern origins, and approximately one per year of American Indian heritage. White students identify themselves as being from a range of European ancestries.

Over four years, we collected several forms of data on students' uses of and reflections on language. Data included personal language inventories, inventories exploring a range of privilege and lack of privilege, visual representations of students' identity journeys, original poems of cultural autobiography, surveys on language profiles and ideologies, and formal essays where students placed their cultural and linguistic autobiographies to date in a socio-political context. In this chapter we highlight the language inventories (260, average 65 collected per year) and reference other data. We developed a system to code inventories for language variations and students' reflections (see Athanases, Banes, Wong & Martinez, 2015). Our process involved repeated reading of inventories, memo writing, practice coding, discussions, refining of codes, side-by-side coding practice, and inter-rater reliability checks, yielding a final coding system.

Language Themes in Education Students' Writings

Drawing upon our analyses of language inventories of 260 undergraduate education students, we isolated inventories of students who identified as bilingual or multilingual (slightly over 50% of 260). We analyzed what this group reported about uses of and reflections on language. We culled themes from our analyses and report several here.

Developing Language Awareness

From conducting language inventories, bilingual students often described increased awareness about language and its uses. A sub-theme of this awareness featured language as tool and process. One student noted how reading 'Mother Tongue' helped her begin to think more critically about language use on a daily basis, noting that she rarely actively thought about language: 'For me, there's never really been a reason to think about it; speaking and language just seemed like an automatic action that never really took any thought at all.' The extensiveness of language in human activity leads to this tendency for teachers to look 'through' language rather than 'at' it (De Jong & Harper, 2005). The heightened attention this student reports is a critically important step in becoming a better English language teacher along the career continuum.

As they reflected on new consciousness about language, students reported awareness of language functions. One function was navigating social situations. The language inventory prompted awareness of varied language uses in varied contexts. One student remarked:

> I make the changes so often and usually fluidly I usually don't take
> a second thought when it happens, but after spending a week
> really thinking about the way I use language and taking notes, I
> realized that the way we change and the amount we change is
> pretty significant.

This student later noted how language 'switches' served as tools to navigate social contexts. Awareness of such tools may aid prospective teachers in their development as they consider the many kinds of language their students will need and use to communicate competently in a variety of contexts.

Among such contexts for bilinguals are those that call for uses of different languages. The language inventory prompted students' awareness of variations within these languages. Examining his language use while visiting friends and family one weekend, one student reported heightened metalinguistic awareness as he described his multiple, integrated uses of varieties of English, Spanish and Spanglish, and how they contribute to a new self-identification: 'It's surprising how I can be multilingual.' Another student echoed this sentiment:

119

I already knew that I use English and Spanish in different contexts, but I never truly paid attention to the several ways I use those two languages alone. The way one speaks defines who they are and I was able to see the diverse ways language helps me play different roles in life.

Another student reported similar new awareness, noting, 'Each type of English I speak serves a unique purpose.' She illustrated: 'I use "proper" English to show how scholarly and educated I am. I use "informal" English and slang to demonstrate my fun and humanlike side.' While we might assume bilingual students already are conscious of multiple ways they use more than one language, a recurring theme was bilingual students' awakening to ways they use language in varied contexts, adjusted for various purposes and audiences. This keen awareness may assist future teachers in their forthcoming careers.

With awareness of language variations and functions came awareness of language linked with culture and identities, and language as power. Students reflected on identities as bilinguals and 'how the world perceives me', as well as on cultural links or what one student called 'hyperawareness over idioms and sayings, as cultural phrases were lost on my mother and I'. While language was cast as tool and resource, one student noted that language can be a bridge or weapon. In a related way, another student reported how her uncle criticized her lack of Hmong fluency, which led to her retaliating by elevating the complexity of her English and speaking in metaphors, and how she would do the reverse (use English words in Hmong sentence structure) to taunt her brother who could not speak Hmong. The self-reflexive inquiry process enabled her to reflect on this 'linguistic bullying': 'I saw my brother and my uncle as having limited, imperfect thoughts because their use of language was limited where mine was fluent.' She reflected on this deficit perspective that had undergirded her bullying of family members: 'This awareness of my use of language will definitely help me become conscious about how I will value language diversity in my classroom.'

This nuanced knowledge of issues of language and power is especially important for those who will embark on English-language career trajectories. This understanding is significant: most teachers across their career trajectories are unaware of widely varying ways they use language in different contexts. Understanding language in their own and their students' lives may be prerequisite to effectively supporting linguistically diverse students (Valdés et al, 2005).

Recognizing the Value of Multilingualism and Cost of Language Loss

Bilingual students reported not only new awareness of their varied language uses, but also strong opinions about benefits of bilingualism. Students' reports describe bilingualism as the ability to facilitate communication that would otherwise be impossible and to express emotions more articulately given two languages from which to choose the most appropriate words. One student reflected on her use of language to communicate different emotions. When talking with her closest friend about day-to-day tasks, school, or family members, they speak in English:

> however, if we are talking about something that is very emotional or expressing feelings towards something extremely important in our lives, I find myself speaking in Spanish with her. I do this because it relates back to my actual background. Since my Guatemalan culture is extremely important to me, expressing my deepest feelings about life is something that I feel I need to express in Spanish.

Related to emotional texture, language uses were tied to family and friendship bonds. One student highlights how use of her home language allows her to relax and feel connected to family: 'When I travel home at the weekend, explaining to my parents about what happened throughout my week, and listening to Cantonese TV shows changes and relaxes my brain.' This student also described a language of intimacy that links families and friends and differentiates them from outsiders. This, too, is critical information that prospective teachers – some of them English-language teachers – should know as they embark on their teaching careers.

Students reported that a further benefit of bilingualism is using different languages to represent different facets of their cultural identities and to support the capacity to see the world from multiple perspectives. One student explained how his two languages 'help identify me as a person'. He reflected, 'I am Mexican American and I have the English from my American part and the Spanish that ties me to my Mexican roots. My family has taught me the importance of that.' Maintaining an awareness of the links between language and identity can serve language teachers.

Other students framed the benefits of bilingualism by reflecting on limitations inherent in using a single language to describe complex thoughts and ideas. One student reported difficulty her mother experienced translating Japanese words or phrases that do not exist in English: 'I go through the same struggle when I talk to my friends. That is why I like talking to my Japanese American friends or my siblings because I can solve that problem by speaking in "Japanglish".' In these ways, bilingual students reported enjoying the flexibility that bilingualism offers and the ability to choose words in either language or combine two or more languages to most aptly communicate thoughts. This awareness has the potential to support future teachers in developing an understanding and appreciation of their students' varied language practices.

Despite benefits, some students reported the gradual loss of fluency in a native language and sadness or shame accompanying this loss. Students attributed decline in fluency to immersion in English-only school environments, attending college far from home, and losing touch with family members who speak the language. One student reported:

> I use my Spanish with extended family, acquaintances who speak
> it, and with the general public who understands it ... I learned
> English at an early age and have been using it consistently. This
> meant that my knowledge of Spanish became limited and I had to
> relearn much of it, giving it a 'textbook' aspect.

Another student reflected on how gradual language loss created a 'communication barrier' from being away from home while at university: 'I find myself losing touch with my Cantonese little by little and it's quite saddening. Language is so important and I feel if I lose my Cantonese, I've lost connection with my family.' Loss of culture, family and identities all were tied to language loss. These insights also are vitally important for future teachers as they embark on their career trajectories.

Recasting Language Shame to Resist Linguicism

Across language inventories, we found many bilingual students reflected on experiences with linguicism, often internalizing hegemonic perspectives that one's emerging second-language proficiency is deficient. One student who worked as a restaurant server described linguicism she faced from customers on a daily basis: 'like "I can't understand your accent" and "are you speaking English?"' This student noted that sometimes such remarks are meant to be 'benignly funny' but this is not how it feels to the speaker: 'Because I clearly do not look Caucasian, my English fluency has always been questioned, predetermined, and/or linguistically profiled throughout my life as lacking language proficiency or other skills.' This student reflects on the linguicism but in such situations does not challenge it; instead she rationalizes the speaker's intent, unequipped to disrupt these linguistic microaggressions.[2] Awareness of linguistic microaggressions also is a tool that can be invaluable to future teachers across their careers.

Bilingual students often recount a shift in feelings toward their families' use of a non-English language. A sense of deficit, shame or embarrassment about 'imperfect English', situated in a linguicism context, gave way to feelings of cultural pride, family unity and appreciation of diverse linguistic skills, as in this student reflection:

> When I was younger I would sometimes feel embarrassed of my
> parents' limited English, but as I grew older I learned to
> understand that their ability to communicate themselves in a
> foreign language was not a representation of their intelligence.

Similarly, in their language inventories students reported a growing recognition that 'flawed' English does not represent a 'flawed' intellect and often belies true intelligence. Students drew on their own experiences to better understand perspectives of language learners and to envision ways of disrupting linguicism for potential students in their future roles as teachers. One student reported a renewed sense of agency as a result of better understanding the language acquisition process: 'Nowadays I stand up for myself and not let anyone look down upon me because I am not capable of fully expressing myself in impeccable English.' By recasting their experiences of linguistic marginalization into an honoring of linguistic diversity and non-mainstream literacies, teachers of color are then able to create counter-narratives that serve as resources for teaching their own students (Fránquiz et al, 2011). As students engaged in processes of inventorying and reflecting on language use, many shared narratives of how they exhibited agency to recast instances of language shaming to counter acts of linguicism or developed new insights into how to resist and disrupt language discrimination. This, too, represents a tool for prospective teachers' toolboxes, one that can be utilized when needed in the future.

Students drew on their own negative schooling experiences to describe the important part teachers play in either perpetuating or counteracting language discrimination in classrooms. One described 'jumping to conclusions' about students' abilities based on their language use as 'the worst type of prejudice' and explains, 'This is an issue that needs to be addressed among teachers and others working around children, do not unintentionally teach to judge based on language.' This student acknowledges the often-overlooked assumptions teachers make about students based on their use of language. These assumptions have crucial consequences for linguistically diverse students as teachers' expectations determine, in large part, which students are listened to and supported, and which are dismissed, discredited or ignored (Milroy & Milroy, 1985; Hill, 2009).

Teachers who understand and reflect on the language acquisition process may be less likely to make assumptions about students' cognitive abilities based on an 'accent' or use of 'imperfect English', and they may be better able to recognize and question assumptions when they do arise.

In a survey item asking them to describe ideas to help teachers address language diversity in classrooms, many participants indicated importance of preventing bias and prejudice toward students who speak languages other than English or who 'speak with accents'. Similarly, many emphasized a need for the teacher to be 'open-minded' or 'not to have any biases or stereotypes toward any language'. Others highlighted the role of the teacher in creating a safe classroom environment, teaching students to respect each other. One student indicated the need for teachers to emphasize 'that everyone is unique and their language is special' and that 'everyone should be able to feel comfortable being different and being able to talk about the differences'. Many participants also suggested that teachers should teach students about languages other than English, with the most common suggestion being students presenting words and sayings in their L1 to their classmates, positioning them as valued experts on their L1. One student suggested that teachers address language diversity by 'asking all the students to share about the languages they know or speak at home as an activity for the students and teacher to learn about a language'. Together, these insights illustrate how bilingual students' reflections on their own language experiences may be leveraged to shape their future instructional practices as they embark on career trajectories as English teachers, bilingual educators and teachers of content courses in which uses of English language will inevitably play key roles in academic learning.

Conclusion

In this chapter, we argued that prospective teachers of English language, including bilingual educators and content teachers serving linguistically diverse students, need opportunities in teacher education to engage in self-reflexive inquiry into culture, language and identities, and to explore ways to leverage their experiences and knowledge for use in their future teaching careers. We described a language inventory process as one tool we found promising in promoting metalinguistic awareness and in fostering ideas for use in teaching, a tool that can serve teachers of English as a Second Language along the career continuum. Potential teachers of color who are bilingual in the US context, in particular, may have experiences and histories that can be explored and mined for ideas related to linking the personal with the pedagogical (Athanases, Banes & Wong, 2015). From language inventories and surveys of this group, many of whom identified teaching as a definite or potential career, we uncovered three overarching themes we illustrated with samples of students' reflections: developing language awareness; recognizing the value of multilingualism and cost of language loss; and recasting language shame to resist linguicism. While dimensions of these themes are not new to literature on language development and education, important here is that students reported the themes grounded in their personal histories and embedded in larger socio-political themes. This kind of early-career attention and self-reflexive work may serve future teachers of English language by anchoring them in their own lived histories and helping them to foster a sense of agency to bring a critical lens to language teaching, as they are the ones who ultimately will negotiate and implement language policies in their classrooms as their careers unfold.

Drawing upon our research, we offer two recommendations for practice and policy. First, we recommend that all prospective and in-service English language teachers of linguistically diverse students engage in self-reflexive inquiry into culture, language and identities with two goals in mind. One goal is to understand the dynamic and situated nature of language use through personal reflection informed by additional sources; a second goal is for teachers to leverage understandings and experiences as resources to serve linguistically diverse students in their current and future teaching practice.

We argue that self-reflexive inquiry heightens awareness of the socio-political context of language learning and teaching and that this awareness establishes a critical foundation for one's trajectory of teaching English language along the career continuum. Without developing this awareness, English-language teachers may continue to reproduce English-only ideologies that privilege a 'Standard English', contributing to students' language and cultural loss. Such experiences were reported by many of our students who had internalized linguistic shame and deficit-thinking about themselves. As illustrated, many successful multilingual undergraduate students continue to struggle with their linguistic identity. These students often refrain from participating in class discussions for fear of being judged for how they speak. Teachers who develop a critical framework for teaching English are more cognizant of how English instruction may perpetuate hegemonic practices and ideologies that subordinate students' home languages and cultures, and are likely to be better equipped to balance these tensions throughout their careers as they provide students with access to the linguistic capital associated with English.

Our second recommendation is for teacher education to make visible the agency of English-language teachers to shape local language policies. Such agency may help teachers at various points on their career trajectories to critique mandates and discourse that subordinate non-mainstream students and to instill a mission of advocacy in their students and a fostering of self-advocacy by them as language learners. Ultimately, teachers are the ones who establish educational contexts and negotiate education and language policies that directly impact how students learn English (Palmer & Martinez, 2013). Teacher agency too often is neglected in teacher education, especially when factory models of teacher preparation and K-12 education are reinforced. However, teacher educators may prepare teachers to serve linguistically diverse students by helping them identify the deficit-thinking many of their students have internalized. One way is by facilitating opportunities for language teachers to mine and examine their prior literacy experiences through a framework that problematizes mainstream linguistic norms and creates spaces that honor students' linguistic identities and uses of language. Many teachers still do not understand how to create supportive, language-rich learning spaces; however, through understanding their agency and selves as dynamic language users, they may be better prepared for a career's worth of teaching to resist English-dominant norms and ideologies and create different types of communities for language learning.

We argue that preparation for a career in English-language teaching begins with activities that facilitate looking to the self, drawing on one's own experiences, and problematizing linguistic norms that subordinate oneself and/or others. Although not all students in our classes will become teachers, their reflections nonetheless highlight themes that are valuable for embarking on careers in English-language teaching that actively resist linguicism and cultivate bilingualism.

Notes

[1] English Learners is a label used in US educational policies to identify students who speak a primary language other than English at home and are learning English as an academic language in school. As authors, we problematize how this label positions individuals only in relation to their proficiency in English.

[2] Microaggressions are brief and subtle denigrating actions premised on stereotypes (Sue et al, 2007).

References

Asher, N. (2007) Made in the (Multicultural) USA: unpacking tensions of race, culture, gender, and sexuality in education, *Educational Researcher*, 36(2), 65-73. http://dx.doi.org/10.3102/0013189X07299188

Athanases, S.Z., Banes, L.C. & Wong, J.W. (2015) Diverse Language Profiles: leveraging resources of potential bilingual teachers of color, *Bilingual Research Journal*, 38(1), 65-87. http://dx.doi.org/10.1080/15235882.2015.1017622

Athanases, S.Z., Banes, L.C., Wong, J.W. & Martinez, D.C. (2015) Toward Leveraging Discoveries about Language Use for Teaching Linguistically Diverse Students. Paper presented at the American Educational Research Association annual meeting, Chicago, and submitted for publication.

California Department of Education (2015) English Learner Students by Language and Grade. March. http://dq.cde.ca.gov/dataquest/SpringData/StudentsByLanguage.aspx?Level=Stat e&TheYear=2014-15&SubGroup=All&ShortYear=1415&GenderGroup=B&CD SCode=00000000000000&RecordType=EL

De Jong, E.J. & Harper, C.A. (2005) Preparing Mainstream Teachers for English-language Learners: is being a good teacher good enough? *Teacher Education Quarterly*, 101-124.

de Oliveira, L.C. (2011) In Their Shoes: teachers experience the needs of English language learners through a math simulation, *Multicultural Education*, 19(1), 59-62.

Fránquiz, M.E., Salazar, M.D.C. & DeNicolo, C.P. (2011) Challenging Majoritarian Tales: portraits of bilingual teachers deconstructing deficit views of bilingual learners, *Bilingual Research Journal*, 34, 279-300. http://dx.doi.org/10.1080/15235882.2011.625884

Hill, J.H. (2009) *The Everyday Language of White Racism*. Oxford: Wiley-Blackwell.

Lucas, T. & Grinberg, J. (2008) Responding to the Linguistic Reality of the Mainstream Classroom: preparing classroom teachers to teach English language learners, in M. Cochran-Smith, S. Feiman-Nemser & J. McIntyre (Eds) *Handbook of Research on Teacher Education: enduring issues in changing contexts*, pp. 606-636. Mahwah, NJ: Lawrence Erlbaum Associates.

Milroy, J. & Milroy, L. (1985) *Authority in Language: investigating language prescription and standardisation*. London: Routledge. http://dx.doi.org/10.4324/9780203267424

Palmer, D.K. & Martinez, R. (2013) Teacher Agency in Bilingual Spaces, *Review of Research in Education*, 37, 269-297. http://dx.doi.org/10.3102/0091732X12463556

Skutnabb-Kangas, T. & Cummins, J. (Eds) (1988) *Minority Education: from shame to struggle*. Clevedon: Multilingual Matters.

Sue, D.W., Capodilupo, C.M., Torino, G.C., Bucceri, J.M., Holder, A.M.B., Nadal, K.L. & Esquilin, M. (2007) Racial Microaggressions in Everyday Life, *American Psychologist*, 62(4), 271-286. http://dx.doi.org/10.1037/0003-066X.62.4.271

Tan, A. (1999) Mother Tongue, in S. Gillespie & R. Singleton (Eds) *Across Cultures*, pp. 26-31. Boston: Allyn & Bacon.

Valdés, G., Bunch, G., Snow, C. & Lee, C., with Matos, L. (2005) Enhancing the Development of Students' Language(s), in L. Darling-Hammond & J. Bransford (Eds) *Preparing Teachers for a Changing World: what teachers should learn and be able to do*, pp. 126-168. San Francisco: Jossey-Bass.

Zeichner, K.M. (2009) *Teacher Education and the Struggle for Social Justice*. New York: Routledge.

Zumwalt, K. & Craig, E. (2005) Teachers' Characteristics: research on the demographic profile, in M. Cochran-Smith & K.M. Zeichner (Eds) *Studying Teacher Education: the report of the AERA panel on research and teacher education*, pp. 111-156. Mahwah, NJ: Lawrence Erlbaum Associates.

CHAPTER 10

Using VideoWeb in EFL Teacher Education: do the benefits differ between teachers with and without previous teaching experience?

EVA MINAŘÍKOVÁ, MICHAELA PÍŠOVÁ & TOMÁŠ JANÍK

SUMMARY Due to the changes in educational policy and the lack of English as a Foreign Language (EFL) teachers after the fall of communism in 1989, unqualified teachers were (and still are) allowed to teach in the Czech Republic. Some of these experienced teachers now seek to gain formal qualifications, which is why the professional biographies of teacher education programme participants vary greatly. This chapter reports on the benefits of a video-based e-learning environment (VideoWeb), which is a part of a teacher education programme for student teachers with and without prior teaching experience (*n* = 37). Their comments on video sequences were analysed to determine how they evaluate classroom situations before and after VideoWeb. Furthermore, their comments on the benefits of VideoWeb were investigated. The analysis showed that there are differences for the more and less experienced group in both these respects. The authors hope to open a discussion on the varying needs of teacher education programme participants with different career trajectories.

Even 25 years after the fall of the communist regime, the career trajectories of teachers of English as a Foreign Language (EFL) in the Czech Republic continue to be shaped by this crucial change. Before 1989, mostly the Russian language was taught in Czech schools at all levels due to the ties with the Soviet Union. This, however, changed rapidly. After the Velvet Revolution (i.e. the non-violent transition from the communist regime to democracy) in 1989, Russian ceased to be an obligatory subject and even evoked negative emotions. Schools started offering other languages (mostly English and German). By the mid-1990s English had become the most widely taught foreign language in the Czech Republic (Hanušová & Najvar, 2007, p. 43). However, qualified English teachers were scarce. There was almost no need for them before the revolution, but they were in great demand afterwards. Many Russian teachers upgraded their qualifications and there were many courses offered for those interested in teaching languages. The greater demand for language teachers went hand in hand with a greater offer of university programmes in teaching languages. These could be studied full time or part time. Despite this, there were still not enough (English) language teachers to satisfy the demand. A new law introduced another exception in 1997 – all university graduates (including those from non-teaching tracks) who had passed the state language exam (approximately today's level C1 according to the Common European Framework of Languages) were allowed to teach language (Čermáková, 2014, p. I). This exception was initially valid for two years but was prolonged repeatedly and, with certain modifications, is still in effect today. This ultimately led to a high number of unqualified teachers at schools. According to Faklova (1999), 76% of all foreign language teachers in the school year 1996/1997 did not have language teaching qualifications. Even ten years later, the situation was far from satisfactory. According to the Czech School Inspectorate (Česká školní inspekce, 2010, p. 8), between the years 2006 and 2009, only approximately 38% of language teachers at primary and lower-secondary schools were qualified to teach language, while 34% were qualified to teach other subjects and more than 25% had no teaching qualifications at all (Česká školní inspekce, 2010).

The discontinuation of the exception has been discussed for many years now. That might be one of the reasons why unqualified but practising English teachers seek to gain formal qualifications at university. However, the programmes offered are not usually designed for them as they can be and are attended by people from all walks of life. Any course can, for example, be frequented by unqualified practising EFL teachers, by students who have just finished secondary education, by (prospective) career changers with no prior teaching practice, and by private language school teachers experienced in teaching adults.

At first glance, this might not seem problematic. All the participants in the programme, no matter what their biographies are, are aiming towards the same qualifications and thus should receive the same instruction. Research on teacher development (e.g. Fuller & Bown, 1975; Kagan, 1992; Berliner, 1995), however, tells us that, with experience, teachers, their knowledge, thinking and practice, do change.

Some models of professional development describe the first period (novice teacher) as the 'survival stage' (e.g. Richardson & Placier, 2001). This stage entails first encounters with pupils, colleagues and the principal, and can be accompanied by feelings of insecurity and doubts about one's own professional qualities. It is characterised by concerns about class control and adequacy of fulfilling one's role (Fuller & Bown, 1975). Teachers are preoccupied with their relationship with students and, as they are still less secure in their role, they are more attuned to negative reactions from students (Gatbonton, 2008, p. 174). Berliner (1995, p. 47) notes that it is a period when general context-free rules are acquired. According to Kagan (1992, p. 156), professional growth of novice and beginning teachers is marked by an increase in metacognition, the acquisition of knowledge about pupils, a shift in attention from self to the design of instruction and to pupil learning, the development of standard procedures, and growth in problem-solving skills. With experience, teachers learn to recognise what is and is not important in a classroom situation; general rules are applied in context-specific conditions and teachers learn to recognise when to break them. They develop a 'more intuitive sense of the situation' and a more holistic way of seeing the situation (Berliner, 1995, pp. 47-48). However, not all teachers reach higher stages of professional development and 'might remain fixed at a less competent level of performance' (Berliner, 1995, p. 47).

It follows that teacher education (pre-service and in-service) has different tasks at different stages of individual teachers' professional development (Feiman-Nemser, 2001). At first, during the preparation phase, it can help them analyse their beliefs and form new visions, develop their subject-matter knowledge for teaching, their understanding of learners and learning, their repertoire of teaching techniques, and tools to study teaching. During the induction phase, teachers need support in gaining local knowledge of students, curriculum and school context, designing responsive curriculum and instruction, enacting the beginning repertoire in purposeful ways, creating a classroom learning community, and learning in and from practice. Further professional development can then focus mainly on deepening and extending subject-matter knowledge for teaching, as well as extending and refining the teacher's repertoire (Feiman-Nemser, 2001).

However, this approach presupposes that all teachers go through the first stage – that is, that they first obtain qualifications in pre-service teacher education, and that the following stages build upon this and their growing experience. What happens when participants of teacher education have (considerable) practical teaching experience but have never participated in a teacher education programme? What are the tasks and goals of such a programme? And what would be tasks and goals of a programme that has to cater for (prospective) teachers with varied biographies (as described above)?

In our context, these are issues that language teacher educators encounter every day. However, they often remain unaddressed. In this chapter we would like to open the discussion by exploring how the benefits of a specific teacher education course differ between students with and without prior teaching experience. The specific context and aims of the course and the research will be introduced in the following section.

Context of the Study

Our interest in exploring the differences between student teachers with and without prior teaching experience stems from our direct experience with teaching a course for 'mixed-biography' participants. This course was optional and was offered to all students in the English department at our institution (Faculty of Education, Masaryk University, Brno, Czech Republic). As a result, there was a mixture of bachelor's and master's degree students; some had studied EFL methodology and some had not; some had experience in teaching and some did not. Working with such groups proved demanding but rewarding, and gave rise to the above-mentioned questions. The course, entitled VideoWeb, was designed to help student teachers develop their professional vision, or the way they perceive classroom situations and the reason for this (Sherin & van Es, 2009; Stürmer et al, 2013; Minaříková et al, 2015). The following section introduces the VideoWeb course in detail.

VideoWeb

VideoWeb is an online course organised by the Department of English language and literature at the Faculty of Education, Masaryk University in Brno, Czech Republic. It lasts one semester and is open to all the students in the department. The participants in this course form a diverse group, as noted above. The online e-learning environment uses video cases to help student teachers develop their professional vision. The students work independently through five online modules that focus on five salient issues in English-language teaching methodology – namely: teacher questions; aims of activities; giving instructions; giving feedback; and developing key competencies in pupils.[1] Each module consists of two or three video cases that elaborate upon the given topic and provide opportunities for analysing video sequences from EFL classrooms (1-to-4-minutes-long self-contained classroom situations), in addition to studying excerpts from EFL methodology books and other sources. When analysing videos, students are guided by a set of questions aiming to focus their attention. After answering each of the questions, the students can compare their replies with the so-called expert opinion; they are advised, though, that this represents a 'possible' answer, not the one and only correct response. Throughout the course the students can contact the course teacher with any questions or comments. They can also start a thread in an (asynchronous) course forum to discuss any issues they encounter with all the other participants. After completing each of the modules, the students are asked to summarise what they have learnt.

Altogether 37 students completed VideoWeb between autumn 2011 and autumn 2012 (3 semesters). The average age of these students was 28 years. There were 27 women and 10 men, 23 in the bachelor's programme, 14 in the master's programme. There were 13 participants who reported having either no or limited teaching experience (usually only compulsory teaching practice, up to 50 hours), and 24 participants who reported that they had been teaching for a longer period of time (above 50 hours). These details are summarised in Table I. Participants gained their teaching experience in various settings: state schools (primary or secondary), private tutoring, or private language schools teaching adult learners.

	Number of participants	Bachelor's programme	Master's programme	Average age	Male	Female
Limited experience	13	9	4	23.5	4	9
Experienced	24	14	10	30.0	6	18

Table I. VideoWeb participants.

The present study is embedded in a larger research study on student teachers' professional vision and its development through VideoWeb (Minaříková et al, 2015). In particular, in this chapter we focus on different benefits of participation in VideoWeb for two groups of students – those with and those without prior teaching experience. The gains were explored on two levels: changes in participants' comments on classroom videos, and the benefits of participation that they themselves report. Specifically, we were interested in whether there were any differences between the two groups, with regard to their changes pre- and post-VideoWeb, in the following areas:

1. how the participants evaluate educational reality captured in video sequences (as evident in their statements regarding giving instructions);
2. participants' reported benefits of working with VideoWeb.

Methods

The data for the main study were collected using a web-based questionnaire that VideoWeb participants completed at the start and the end of the course. The questionnaire consisted of four video sequences from EFL classrooms (1 to 4 minutes long) supplemented by context information and, when necessary, classroom materials (worksheets, textbook pages). Each video sequence was followed by a prompt: *Please comment on the video you have just observed.*[2] In the questionnaire at the end of the semester, two videos were repeated from the pre-test (videos B and C) and two new videos were included in order to address the issue of repeated viewing effect.

For the purpose of tapping into the changes in participants' evaluations of classroom situations, the scope of the analysis was limited to the theme *giving instructions* and only conducted for responses to one of the video sequences used in the questionnaire (video B). The focus on a well-defined area of instruction allowed us to explore how participants' views changed, which might be indicative of changes not only in their professional vision but also in their professional knowledge. Comments on video B were selected as the video portrayed the start of a classroom activity – that is, teachers' instructions and also pupils' reactions. The video provided ample opportunities for discussing *giving instructions* as there were a number of instances where the teacher's approach could have been changed for the better. Comments to video sequence B were analysed in terms of whether they mention *giving instructions*. If yes, the comment was then assigned a category depending on whether it was overall *positive*, overall *negative*, or *neutral*. The content of video sequence B is described below.

> *Video Sequence B (2:09)*
> A sequence from the end of a lesson for intermediate students at a grammar school. The teacher introduces a pair work activity – an interview with a music star (based on previous reading and grammar exercises). It is not clear if the students are following. After setting the tasks, the teacher monitors and corrects mistakes of individual students.

The second source of data was participants' evaluations of individual modules. After completing each module, the participants were asked: *What have you learnt in this module (not necessarily only theoretical information)?* Their responses were inductively analysed and five categories emerged that will be presented in the following Results section.

Results

In this section we are going to introduce the results of the two analyses. The data presentation follows the structure set by the research questions mentioned above.

Evaluation of Educational Reality Captured in Video Sequences

Evaluation of educational reality captured in video sequences was investigated with regard to the topic of *giving instructions*. As noted earlier, comments responding to video sequence B that contained statements regarding giving instructions were divided into three categories – positive, negative and neutral (see Table II, which shows the percentage of comments in each category). Afterwards, how the evaluation changed for individual participants was determined (see Table III for the percentage of comments in each change category).

Most of the comments in both the experienced and inexperienced group were negative before as well as after VideoWeb. This is likely to be connected with the content of the video sequence that had some negative features (unclear hurried instructions, confused pupils). The groups differed in positive evaluations and neutral comments. Before VideoWeb, many students in the inexperienced group did not mention giving instructions at all and many commented on them in a neutral way. On the other hand, many students in the experienced group evaluated them positively. This might have been caused by their focus on the more positive features of the situation – for example, that the teacher spoke mostly English and helped the students when needed. However, after VideoWeb the experienced group's positive comments became less common. The neutral comments were also more frequent in both groups after VideoWeb.

	No experience		Experienced	
	Before %	After %	Before %	After %
Not mentioned	23.08	7.69	4.17	0.00
Neutral	23.08	30.77	12.50	37.50
Positive	7.69	15.38	29.17	4.17
Negative	46.15	46.15	54.17	58.33

Table II. Evaluation of video sequence B (topic: giving instructions).

		No experience %	Experience d %
The same	Evaluation before and after was the same	15.38	45.83
Opposite evaluation	Evaluation changed from positive to negative or vice versa	0.00	16.67
To neutral	From evaluating or not mentioning to neutral comments	30.77	29.17
To evaluation	From neutral comments or not mentioning to evaluating	46.15	8.33
To nothing	In post-test, instructions not mentioned	7.69	0.00

Table III. Changes in evaluation of video sequence B (topic: giving instructions).

If the changes for individual students are considered, major differences between groups are evident. In the inexperienced group, only 15% of the students commented on giving instructions in the same way (in this case, negatively) after participating in VideoWeb. On the other hand, almost half of the experienced group stood by their original evaluation (mostly negative). About 30% of the comments in both groups became neutral. Interestingly enough, almost half of the inexperienced group started evaluating the instructions after participating in VideoWeb (as opposed to not mentioning this aspect at all or being neutral before VideoWeb).

Reported Benefits of Working with VideoWeb

After completing each module the participants formulated what they had learned when working with it. For this analysis, only data from one semester (one group of participants; *n*=16) were considered. Through inductive analysis, five categories emerged. Some of the respondents claimed that they acquired (1) new *Information* or (2) a new *Rule* (or were reminded of it). Sometimes the respondents claimed that the module provided them with (3) an *Impulse to think* or (4) an *Impulse to act*. On rare occasions, the respondents reported (5) *No benefits*. Acquiring a new rule means that the students reported learning that *you should* or *it is good to* do a certain thing (normative statements); for example: *You should get students' attention before giving instructions*. Value-neutral statements were categorised as acquiring new information (e.g. *I learned about wait time*). The responses of the experienced group were more varied (i.e. there was a bigger difference between the maximum and the minimum values, except for the *Information* category). This might have been influenced by the fact that there were more participants in this group. Figure 1 shows average number of comments in each category. On average, the more experienced participants stated less often that they gained new *Information* or learned a new *Rule* but more often that the module gave them an *Impulse to think* (in general or about their own practice). These results will be discussed in the subsequent section.

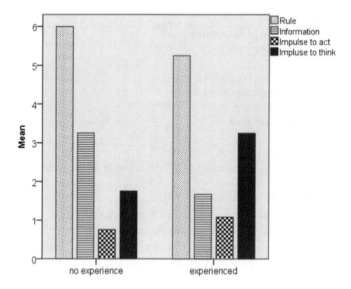

Figure 1. Mean values of reported benefits of working with VideoWeb.

Discussion and Conclusion

This study was inspired by our experiences in a university teacher education course that has to cater for participants with different professional biographies. Based on the research on professional development of teachers and its various stages we assumed that teachers with different backgrounds come to our course equipped differently. It is then to be expected that their learning and learning experiences in the course will vary.

When Berliner (1995) talks about the different stages of teachers' professional development, he mentions the different approaches teachers at various stages take to rules. For example, at the beginning of their careers teachers acquire general (context-free) rules and as they progress, they learn to apply them (or break them) depending on the context.

Different approaches to rules were evident in the perceived benefits the participants reported. The inexperienced group reported *Rule* acquisition on average slightly more often than the experienced group. Also, the number of statements was similar for all of the participants in the group (with just a small variation). Contrastingly, the difference between maximum and minimum values was substantial for the experienced group, suggesting that there were big differences between the individual participants in the group. This might have been caused by the wide range in the years of experience within the group and also by the fact that each individual's learning experience differs and that they learn from experience differently (compare Berliner's notion that not all teachers progress to higher levels of professional competence; see above). When we group the *Rule acquisition* with the *Information acquisition* benefits and the *Impulse to think* with the *Impulse to act* benefits, the results seem to be in line with Berliner's conclusions. The more experienced teachers did not report acquiring many context-free rules, but rather VideoWeb made them think about teaching and learning in general and about their practice in particular.

The fact that the less experienced participants acquired new rules that they applied to the observed situations is also evident in the changes in evaluation of the video sequences. Whereas the experienced group stood by their original evaluation of the situation half of the time, only about 15% of the comments from the inexperienced group contained the same evaluation pre- and post-VideoWeb. The dominant tendency for the inexperienced group was to start evaluating (as opposed to not mentioning instructions or being neutral). This might suggest that VideoWeb helped the less experienced participants acquire new rules about giving instructions and applying them to evaluating situations. On the other hand, it would seem that the more experienced students had acquired the rules beforehand and used them in their comments in a more consistent way. Unfortunately, our analysis does not show how relevant these evaluations (and thus the applied rules) were. This lack of change could therefore be either positive (if their initial evaluations were relevant) or negative, in that VideoWeb did not succeed in making the experienced teachers see the situations in a new light.

However, for any change to be established, more analyses would be needed that would consider the quality of the comments. The analysis presented in this chapter has only dealt with the comments on a descriptive level, which could be regarded as one of the limitations of the study. The other limitation is the sampling method used (convenience sampling) and the limited number of participants. Because of this, we have interpreted our results as tendencies, and our aim is to collect more data to further explore these findings.

Nevertheless, we believe that this study has achieved its aim – to open the discussion on the influence that the diverse population of students attending language teacher education courses (in the Czech Republic) has on the courses themselves, and on the benefits for the students. We have shown that experienced and inexperienced participants of language teacher education courses learn differently from the same content. Their approach to rules differs, which might have an impact on their teaching practice, in that what teachers evaluate as positive or negative influences how they (aim to) behave when they are teaching. Thus it is imperative for language teacher educators to bear this in mind when working with the diverse population of EFL (student) teachers.

The diversity of the student population has its roots in the changes following the Velvet Revolution in 1989. However, the lack of qualified English language teachers is a worldwide phenomenon. It goes hand in hand with the diversification of paths to the teaching profession. Therefore this study might be relevant also outside the Czech context.

Acknowledgements

The preparation of this chapter was supported by a Czech Science Foundation project, GA13-21961S.

Notes

[1] The last topic focuses on the opportunities English lessons provide for developing key competencies in pupils (problem-solving competence, learning to learn, etc.). This topic was included as it relates to one of the innovations that was introduced by the recent curricular reform in the Czech Republic.

[2] The task was set in English as the whole course was organised by the Department of English that follows an 'all-English policy' (i.e. all communication – in or outside of lessons – must be conducted in English). However, the students were instructed that they could write their answers in either English or Czech, or they could combine both languages. This approach was chosen in order to allow the students to express their ideas freely. The fact that the ideas are important, not the language, was stressed

repeatedly. Many students used the opportunity to select the language they preferred to use (and also to switch languages).

References

Berliner, D.C. (1995) Teacher Expertise, in L.W. Anderson (Ed.) *International Encyclopedia of Teaching and Teacher Education*, pp. 46-52. Oxford: Elsevier.

Čermáková, H. (2014) *Výuka cizích jazyků a proces přípravy učitelů cizích jazyků v období 1990-2012* [The teaching of foreign languages and the process of preparation of teachers of foreign languages in the period 1990-2012]. Unpublished diploma thesis, Charles University, Prague.

Česká školní inspekce [Czech School Inspectorate] (2010) *Souhrnné poznatky o podpoře a rozvoji výuky cizích jazyků v předškolním, základním a středním vzdělávání v období let 2006-2009* [General information on the support and development of foreign language teaching in pre-primary, primary and secondary education between 2006-2009]. Prague: Česká školní inspekce. http://www.csicr.cz/cz/85027-podpora-a-rozvoj-vyuky-cizich-jazyku

Faklová, Z. (1999) Baseline Study on FLT to Young Learners in the Czech Republic, in M. Nikolov & H. Curtain (Eds) *An Early Start: young learners and modern languages in Europe and beyond*, pp. 79-92. Strasbourg: Council of Europe Publishing.

Feiman-Nemser, S. (2001) From Preparation to Practice: designing a continuum to strengthen and sustain teaching, *Teachers College Record*, 103(6), 1013-1055. http://dx.doi.org/10.1111/0161-4681.00141

Fuller, F. & Bown, O. (1975) Becoming a Teacher, in K. Ryan (Ed.) *Teacher Education (74th Yearbook of the National Society for the Study of Education, Part 2)*, pp. 25-52. Chicago: University of Chicago Press.

Gatbonton, E. (2008) Looking Beyond Teachers' Classroom Behaviour: novice and experienced ESL teachers' pedagogical knowledge, *Language Teaching Research*, 12(2), 161-182. http://dx.doi.org/10.1177/1362168807086286

Hanušová, S. & Najvar, P. (2007) Výuka cizího jazyka v raném věku [Teaching English as a foreign language to young learners], *Pedagogická orientace*, 17(3), 42-52.

Kagan, D.M. (1992) Professional Growth among Preservice and Beginning Teachers, *Review of Educational Research*, 62(2), 129-169. http://dx.doi.org/10.3102/00346543062002129

Minaříková, E., Píšová, M. & Janík, T. (2015) Using Video in Teacher Education: an example from the Czech Republic, in L. Orland-Barak & C.J. Craig (Eds) *International Teacher Education: promising pedagogies (Part B)*, pp. 379-400. Bingley: Emerald Group Publishing.

Richardson, V. & Placier, P. (2001) Teacher Change, in V. Richardson (Ed.) *Handbook of Research on Teaching*, pp. 905-947. Washington, DC: American Educational Research Association (AERA).

Sherin, M.G. & van Es, E.A. (2009) Effects of Video Club Participation on Teachers' Professional Vision, *Journal of Teacher Education*, 60(1), 20-37. http://dx.doi.org/10.1177/0022487108328155

Stürmer, K., Könings, K.D. & Seidel, T. (2013) Declarative Knowledge and Professional Vision in Teacher Education: effect of courses in teaching and learning, *British Journal of Educational Psychology*, 83(3), 467-483. http://dx.doi.org/10.1111/j.2044-8279.2012.02075.x

CHAPTER 11

Innovating in Initial Teacher Education: a new integrated curriculum for meaningful English learning

MARY JANE ABRAHAMS & PABLO SILVA RÍOS

SUMMARY Although school students in Chile have a minimum of eight years of English with an official curriculum which clearly focuses on communication skills, national English tests prove they leave secondary school without having reached even the language competence level prescribed for primary education leavers, CEFR A2. A wide variety of factors can be claimed to account for such disastrous results. English teachers' classroom practices can be evidently claimed as one of the most influential of those factors. The consequent question would be what has their teacher education program been like, and how could they be improved in order to safeguard English teaching/learning effectiveness in schools? This chapter reports on the teacher education program at Universidad Alberto Hurtado in Chile, which proposes the integration of program components, giving special attention to integrated English language learning. This proposed change is based on the understanding that an English teacher education program with disconnected and fragmented subjects will never offer pre-service language teachers the opportunity to experience and understand that, beyond its complexities and varied facets, when the aim is communication, learning a foreign language is indeed a unitary subject that needs to be understood as such.

Introduction

We have worked as teachers of English in Santiago, Chile and abroad for a long time, putting all of it together approximately during the last forty-five years. Early in our professional lives we opted for teacher education to be able to address and find solutions to the problems related to school teachers'

141

pre-service education and the unsuccessful results obtained by secondary school leavers in the use of the English language.

For seventeen years, schools and universities were in the hands of the military or people designated by the military junta. Faculties of education were removed from universities and turned into technical institutes. Teaching ceased to be considered an academic profession and those graduates became technicians. The obvious result was a loss of quality and dignity, evidenced in the school results of the vast majority of the population. Once we returned to a democratic form of government in 1990, pedagogy programs became university faculties once again. But, by law, universities continued to be autonomous, so the Ministry of Education did not have the authority to set guidelines for the teacher training programs they offer. Therefore, educational reform, the crucial goal for the Ministry of Education, focused on primary and secondary schools only.

This reform affected English significantly. English had become the language of globalization. Therefore, for the government it became obvious that promoting the teaching and learning of the language was a national priority. One of the main measures was to move the start of the teaching of English from seventh grade down to fifth grade in order to extend students' exposure to the language to eight full years. This was implemented in classrooms in 1998 with a new curriculum, new programs, new free textbooks and a totally different approach to the teaching–learning process. Unfortunately, one of the most important obstacles for this new policy to be effective was that no provisions had been made about the number of English teachers available to cover fifth and sixth grades. As a result, many schools in the country had to hire teachers of other subjects who did not even speak the language. The urgency for universities to strengthen and expand Teaching English as a Foreign Language (TEFL) programs was evident, but it took them years to react and offer programs to train teachers for primary schools. Another consequence was that English became the only foreign language that had official programs for each school year and free official textbooks. This resulted in teachers of French, for example, having to switch over to becoming teachers of English, with very little support from their schools or from the government.

On the other hand, the new curriculum also set guidelines for moving from grammar translation to a more modern and communicative text-based approach developing the receptive skills with less emphasis on the productive skills. By that time, English was seen mainly as a tool that would allow citizens to have access to information (MINEDUC, 2005, p. 65) and to better jobs. After about 850 hours that the whole program offered, the idea was that students would be able to, with enough learning strategies, understand written and oral texts, plus have a basic command of spoken English. Voluntary training, organized by the Ministry of Education, was given to classroom teachers by universities during the summer of 1998, plus a two-week workshop during their winter holidays. The authors participated in this project and felt the impact of classroom teachers' despair at having to change their ways and practices so drastically. This was another sign for us to start thinking about getting involved in teacher education and trying to find out what it was that we needed to improve, remove or adjust in a pre-service teacher education program.

The precise moment came when we were asked to design an initial teacher education program for English at Universidad Alberto Hurtado (UAH), a Jesuit university, in 2004, and then later to develop and implement it in 2005. This led to the design of a five-year curriculum where the emphasis was placed on language as a complex but unitary phenomenon, and on the process of language teaching and learning. The central idea was to reduce the fragmentation of traditional Chilean curricula present in most local universities. We observed that one of the consequences of such fragmentation is an excess of grammar, phonetics and vocabulary subjects. This distracted from the main aim of enabling teachers to speak English at an advanced level and, at the same time, giving them the knowledge to teach it with enough methodology and pedagogy as well as theoretical knowledge and classroom practice. Julian Edge (2011) explains that separating areas to be analyzed and categorized can take us a long way. However, the world is not just a number of its constituent parts - the purpose remains to understand the whole a little better. In his own words, Edge asks: 'Isn't that, for instance, what grammar is all about?' (2011, p. 12). Our design did not give less importance to linguistic knowledge but integrated areas like this into the English language strand.

Therefore, we proposed three major strands – (a) English language; (b) linguistics and methodology; and (c) work experience, practicum and reflection workshops – but in addition retained two lexico-grammar subjects, one phonetics subject, two culture and civilization subjects, and four literature subjects. We also had humanistic subjects as a university requirement – such as philosophy, history, math, Spanish, etc. The program was divided into a two-year foundation stage followed by a three-year disciplinary, pedagogical stage. By the time students finished their second year, their level of English was expected to be B2, since they would have had twenty hours of English a week and 850 hours in two years. We felt this was a huge leap from the way we had been educated as teachers, but there was still something missing that prevented our students from becoming the professionals we expected them to become. Program integration was still unsatisfactory, not enabling our students to relate the different contents to one whole. Teachers, on the other hand, had not yet grasped the full concept of 'integration', so each concentrated on their own topic or discipline without connecting with the rest. As Ornstein and Hunkins (2004) state, knowledge is not separated from its reality, people cannot really disconnect themselves from their enquiry; the curriculum cannot really exist as separate bits. We needed our teachers of English to be imbued with the complexities of the teaching and learning process. Academic education is meaningful inasmuch as it contributes to a more effective practice because the future teacher fits into the exit profile and they have understood that theory and practice need to go together.

New Developments

By the time our students were in their fifth year in 2010, an important review of our program had to take place. The team (comprised of the Head of Program, and methodology, language, practicum, and information and communication technologies [ICTs] coordinators) met during that year to reflect, discuss and interview focus groups of students, alumni and stakeholders to share issues, adjustments and new ideas on how to answer the challenge of educating our students according to our new exit profile. The project was finally approved by the university authorities and implemented in 2011 with the name of 'Integrated Curriculum'. The core principle underpinned in our proposal is clearly stated by Norton and Toohey (2004, p. 1): 'language is not simply a means of expression or communication: rather, it is a practice that constructs, and is constructed by, the ways language learners understand themselves, their social surroundings, their histories, and their possibilities for the future'.

At the same time, after twelve years of the reform in the teaching of English in Chile, the Ministry of Education decided to evaluate the level of English students were graduating with. Unfortunately, international English tests given by the Ministry to the whole population of eleventh graders in the country in 2010, 2012 and 2014 proved beyond a doubt that students, around 85% to 90%, were leaving secondary school without having reached even the language competence level prescribed for primary education leavers, CEFR A2.

The English team at UAH, very much aware of the seriousness of what was disclosed, felt and accepted the challenge for an urgent and drastic innovation in how future teachers should be educated in our pre-service program. Namely, we needed to come to terms with and find answers to several issues we had not been able to address up to then. As Widdowson (2003) asks, what kind of options are there in language pedagogy, and how might we theorize about them? This led us to think that a protected time and space were needed to effectively sit down and reflect about our options, and to rethink our curriculum with the exit profile in mind. Therefore, in December 2013, a three-day academic retreat was held for all the staff involved in teaching the discipline subjects. This event took place in Leyda, a holiday resort about an hour away from Santiago, so that the work could be done without interruptions of any kind and concentrating on the discussion. The objective of the meeting was to reflect on how we were implementing the new curriculum, identifying strengths and weaknesses and creating strategies that would help us enhance the education of our future teachers and ensure their achievement of the exit profile. One crucial unexpected product was a *halfway profile* at the end of the second year to account for expected outcomes at the foundation stage. This profile sets the guidelines and builds a bridge to allow progress monitoring, thus avoiding knowledge and practice gaps in our newly qualified teachers. This halfway profile was stated as follows:

> A student who begins the third year of the English Pedagogy Program at Universidad Alberto Hurtado, is inquisitive about academic learning; able to raise questions and propose solutions from a critical perspective to complex issues emerging from their own reflection and from the classroom. This reflects a student with committed and well-founded opinions, with a clear sense of social participation and who is active in the English Pedagogy program. The student has developed professional attitudes of responsibility, autonomy and flexibility; and ethical attitudes of respect, justice and honesty. At the same time, the student is able to work in teams in a collaborative manner, with assertiveness and respect for diversity. In terms of their English language competence, the student who begins third year is able to demonstrate a higher intermediate level equivalent to CEFR B2.

Another product was a *set of projects* to improve our integrated curriculum program. First of all, a *code of practice* was planned to be developed in order to address our students' lack of inquisitive knowledge and academic attitude, plus low self-esteem. Also, a *portfolio* was considered to be necessary in order to facilitate students' awareness of their own learning progress with hard evidence in terms of standardized tests, essays, papers, videos and reflections on their practice. In addition, *student participation* was encouraged with invitations and access to academic and professional events and activities, such as designing and implementing free subjects for 16-18-year-olds with logistic and academic support from the team; publishing a bulletin board, an academic gazette, and/or a virtual magazine/blog, etc. With regard to *integrated language,* three different strategies were considered: (1) the design and use of an instrument to monitor proficiency levels across the nine semesters; (2) the design and use of an instrument to measure the effect of explicitly discussing with students the methodology used in Integrated English Language (IEL); and (3) coordination/integration of other relevant subjects with language and among themselves. Another project was to design a map of *critical thinking* to be applied to all subjects in the ten semesters of our program. Such a map was necessary so students would be able to build their own arguments. In the halfway profile, the expectations were for students to raise issues and propose solutions, be accountable for their actions and propose actions for participation, critically. And finally, the exit profile specified that our students should be able to identify intervention needs for cultural change. Considering our first-year students' feelings of inadequacy, their low self-esteem, and their lack of study habits and cultural wealth, our proposal is to have a *tutorial program* to help them to integrate themselves into the university community. Groups of ten students with a tutor, a first-year teacher, meet every two weeks, with activities and topics chosen by an educational psychologist, who is the coordinator of this program. Finally, the belief that our four strands have to be interactive and interrelated is addressed by designing and providing guidelines to unify strategies, methodologies and assessment criteria for all subjects.

The team decided we had two years to carry out this set of projects, ending with a full review of the new program in 2015. In the next section we explain what happened in the interim period.

2011 Program

Our UAH team developed a program that aims at educating a professional as described in the following exit profile:

> A teacher of English graduated from Universidad Alberto Hurtado is a professional who seeks to permanently enrich the development of their thoughts from multiple perspectives in order to comprehend social dynamics present in school contexts, and to identify intervention needs for cultural transformation. In this pursuit, they offer creativity, advanced English language competence, both orally and in written form, and expert management of its teaching at the service of such transformation. In this way, they can generate significant social changes in the school context using the teaching of language as a tool to diminish inequity and educate critical citizens with self-esteem and dignity.

In order to educate a professional with those characteristics, the five-year program consists of a total number of 46 subjects and workshops organized in four strands (see Appendix 1): (1) Integrated English Language; (2) psychology, linguistics and TEFL methodology; (3) work experience, reflective workshops and practicum; (4) education and humanities; and elective subjects.

The IEL strand consists of a single subject each semester. The first two years this subject has ten modules (20 hours), which go down to five modules (10 hours) from the third to the fifth year. This subject serves the purpose of developing communication skills as well as critical thinking and social skills. Additionally, in this subject students learn the structural components of language: grammar, pronunciation and vocabulary. Literature is also another component of this subject. All of the above are taught in topic units where students have the opportunity to learn English while reflecting on issues of relevance to their personal growth and to their education as future teachers: identity, professionalism, school culture, citizenship, teenage issues and inclusive education are among the discussed topics. At the end of each unit, students are expected to provide hard evidence of their learning. They are given different tasks like designing and producing a magazine or recording a video, within certain constraints but as professionally as possible; these are projects offering reflective proposals to issues raised in the discussions of the different topics, etc. They also have to produce a multimodal journal recording their learning related to the contents of each unit, as well as the language they have learnt and the teaching – methodological strategies – they have been exposed to.

Since Chile fits in the 'expanding circle' of teaching world Englishes in Kachru's model (1989), English is considered a foreign language in our context. This means that the need for English has a global as well as a local dimension. In other words, we need to speak English to communicate with the rest of the world, standing from our own cultural identity. Therefore, our future graduates, from their 'Chileaness', their advanced communicative English competence and their newly developed exit profile, will teach their students accordingly.

The TEFL methodology strand provides the theoretical foundations and practices of language teaching. This strand includes psychology, and the linguistics and language teaching theory that supports both how students learn a language and how English as a foreign language should be taught. On the other hand, work experience, reflective workshops and practicum is the strand that offers students opportunities to put their methodological knowledge and skills into practice in real school contexts. Reflective workshops give students the opportunity to relate theory and practice, to develop more awareness through exploration, to discuss their classroom experiences, issues and findings among themselves and with a tutor, who usually is the practicum teacher. This subject aims at developing in our students the need to challenge the reality of classrooms today. They bring real cases for analysis and exploration to come up with their own alternatives. Gebhard and Oprandy (1999) suggest that we explore what we actually do in our teaching as opposed to what we think we are doing. Awareness leads to a common consequence of these activities in our students; they feel the shock of poverty, of vulnerability, and, in general, of a neoliberal system which cannot provide fair, democratic opportunities for quality and equitable education. The team expectations are that our students will be able to move on to find compensatory strategies to balance out the deprivation of children in vulnerable schools through the teaching of English, as one of the tools they can develop to have better future opportunities. They will be able to do it because the program has used theory-informed practice as an approach to methodology, so they can seek to define problems as explicitly as possible so that they are amenable to finding solutions reactively in the teaching/learning process (Widdowson, 2003).

The education strand aims at giving students the opportunity of learning and reflecting on education in a broader sense, and those subjects are offered during the first two years of our program. The students are introduced to a general perspective of the role of education in society; the different educational approaches from a historical and philosophical point of view; Chilean public educational policies and curriculum; discussions about ethics and education, philosophy and education, school culture and the role of teachers in the educational system; and a critical overview of the social history of Chile and Latin America. This is a Jesuit university with an explicitly social mission we agree with. As a consequence, we believe humanistic subjects will make students reflect about themselves and others, and that these subjects will allow them to develop a deeper understanding about the complexities they will be faced with in their classrooms, so students can then become effective agents of social change. We therefore connect this with the discipline, thinking that through English as their instrument, they will truly cause a positive impact in their own students.

In relation to the elective subjects, students can choose topics from a wide variety that aim at giving them the chance to experience university education in an even broader sense. The subjects offered include theological and ethical topics, sports and physical fitness, the arts (music, visual arts), social skills and self-esteem.

The first four strands of our new curriculum have a common cross-curricular denominator which reveals where we stand now as teacher educators in Chile. We work under the methodological principle that reflective critical-thinking skills applied to social groups in the classroom, school communities and society are the key to what Freire and Macedo (1995) define as 'epistemological curiosity' – a balance between theory and practice that helps students exercise well-founded observation of reality that leads to its problematization and subsequent proposals for changes.

Our Students

A fundamental consideration we had in mind in the design of the 2011 program is the characteristics of the student who enter the program. During our retreat we spent a good deal of time identifying such characteristics. The result was the following *entry profile*:

> The student who is accepted onto the pre-service English teacher education program at UAH tends to be highly motivated to learn and teach English, feel attracted by the idea of becoming a professional and identify with the mission and vision of our University. They expect to receive the correct answer to the questions and problems in relation to knowledge, information and opinions which, according to staff, is reflected in a lack of inquisitive knowledge and are unable to build their own arguments to support, for example, a political stand. They tend to show lack of awareness of their identity and of self-esteem. Therefore, they avoid interaction in heterogeneous groups (lifestyles, beliefs, interests, special needs, etc.). Staff also observe that they lack study skills, autonomy, critical dispositions, responsibility and show a client-oriented disposition.

The above profile does not describe a student who is prepared to face university challenges. However, UAH, our program, and the authors in particular, subscribe to the principle of inclusion; we aim at offering the highest-quality education to students who would not have access to tertiary education otherwise. Some of the strategies we have designed concerning this issue are: tutorials for all first-year students; a drama club organized by them and which is open to students of all levels; students' participation in department governance and IEL program design; language workshops designed and given by IEL teacher assistants where students of all levels can participate according to the topics of their choice, which supposedly are the ones students want.

Our Teachers

One major feature of the teachers in our program is their ability to be flexible, efficient, committed team workers. The authors have created a specific way for teams who teach IEL to work together. They rely heavily on ICTs for this purpose: online documents where they share and build lesson plans, materials, and relevant information about classes and students.

The role of the strand coordinators is key to guaranteeing a continuum in terms of inter-related contents, students' tasks and experiences, CLIL (Content and Language Integrated Learning) projects, and methodological principles such as learning centeredness, learning by doing, autonomy and critical thinking.

Conclusion

The authors feel that, after all the experiences lived while teaching and observing teacher trainees doing their practicum in a wide range of schools and universities and with a variety of classroom teachers, we have gathered enough knowledge and information that allowed us to design the first version of our English teacher education program at UAH in 2005. At some point during the first five years of its implementation, we came across Jack Richards' Curriculum Development in Language Teaching (2001), which made a lot of sense for our needs. His Situation Analysis proposed taking into account societal factors, project factors, institutional factors, teacher factors, learner factors and adoption factors, and these are the identified elements that created a model for readjusting our program, and this made the rest of the process more relevant. We believe that this program will be able to graduate teachers who correspond to our exit profile, and who, in doing so, will not only be able to teach English efficiently, but will be the agents of change Chile needs: teachers who possess a deep understanding that English is primarily our means of communication with the rest of the world; teachers who teach English knowing that grammar and phonetics are just another component at the service of their students in their development of communication skills; and teachers who understand that English teaching and learning offer a rich opportunity to empower their students as citizens who know themselves and value who they are individually and collectively.

References

Edge, J. (2011) *The Reflexive Teacher Educator in TESOL: roots and wings.* New York: Routledge.

Freire, P. & Macedo, D. (1995) A Dialogue: culture, language, and race, *Harvard Educational Review*, 65(3), 379.
http://dx.doi.org/10.17763/haer.65.3.12g1923330p1xhj8

Gebhard, J. & Oprandy, R. (1999) *Language Teaching Awareness: a guide to exploring beliefs and practices.* Cambridge: Cambridge University Press.

Kachru, B. (1989) Teaching World Englishes, *Indian Journal of Applied Linguistics*, 15(1), 85-95.

MINEDUC (2005) *Objetivos fundamentales y contenidos mínimos obligatorios.* Santiago: Ministerio de Educación.

Norton, B. & Toohey, K. (2004) *Critical Pedagogies and Language Learning.* Cambridge: Cambridge University Press.

Ornstein, A.C. & Hunkins, F.P. (2004) *Curriculum Foundations: principles and issues,* 3rd edn. Boston, MA: Allyn & Bacon.

Richards, J.C. (2001) *Curriculum Development in Language Teaching.* Cambridge: Cambridge University Press.

Widdowson, H. (2003) *Defining Issues in English Language Teaching.* Oxford: Oxford University Press.

CHAPTER 12

Knowing as Embedded in Action: preparing preservice teachers to develop career trajectories as English language teachers in China

ZHILIAN ZHENG & JIANFEN YING

SUMMARY This chapter explores the modes of knowing underlying a decade-long RICH curricular innovation. It is an approach to preparing preservice teachers for their career trajectories as English language teachers. *City Learning Story* is a narrative account of four separate but continuous learning events that emerged as a result of interpreting and reinterpreting various data in context. Four perspectives of knowing in this curricular innovation are examined: (1) connection to learners' inwardness; (2) learning through participation in shared practice; (3) learning objectives as road signs; and (4) teacher as curriculum. RICH knowing accommodates context-situated and relationally distributed dimensions of knowing in practice. It concludes that RICH preservice teachers primarily endeavor to understand the reality of English language teaching and of the world rather than to acquire linguistic knowledge.

Introduction

The authors graduated as English majors and became teachers in a provincial teachers' university in Zhejiang Province, China, which provides training for K-12 teachers of all subjects. The English Department of the Foreign Languages College was started in 1978, and its English teaching has basically undergone three stages. First, English was taught as a subject by following the grammar-translation method as language proficiency was seen as the most essential quality of prospective English teachers. Second, due to the popularity of communicative competence, which is reinforced by China's National English Curriculum (Ministry of Education, 2003), language teachers were exposed to theories of communicative language teaching

(CLT) and task-based language teaching (TBLT), and required to experiment with these new ways of teaching English, through the initiation of a curricular innovation named RICH (an acronym for research-based learning, integrated curriculum, cooperative learning, and humanistic outcome). The RICH approach has become a typical teaching model for integrating preservice language teacher formation into the daily language skill training courses (Wu et al, 2005). Third, language teachers were nourished through increased awareness of enrichment in their lived experiences (Wu, 2005), and narrative inquiry was adopted to explore the modes of knowing underpinning RICH exploratory practice (Zheng, 2005). In this study, narrative inquiry is also adopted as the primary research method and data are collected through classroom observations, interviews in the form of videotapes, records, field notes, lesson plans, emails, pictures and other artifacts.

Before moving on, it is useful to provide some insights into the field of pre-service English teacher education in China. This field has a relatively short history of about 60 years, compared with that of general teacher education, which has a history of around 110 years (Zheng, 2004). However, language teacher education still centers on the acquisition of language knowledge rather than the learning of teaching techniques or the cultivation of teachers' qualities (Chen, 2000, p. 7). In fact, 73% of teachers' universities claim the acquisition of language knowledge should be prioritized among the objectives of English majors (Zhang & Wang, 2000). Zou (2009) investigated the course settings of eleven normal universities and found that the percentage of training courses for English language skills accounts for 65% of the programme, courses focused on general knowledge and general pedagogy account for 31%, and those that deal with English pedagogical content knowledge account for just 4% of the programme. In addition, the classroom teachers in normal universities lack awareness of their role as teacher educators and of teachers' professional qualities. Consequently, teachers often ignore their own demonstrative modeling as teacher educators or are not aware that their own teaching methods will influence their students as 'hidden education' (Zou, 2009). Finally, research on language teacher education is generally paid sparse attention in current Chinese academia. In other words, research on language teaching and classroom teaching is not considered as academic as the studies on linguistics and literature.

Since the late 1990s, 'English teaching' has been gradually shifted into 'English education' in teachers' colleges. It is accepted that many difficulties that emerge in the process of language learning are caused by cultural differences. Furthermore, in the current era of information explosion, what matters most for language learners is to acquire suitable learning strategies and know how to obtain information from diverse sources. Ultimately, language teaching in teachers' colleges aims to cultivate prospective teachers with independent, critical and creative thinking skills (English Section of the

Advisory Committee of Foreign Languages Programs in Higher Education, 2000).

The question remains, however, of how the routine English language skill training can be transformed into a process of improving preservice English teachers' qualities and cultivating their teaching techniques. In the field of preservice English teacher education, RICH exploratory practice (Wu et al, 2005) evolved from an earlier approach called RICH and Exploratory Practice (Allwright, 2003). In 2006, RICH became a sub-project of the MOE Supported Projects of Key Research Institutes of Humanities and Social Sciences in Universities, headed by Wu Yi'an (2007). Two key sections published in this national project were *Exploratory Language Curriculum: RICH Curricular Praxis* and *RICH Teacher Development*. In 2011, Zhejiang Normal University hosted the Fourth National Language Teacher Development Conference.

Language teaching in China has been undergoing a shift from curriculum as product to curriculum as process (Stenhouse, 1975). Notions of curriculum as praxis and teachers as curriculum makers (Wu, 2005, p. 60) are by far the most theoretically advocated approaches and are being experimented with by some leading schools. Indeed, RICH was initiated in 1997 and has been practised by RICH group teachers ever since, yet it has still not been accepted by all teachers in the English Department. Therefore, instruction as a knowing process is still a relatively new field of research. It is valuable therefore to explore the modes of knowing embedded in RICH in order to understand how this approach provides teachers with better understanding.

Theoretical Framework for RICH Knowing

The present inquiry is based on 'knowledge-constitutive interest' proposed by Habermas (1972), a theory about the fundamental human interests which influence how knowledge is constituted or constructed. Related to this, Habermas identifies three basic cognitive interests: technical, practical and emancipatory interest.

RICH is basically influenced by the practical interest, which has a basic orientation towards understanding. In RICH learners are empowered with equal rights with the teacher for identifying course objectives, selecting learning experiences, organizing ways of learning, and assessing learning outcomes. During the teaching process the learners and teacher often interact in order to make meaning of texts, so as to foster an interest in taking the right action in dealing with daily problems on the basis of understanding.

RICH is partly influenced by the emancipatory cognitive interest for autonomous action arising out of critical insights. In teaching practice, it is important to bear in mind that not all the accepted practices are true, that knowing is generated between self-reflection and action, and that learning is a social construction. In addition, RICH knowing implies a basic orientation

153

towards understanding of realities of English teaching and learning and of the world. The RICH curriculum develops through dynamic interactions and reflections so as to achieve the promotion of 'right action' in learners. This is also a process of personal and social constructive knowing in informed and committed actions.

Constructing a Story from Collected Data

Hafen (pseudonym), one of the instructors of Basic English, was chosen as a research participant because of her typical teaching methods and close personal relationship with the researchers. As participant researchers, our collection of data underwent three stages as follows:

Stage 1. Find out as much as we could about Hafen's teaching practice. After we decided to conduct the research in Hafen's class, we kept ourselves constantly informed about her teaching activities through various means, such as casual talks whenever and wherever possible, conversations in meetings, telephone conversations, class observation, and after-class coach observations.

Stage 2. Self-selected topic learning activities. First, we asked Hafen for teaching schedules concerning topic learning. We observed how Hafen coached the students after class before the presentation. Then, we attended nine hours of presentation given by them. In addition, we collected students' portfolios and found out what the students did in independent learning time. These data became the focus of the study

Stage 3. The *City Learning Story* emerged as the story-writing process proceeded. This story was initiated in a talk with Hafen. Hafen recorded every class and videotaped every presentation, so we transcribed part of the lesson on *Unit 3 Cities*, and watched the videotape of favorite city presentations. We often called Hafen on the telephone for more details, and we also interviewed Hafen; in addition, we conducted email interviews with her students to gain insights into their impressions.

The procedure above followed a narrative inquiry process. The rationale of narrative inquiry is based on the hermeneutic philosophy that teachers' knowledge emerges as they present themselves in the stories they tell about their work. The stance adopted in narrative inquiry regards teachers as thinking persons who are oriented towards action and change. Teachers are holders of knowledge, assuming a position of autonomy over curricular innovation (Wu, 2005, p. 60). Through story writing and narrative analysis we made meaning of the curricular stories and relived them in our own teaching practice. The story below is presented in the present tense. It is an interpretative reconstruction from the empirical data, and therefore represents a step in the movement from field notes to interpretation and research knowledge (Wu, 2005, p. 65). The final story that we constructed was given to Hafen for revision.

City Learning Story: knowing embedded in action

On Wednesday morning, Hafen starts the first lesson of *Unit 3 Cities* by introducing the capital of the United States with her personal experiences:

> I once visited Washington D.C. I stood right in front of the White House where the American presidents work and live. I saw a very tall monument, where Martin Luther King, Jr. once gave a wonderful speech 'I have a dream'. I also visited Lincoln Hall. Something interesting here is a river that carries an Indian name. (Hafen's class record)

The students are immediately attracted by Hafen's gentle voice and fluent English. *Unit 3 Cities* involves some information about Seoul, New Orleans, Kyoto and Salvador. In the lesson plan, Hafen connects them with the ten cities listed in the *American Manual* (unpublished book) – namely, New York City, Chicago, Los Angeles, San Francisco, Washington, DC, Boston, Philadelphia, New Orleans, San Antonio and Orlando. Then Hafen moves on to her experience in New York City, her friend's story in New Orleans, and other related stories. As she notices her students are showing greater interest in listening to these stories, she promptly says, 'Each of you is to select one favorite city and give a presentation in three weeks.' After a pause, Hafen convinces them, 'Of course you can choose a city you like best. The writer of the *American Manual* chooses the ten cities out of his own view, so is the textbook writer of this Unit.' Students all willingly accept the task of presenting a favorite city but wonder 'how'. Hafen reads their minds and asks, 'If one hopes to introduce a city, what will be the best way to do it?' With this question Hafen begins to show 'the story ways employed in *Unit 3 Cities*, like riddles, relative clauses, and the content including topics such as air quality, unemployment, and night life'. Concerning the ways to present cities, she suggests students use posters instead of PowerPoint and decide the size and color by themselves. Maybe two or three students could form a group, and the time limit is five minutes. In this way the learning task is generated, moving from textbook learning towards students' inwardness and knowing process.

In three weeks thirteen cities are introduced, including Hangzhou, well known for West Lake, and Wuzhen, a small town famous for its ancient architecture. Also eleven foreign cities are presented – Melbourne, Sydney, Athens, Cairo, London, Copenhagen, Paris, Pompeii, Rome, Milan and Lausanne. In constructing presentations, learners have referred to various resources such as websites, encyclopedias, booklets and newspapers, consulted new words concerning climate or specialties, summarized key words, edited materials, finished written reports, made posters, learned pronunciation of unfamiliar words, and practised delivering the speech. All of these activities are done autonomously and basically in groups in their spare time. In class, Zhanghua (pseudonym) distinguishes herself in pronunciation, intonation and the clear logic of organizing the speech. However, the majority of students are not confident when speaking in public, with some reading notes, while others speak with trembling voices, uneasy gestures and an absence of eye contact. After sharing city stories, they come up to Hafen and ask politely, 'Teacher, my pronunciation is awful, how can I improve it?', 'Madam, I feel so nervous when I speak in class, what should I do? How can I become a teacher in four years?' A few students complain in low voices, 'Our middle school English teachers paid little attention to our oral English because it is not included in the college entrance examination. We have difficulties in speaking fluent English.' Hafen can clearly perceive these anxieties and worries, so she makes an instant decision that all the students should improve their presentations and continue to work on these, and that this activity will develop into a test for the course on phonetics in four weeks.

In a two-hour session on phonetics that occurs two weeks later, Hafen diagnoses faults in students' pronunciation, intonation, rhythm, eye contact, body language, and the like. Six students come voluntarily to the front. The first two students deliver speeches and the teacher undertakes diagnosis, pointing out the strengths and weaknesses, while all of the other students are required to give a score out of 100%. The other three students work together with Hafen to give a phonetic diagnosis of the third volunteer's presentation. They give very good comments and sometimes even point out some aspects beyond Hafen's expectation. The scores given by them are reasonable and can be justified. And when it comes to the following three volunteers, the other students make all the diagnoses, while Hafen keeps silent and just gives scores. The fact that students can diagnose and give reasonable scores pleases Hafen greatly. This incident takes her by surprise and inspires her to invite students to give scores for themselves in the coming test.

During the test, Hafen and the other teacher assigned by the English Department assess each speech in terms of pronunciation, intonation, and so on. In addition, Hafen encourages each student to write down a one-sentence comment on which factor impresses him/her most, and to give a score for him/herself. The final score for each student in phonetics is the average of the three scores respectively given by the teacher, the peer teacher and him/herself. When the sheets are handed in, Hafen finds one student writing, 'Today I feel terribly sad, for my spoken English is awfully bad. I will practice my oral English madly during the coming winter vacation.' Another student writes: 'If I were given another opportunity, I could speak better.' And some others, including, 'We need more opportunities like this.' Because of these feedback comments and Hafen's understanding that the classmates need more opportunities to get familiar with each other, Hafen gives the next assignment promptly. During the coming winter vacation, all students are asked to prepare a poster introducing their hometowns and families. As soon as new term starts, another presentation of hometown and family will be given. In this way students can do some investigation and make posters during the winter vacation at home.

Discussion: four perspectives of knowing in RICH

As indicated above, RICH knowing is mostly informed by practical interest, and partly by emancipatory interest. By examining the story, we have come to realize the process of understanding can be demonstrated from four perspectives: (1) connection to learners' inwardness; (2) learning through participation in shared practice; (3) learning objectives as road signs; and (4) teacher as curriculum.

Learning as a Mode of Knowing towards Learners' Inwardness

The choice of a favorite city makes learners inquire more profoundly into the heart and make personal decisions rather than memorize information and output this by paper and pen for examinations. Hafen urges them to choose a city they like best, just like the writers of the *American Manual* and the textbook. *My Favorite City*, that was constructed with personal opinions, involves decisions about which city, reasons for choosing, and ways of presenting. This connection arouses learners' intrinsic motivation for learning and ultimately redirects textbook learning in a more promising direction. Thus, English is regarded as a knowledge carrier (Allwright, 1981) and can be acquired by using it. The significance of choosing a favorite city in the Chinese context goes far beyond the prevailing test-oriented teaching, which is often removed from students' subjective knowledge. Learners, rather than texts, are at the center of the curriculum, and knowing is first and foremost a personal constructive process.

Learning through Participation in Shared Practice

Presenting favorite cities by groups with posters in this case may be termed as 'learning through participation in shared practice'. This approach greatly engages everyone in learning. As indicated above, Zhanghua's demonstrative speech is so impressive that all the others regard her as a model to follow. For example, they like her approach to introducing Melbourne by acting as a tourist guide in a plane, and her style of organizing her speech with topic sentences: 'Now please look at the poster and know some facts about Melbourne. Next, let's come to the final part – shopping and sports part.' Sharing information concerning 13 cities with the aid of colorful posters delivered by classmates is a new experience of learning, to which they can have easy access, and utilizes the concept of ZPD, or the zone of proximal development (Vygotsky, 1978). Knowing, in this case, becomes exchanging the city information and understanding local historical customs to broaden students' horizons. Furthermore, as pre-service teachers, watching counterparts' performances may assist in making them reflect on their own. This can be seen in the increasing number of students who turn to Hafen for suggestions after their presentations, for they become more clearly aware of their own levels. Finally, the engagement in activities such as city choosing, topic editing and speech presenting may actually embody a large part of the tacit dimension of knowledge (Polanyi, 1966), which cannot be articulated, yet which is fundamental to understanding the knowing process.

Objectives as Road Signs

The learning objectives prescribed in *Unit 3 Cities* are found to act as road signs. That means the preset goal may direct teaching towards certain ideas, but it may not necessarily mean that teachers will simply follow the course as planned. Hafen does not plan to assign students the task of presentation, but generates it on their emerging interest in various cities. Again, after the first presentation, Hafen argues that there is no preset plan that students need to work on but she explains that the activity will be developed into a test on phonetics. It is also true that Hafen, as the head teacher, invites students to explore their hometowns and families, and share their findings in the coming term after the test is over. In this way, the presentation practice is continued and expanded, generating new ways of learning from the original semi-transparent teaching goals. In Hafen's mind, knowing in unknown territory is full of uncertainties, but the objectives are the signs for direction instead of the ends that must be met through 'certain' means. As a whole, the learning process evolves through social construction by teachers and learners.

Teacher as Curriculum

Finally, the teacher as curriculum refers to Hafen's teacher autonomy. In this case, Hafen decides to use her own experience in the USA as the learning content, to render learners' presentation as the final test form in phonetics, and to extend presentation of favorite cities into that of hometown and family. Most surprisingly, she is able to invite the learners to give a score for themselves in the final test, which is normally considered unacceptable. After Hafen demonstrates how to diagnose a peer's oral performance, students acquire the diagnosing skills and understand that scores are only an indication of their present proficiency, and that if they hope to move beyond this they need to continue working. Only if they assess their levels correctly can they make greater achievements in oral English. That's why they are able to make a 'just assessment' for themselves and conduct this within a frame of 'right action'. Therefore, teacher autonomy is built on sufficient understanding about learners' knowing and acting processes.

Conclusion

To conclude, the trajectory of preparing preservice teachers in RICH is to understand teaching through knowing in informed actions rather than approaching learning language skills and teaching techniques separately. In contrast to the traditional textbook-oriented instruction, knowing in RICH is action oriented. Teachers and learners enjoy autonomy in determining the learning content, the ways of learning, and the means of assessing, on the basis of self-exploration and social interaction. It is crucial for teacher educators to acknowledge that preservice English teachers need to understand how to teach language skills through the trajectories they discover in the course of action (Korthagen, 2004). Learners' realities, especially their inner landscapes, should be spoken to, and become the vital and critical resource from which to generate unplanned activities. Administrators will also need to bear in mind that teachers need autonomy to weave themselves, the subject and the students together in classroom teaching (Palmer, 1998). Both teachers and students ought to be authentic to their utterances in class in order to have a better understanding of the reality. This process of interaction between teachers and learners can then have a great impact on preservice teachers' formation, both in developing teaching techniques and in personal growth as teachers.

References

Allwright, D. (1981) What Do We Want Teaching Materials For?, *ELT Journal*, 36(1), 5-18. http://dx.doi.org/10.1093/elt/36.1.5

Allwright, D. (2003) Exploratory Practice: rethinking practitioner research in language teaching, *Language Teaching Research*, 7(2), 113-141. http://dx.doi.org/10.1191/1362168803lr118oa

Chen, G. (2000) Preface, in J.C. Richards & D. Nunan (Eds) *Second Language Teacher Education*. Beijing: Foreign Language and Research Press. http://dx.doi.org/10.1017/cbo9780511486364.001

English Section of the Advisory Committee of Foreign Languages Programs in Higher Education (2000) *National Teaching Syllabus for English Majors in Higher Education*. Shanghai: Shanghai Foreign Language Education Press.

Habermas, J. (1972) *Knowledge and Human Interests*. London: Heinemann.

Korthagen, F.A.J. (2004) In Search of the Essence of a Good Teacher: towards a more holistic approach in teacher education, *Teaching and Teacher Education*, 20(1), 77-97. http://dx.doi.org/10.1016/j.tate.2003.10.002

Ministry of Education (2003) *National English Curriculum for Senior High School*. Beijing: People's Education Press.

Palmer, P.J. (1998) *The Courage to Teach: exploring the inner landscape of a teacher's life*. San Francisco: Jossey-Bass.

Polanyi, M. (1966) *The Tacit Dimension*. London: Routledge.

Stenhouse, L. (1975) *An Introduction to Curriculum Research and Development*. London: Heinemann.

Vygotsky, L. (1978) *Mind in Society*. Cambridge, MA: Harvard University Press.

Wu, Y. (2007) *Research on China's Higher Institutional English Teacher Education and Development*. Beijing: Foreign Language Teaching and Research Press.

Wu, Z. (2005) *Teachers' Knowing in Curriculum Change.* Beijing: Foreign Language and Research Press.

Wu, Z., Huang, A., Zheng, Z., Ying, D. & Hu, M. (2005) *Foreign Language Curriculum and Teacher Development – From RICH Perspective.* Hefei: Anhui Education Press.

Zhang, Y. & Wang, Q. (2000) Teacher Training Model and Teacher Qualities, *Foreign Language Teaching Abroad*, 3, 10-16.

Zheng, S. (2004) On the Transformation of Teacher Training Institutions and Universities, *Teacher Education Research*, 16(1), 3-7.

Zheng, Z. (2005) Understanding Ways of Knowing in the Exploratory Practice of RICH Curricular Innovation. Unpublished MA thesis, Zhejiang Normal University.

Zou, W. (2009) China's Elementary Phase FLT Preservice Education Research, *Foreign Language Learning Theory and Practice*, 1, 1-17.

CHAPTER 13

Overcoming Isolation as ESL Professors and the Challenges of Doing Research Collaboratively across Continents

TELMA GIMENEZ, NORA BASURTO-SANTOS, AMANDA HOWARD, AMIRA TRAISH & MICHAEL F. McMURRAY

SUMMARY Contrary to the discourse that teaching is an individual activity, sociocultural approaches to teacher education have emphasized the importance of collaborative efforts by groups of teachers as a way of improving professional practices. One of the theoretical concepts that stress the situated nature of professional learning is 'communities of practice'. Professional networking is considered an essential aspect of professional development and a necessary condition in a globalized world. As a group of teachers/researchers operating in different parts of the world, in this chapter the authors reflect on their individual trajectories and explore how they came together as a team to develop a comparative large-scale investigation into the processes of employment and professional development of English language teachers in the public sector in Latin American (LA) and the Middle East (ME). Their narratives point to their professional development as a mosaic of experiences that reveal the value of networks created by serendipitous circumstances prompted by initiatives such as attending postgraduate programs and conferences. The work they are developing as a small international community can be seen as a micro-cosmos of the potential to bring teachers together to develop joint research and advance in their careers.

Introduction

Despite the advances generated by reflective approaches to teacher development, one of their unintended consequences was the reassurance that teaching is an isolated activity that can be improved by 'looking at oneself in the mirror' (Fendler, 2003). More recent criticisms of this particular version of reflective teaching have been grounded on the notion that learning is a sociocultural practice that can only succeed if developed collectively, and for this reason the notion of communities and networks has started to make sense when professional development is a goal (Wenger et al, 2011). The concept of 'communities of practice' has become a useful one to guide bottom-up initiatives by professionals in different fields of expertise, and especially in education (Kimble et al, 2008).

Another proposal that has become popular in professional development is teacher research or action research, which, combined with the notions of communities and networks, represent a powerful way of promoting teacher learning while contributing to the advancement of the profession as a whole. Thus, research carried out by communities of practitioners stands a good chance of strengthening the ties among the participants and fostering affinities (Wenger, 1998). In communities, the researchers themselves are able to maintain links with one another, as these links allow them to explore environments beyond their own and to learn from practice and experience in different contexts. This is particularly true in contemporary international networks, as it is the case of this group. The five authors of this chapter are all university professors working in different parts of the world (Latin America, the United Kingdom and the Middle East), and who came together to develop research collaboratively, in order to understand how English language teachers are recruited, what kind of teacher education opportunities they engage with and what explains their commitment to stay in the profession, a topic very much in tune with this collection.

In this chapter we will reflect on our individual trajectories that brought us together in 2014 to submit a proposal for a joint project funded by an international agency. These stories point to our professional development as a mosaic of experiences, and our individual trajectories can shed light on some of the challenges of our profession as it faces new demands and pressures. Each narrative (Barkhuizen, 2013) will be named after the writer/teacher/researcher, alongside the country: Telma, from Brazil; Nora, from Mexico; Michael, from Kuwait; Amira, from the United Arab Emirates; and Amanda, from the United Kingdom.

From Brazil: Telma

I have been a public university professor since 1986, after graduating as a teacher of Portuguese and English for secondary schools from the same institution. Before that, I had worked as a secretary for a multinational company, an experience that gave me insights into the world of businesses, a completely different one from education, at the time. Or so I thought. Nowadays, these distinctions are blurred, as public universities face the challenge of meeting international standards and are losing control of their role as institutions with social responsibility in their local contexts. The push for internationalization has brought new challenges to administrators and professors/researchers alike, and many private higher education institutions look like businesses as they try to attract students/customers. The English language plays an important role in this process and invites us, teacher educators, to consider the consequences of the global imaginary (Kamola, 2012) in our work.

As a recent graduate (MA in Applied Linguistics) from the Catholic University in São Paulo, I joined the department of foreign languages in a state university in the south of Brazil with eagerness to teach. Previously, I had already taught there for a brief period of time but had no specific training, and followed what I had learned during my 'apprenticeship of observation' (Lortie, 1975). In terms of English language teaching we were supposed to follow the communicative approach and use a textbook. The institutional culture allowed, but did not encourage, collective learning. We tended to plan and teach in isolation, sometimes comparing notes and sharing bibliography. The university focused largely on teaching, as opposed to research, and there were not many incentives to engage with scientific investigations.

That picture started to change in the 1990s, with more and more postgraduate programs being created and greater motivation to pursue studies further. Thanks to increased public funding for studies abroad, I was able to get a scholarship from the federal government and did a PhD in England. Although I had had some training in doing research in the MA program in Brazil, it was upon my return that I became more involved with research, in addition to teaching. This time I gradually moved into supervision of student teachers, since my thesis had been on teachers' beliefs and teacher education. Still, the focus of my work remained local, by presenting papers and giving talks at regional and national conferences. In the late 1990s, though, I got in contact with a network of Latin American teachers of English through the British Council, when I met Nora, one of the co-authors of this chapter, and Adriana, another professor, from Colombia, who collaborates with this research. Thanks to those connections, I was able to have a better understanding of the similarities and differences in English language teaching in Latin America (Farias et al, 2008). Thanks to those connections, too, I was introduced to the other writers of this chapter, under Amanda's leadership, and I could, once again, confirm the value of sharing knowledge, building on each other's experiences, and seeing myself as part of an international community of English language professionals.

From Mexico: Nora

I never hesitated or had any doubts as to what I wanted to pursue in university studies, since English was my favorite subject in secondary/high school. What I did not plan was to become an English as a Foreign Language

(EFL) teacher: that did not appear to be a very 'sophisticated' career to an 18-year-old girl, but a couple of opportunities arose even before I finished my undergraduate studies. Advanced students were often offered positions to cover those on maternity leave in some private schools. I was invited to do this while I was still studying and I accepted. That meant that my first teaching experiences drew largely on my 'apprenticeship of observation' (Lortie, 1975), which proved insufficient to deal with the challenges of the profession. These brief teaching experiences served to prove to me that I had no idea whatsoever about what EFL teaching entailed, let alone knowing anything about adolescents. In 1981, soon after graduating, I started teaching in the Department of Foreign Languages of my university. Despite the difficult times faced in those first teaching experiences, I discovered that I really enjoyed *trying* to teach EFL to young adult learners. One of the lessons from this time was that the engagement with the practice of the community of English language teachers helped shape my motivation to stay on being a teacher (Wenger, 1998).

Learning continued to be part of my career, and from 1991 to 1993 I was part of the first generation to study for a diploma in EFL teaching together with the Certificate for Overseas Teachers of English (COTE) course for three semesters. Just a few months later, I was offered a scholarship to join the first generation of teacher-students to do the master's programme for EFL teachers in the south-east region of Mexico, provided by Aston University in the United Kingdom, in semi-distance mode. Looking back, I could say that this was the first real opportunity to learn not only with and from other colleagues outside my university and from other parts of the country, but to learn and get to know other academics working in a university outside the Mexican context. In this programme, and as a result of this master's, I became interested in, and started carrying out, my first qualitative research projects. I did so first individually and then working together with some colleagues.

Those formative experiences, coupled with the participation in events organized by the British Council in Latin America, such as the Best of British, in Mexico City, put me in contact with some of the other authors of this chapter. I can say that this was another key moment in my teacher-researcher trajectory. The benefits of attending international conferences and the positive impact on teacher development have recently been confirmed through research by Borg (2015).

In 2003 I moved to England to do my PhD, and at this time Amanda Howard and I had the same supervisor at Warwick University. I can say that both my experience of doing a research programme and living in a foreign country for an extended period of time helped me not only to get to know many EFL teacher-researchers from many parts of the world, but also to develop skills deemed necessary to carry out research collaboratively with researchers with different educational and cultural backgrounds that otherwise would have been almost impossible.

Being responsible for the organization of the first International Conference on Research in Foreign Languages (CIILE) represented a great effort to create an international network. In the second year, Colombian teacher-researchers joined this effort and the CIILE has since been held in venues alternating between Mexico and Colombia. The efforts and all the work involved have been worthwhile as in 2015 we are organizing our seventh CIILE, at which in the last three years we have had not only international keynote speakers but more than 200 teacher-researchers attending from several countries in Latin America, the USA, Spain and Portugal. For the first time, two delegates will also attend from the Middle East, a feat no doubt resulting from my 34-year-effort to engage with other colleagues in the profession.

From Kuwait: Michael

In terms of career trajectory in the field of English and ESL teaching, mine has been a steady line of happenstance. Mentored by a diverse team of teachers united in their commitment and professionalism, I worked as a student assistant (teaching assistant) in a nationally recognized developmental education program in the Dallas County Community College District (Richland College). In this college at that time the cohort was predominantly native speakers in need of remediation or development in reading, writing, and listening for academic purposes. This developmental studies program was and remains for me the ideal actualization of Wenger's concept of community in that the department shared an identity as a consequence of a collective intention (to best equip students with skills necessary to perform tasks required in undergraduate credit courses) and yet, perhaps by design or accident, resisted becoming insulated or hostage to its history and reputation. Its participants are likewise my best example of a network in Wenger's sense in that via this community I established ties that continue, decades later, to be my best source of information and a forum for idea exchange. Because of the caliber of this program and its faculty, I was inspired to pursue this field and earned a BA in English, and then in 1994, an MS in Education (reading specialization).

At this time, I was, like many others, caught in an era of increased competition for a number of jobs that had not increased significantly since the 1970s and that were in fact largely still held by those who had taken those jobs in the 1970s (Adair, 2000). Unable to secure a full-time teaching position in a community or junior college in the United States (and $20,000 in debt), I answered an ad in the *Dallas Morning News* in May of 1994 that offered $45,000 tax free annually to qualified, approved applicants to teach English overseas. Overseas, as it turned out, meant Saudi Arabia, and the job was to train Aramco employees in English, management, and office skills. Qualified, as it turned out, meant having a degree, certificate, or some experience in the field of English. My colleagues were Americans in situations similar to mine (some former full-time public school teachers) and British EFL instructors who had already cowboyed [1] around the Middle East, Africa and East Asia.

Three years later, to the day, I left Saudi, having spent two full years researching and applying for English-teaching jobs in the academic environment elsewhere in the world. Having received but declined offers to teach in language schools in Japan and Saudi, I was offered university jobs in Korea and Kuwait. For personal reasons, I accepted the job with Kuwait University (KU). For the next seven years I worked as an EFL/Developmental English instructor with the Language Center at KU. During these seven years, out of financial necessity, I supplemented my income with outside work at KU's Continuing Education Center, ELS Language Center, the Institute for Banking Studies, and Amideast. In 2004, with an offer for nearly triple the basic KU salary, I accepted a position in the Intensive English Department at the American University of Kuwait (AUK), a start-up institution.

Seven years later, I was recruited by the departing AUK Director of Intensive English to join her at Gulf University of Science and Technology in their Foundation English Program. Throughout most of my time in Kuwait higher education institutions I have been asked to step in and coordinate courses. This has, without fail, manifested itself as curriculum-writing, teacher-training and semi-management positions with heavy responsibility and no power, no security and no recognition.

Although never intending to be an ESL/EFL instructor, to work overseas, or to pursue research, I did intend to perform whatever job I was offered and accepted to the best of my ability. Had I known that the involvement, intelligence and integrity that governed the developmental studies program at Richland College were not typical in higher education both nationally and internationally, I doubt that I would have pursued this career track, and I am certain that I would not have abandoned so soon a lucrative job in training to return to academia.

My involvement in the recruitment and retention project came about after I had chaired a panel during TESOL Kuwait's first annual conference in 2013. Among the panelists was Amanda Howard, who first invited my interim director to serve as the Kuwait team member. Unable to commit to the project, the interim director recommended me.

From the United Arab Emirates: Amira

I have always recognized the need to exploit opportunity, especially in the job market. When I first entered university, I was undecided on a major. I would like to say that a passion for teaching prompted me to major in education; however, that claim would be disingenuous. The truth is that I knew that it was a field in which I would have little difficulty securing employment with a bachelor's degree, and, in addition, my parents would approve of it. Being female and from a Middle Eastern background, I understood that if I wanted to please my parents, I had a limited number of career choices. I could say that, unlike my colleagues, my decision to become a teacher followed pragmatic reasons. Once I graduated with my bachelor's degree in English, I was indeed able to find a job quite easily, and worked for one year as an elementary school teacher. However, eventually I realized that an undergraduate degree was not a guarantee of advancement or financial security. Consequently I opted to return to school to pursue my master's, giving up my teaching position for a teacher assistantship at a university.

After I obtained my master's degree, a move to the Gulf was necessary because my husband was offered a job in the region. I must admit, however, that I was not looking forward to it for several reasons. I would need to begin my job search anew and make the critical connections I needed in the teaching field in a completely different environment and culture. Fortunately, thanks to my adjunct work and other qualifications, I was able to find a full-time instructor position in the English foundation program of a university.

As a new transplant to the United Arab Emirates (UAE), I was immediately impressed by the diversity of the population. When I was in the USA, 90 to 95% of the people I worked with were American, but teaching in the UAE provided me with the opportunity to meet people from different parts of the world. Additionally, this experience exposed me to a great variety of different teaching styles and pedagogies. I see this aspect of operating in a new vocational arena as a tremendous benefit: my instructional personality is enhanced and enriched by exposure to colleagues who operate from a multiplicity of ethnic, cultural and philosophical perspectives, and my horizons are broadened daily as I am required to meld and integrate their various ideals and pedagogies with my own. For example, I have observed instructors who follow the grammar translation approach where others are following a more communicative approach in teaching. This has helped me to realize that no one teaching approach can be termed as ideal. The diversity of this professional community enlarges the repertoire of practices I have access to and benefit from, as well as shapes my identity as a teacher in a multicultural setting.

Although there are a number of benefits to be gained from employment in the UAE, it is not without its challenges. The job market is highly competitive, being populated by competing applicants on an international scale. Furthermore, once one has secured employment, the need to establish a profile of professional development activities is critical. Instructors in this part of the world are strongly encouraged to develop this facet of their career portfolio; at times, heavy engagement in professional development pursuits is even a requirement. Many employees collect certificates, displaying them proudly in family albums. In deference to this emphasis, as well as to the educational and vocational benefit that would accrue, I decided to pursue my doctoral degree, and it was during this process that I had the opportunity to meet Amanda, who became my EdD supervisor, as well as the rest of the research team with whom I will be working on this project.

During my tenure in the UAE, I have found myself in the midst of a generally frenetic, unstable and stress-filled employment dynamic. The employment picture in my industry is highly volatile and insecure; employees are constrained to accept short contract terms and understand that they may be let go at any time with little or no explanation or reason for their release. Turnover rates among teachers are high, and the prevailing rationale seems to be that student success or failure must be directly related to teacher competency, which places a tremendous amount of pressure and stress on instructors.

In this part of the world, I can see that the emphasis is on the individual teacher with little or no effort to build communities of professionals. As my reflections show, this can result in a sense of insecurity that threatens the development of collegiality and joint enterprises. It seems that our institutions are far from taking Wenger's (1998) community of practice concept as a guiding framework for staff learning.

From the UK: Amanda

I have been in the fortunate position of being able to bring the people involved in this project together to form a community of practice and, as can be seen in the previous sections, we have arrived here via long and circuitous routes.

My first career was in catering and hospitality management. However, when the family relocated I found myself in the Middle East and discovered that, at that time, it was inadvisable either for me to work for men, or for them to work for me, which was somewhat problematic. I started looking for something that I was able to do and a friend suggested approaching the British Council, who advised acquiring a Certificate in Teaching English as a Foreign Language to Adults (CTEFLA) as soon as possible. I had always enjoyed the training aspect of my previous career, so approached this idea with enthusiasm, donated my children to my parents on a temporary basis, and enrolled on a 4-week Royal Society of Arts/University of Cambridge Local Examinations Syndicate (RSA/UCLES) CTEFLA. Although some of my companions were seasoned teachers who were highly resistant to much of the classroom pedagogy being presented, I enjoyed the vast majority of the course, particularly the sessions in the classroom, happily applying to the British Council in Doha when I had my qualification. During this time I gained plenty of experience working with Young Learners (YL) as well as adults, whilst having the opportunity to meet, and work with, professionals from a wide range of countries. I was also given the responsibility of setting up the computer training unit, involving several visits to Cairo, the regional hub, also becoming involved in teacher training. I found this particularly rewarding in terms of the differences between teacher nationalities and preferred classroom pedagogies.

In 1995 I moved on to set up a language and computer training school for a national institution in Qatar, subsequently deciding that I needed theory to back up my practical experiences. My professional life has often incorporated family-based travel, so I returned to the UK to do a full time MEd TESOL at Leeds University, which was a very rewarding experience. I was subsequently offered a part-time post there, teaching postgraduate students, which fed my early interest in this particular area of expertise. However, family dynamics again meant that I needed to return to the Middle East, so I began working for a federal college system in the UAE as an ESL teacher. This gradually expanding role soon incorporated tutoring on the RSA/UCLES DELTA programme, as well as becoming involved in the writing and set-up of the first English medium BA TESOL course in the Middle East, provided in conjunction with the University of Melbourne.

These were very exciting times, and it was fascinating to be able to visit YL classrooms in the UAE, feeding my interest in the teaching pedagogies needed for the younger age groups, and enabling me to write and present on the topic. Once again theory needed to catch up with the practice, so I returned to the UK to register for a PhD. In order to support myself during this time I continued to work on a part-time basis for the TESOL faculties of a number of universities, including Leeds, where I was involved in teaching on their BA TESOL in Oman, similar in structure to the BEd TESOL I had worked on in the UAE, and which allowed me to spend time in Omani classrooms.

During my career I have been lucky enough to attend numerous conferences and meet a large number of TESOL professionals with a wide range of specialties, qualifications and nationalities, which has been a continuing pleasure. Nora and I shared the same PhD supervisor and she has introduced me to a number of her colleagues, including Telma, as well as Adriana at a CIILE conference in Mexico. For several years after graduation I continued to be based in the Middle East at the postgraduate British University in Dubai, which provided a vast amount of postgraduate education experience. I became involved in organizing and presenting at conferences and workshops, and met Michael during a TESOL conference in Kuwait when he chaired a panel discussion. When the opportunity arose to apply for research funding it was very satisfying to be able to offer colleagues a part in a project of this significance. Although now based in the UK rather than the Middle East, I am very aware of the way in which my previous experiences and contacts have impacted on my current ability to carry out research that is significant for the international TESOL community and look forward to continuing a long and rewarding partnership with my fellow investigators.

Conclusion

Our narratives support the view that professional learning takes place in communities of practice as well as in formal educational settings. These trajectories reveal the value of networks created by serendipitous circumstances prompted by initiatives such as attending postgraduate programs and conferences. We joined the profession mainly because of the language we learned or spoke and we developed a love for teaching it by engaging with other professionals in the field. We also saw our professional development strongly associated with studies, mainly in English-speaking countries, and we were able to take part in them because of public incentives or individual efforts. We all see research as an integral part of our work. Our stories are a continuum of professional development demonstrating that learning is social and that our identities are constructed through our ongoing engagement with others. In other words, the meanings we attribute to our work as teachers derive from our participation in various communities of practice.

As we look back at our collective reflections, we can see that mobility has been an essential feature of our careers. This mobility granted us access to one another and enabled us to develop a form of professional activity that seems fundamental to being a teacher of English nowadays, irrespective of where we are located. In developing a joint enterprise (an international research project) we are not just a network of English language teachers; our social relations are formed, negotiated and sustained around the activity that has brought us together (Fuller, 2007). The fact that we work in different countries and regions means that we are in a position to make a significant impact in terms of sharing our experiences and comparing outcomes. In this sense, the work we are developing as a small international community can be seen as a micro-cosmos of the potential to bring teachers together to develop joint research and advance in their careers. Needless to say, we were only able to do this because of the connectivity provided by the Internet. Thanks to tools such as Skype and email, we interacted and exchanged insights into the project, thus demonstrating that technology and a shared purpose can be fruitfully exploited in order to overcome isolation. We hope our narratives can illustrate that potential.

Note

[1] A term frequently employed by the British, alluding to the American West and the cowhands who would sign on for a season, possibly complete a contract, then hire on for another such job the following season.

References

Adair, S. (2000) Stars, Tenure, and the Death of Ambition, in P.C. Herman (Ed.) *Day Late, Dollar Short: the next generation and the new academy*, pp. 45-62. Albany: State University of New York Press.

Barkhuizen, G. (2013) *Narrative Research in Applied Linguistics*. Cambridge: Cambridge University Press.

Borg, S. (2015) The Benefits of Attending ELT Conferences, *ELT Journal*, 69(1), 35-46. http://dx.doi.org/10.1093/elt/ccu045

Farias, M., Armendariz, A., Gil, G., Gimenez, T., Clavijo, A. & Abrahams, M.J. (2008) Sociocultural and Political Issues in English Language Teacher Education: policies and training in Argentina, Brazil, Chile and Colombia, in Glória Gil & Maria Helena Vieira-Abrahão (Eds) *Educação de Professores de Línguas: os desafios do formador*, pp. 23-44. Campinas: Pontes Editores.

Fendler, L. (2003) Teacher Reflection in a Hall of Mirrors: historical influences and political reverberations, *Educational Researcher*, 32, 16-25. http://dx.doi.org/10.3102/0013189X032003016

Fuller, A. (2007) Critiquing Theories of Learning and Communities of Practice, in J. Hughes, N. Jewson & L. Unwin (Eds) *Communities of Practice: critical perspectives*, pp.17-29. Abingdon: Routledge.

Kamola, I. (2012) US Universities and the Production of the Global Imaginary, *British Journal of Politics and International Relations*, 16(3), 515-533. http://dx.doi.org/10.1111/j.1467-856X.2012.00540.x

Kimble, C., Hildreth, P. & Bourdon, I. (Eds) (2008) *Communities of Practice: creating learning environments for educators*, vol. 1. Charlotte, NC: Information Age Publishing.

Lortie, D. (1975) *Schoolteacher: a sociological study*. Chicago: University of Chicago Press.

Wenger, E. (1998) *Communities of Practice: learning, meaning, and identity*. Cambridge: Cambridge University Press. http://dx.doi.org/10.1017/CBO9780511803932

Wenger, E., Trayner, B. & de Laat, M. (2011) *Promoting and Assessing Value Creation in Communities and Networks: a conceptual framework*. Report 18, Ruud de Moor Centrum, Open University of the Netherlands.

CHAPTER 14

Rise or Fall of the EFL Teaching Profession in Thai Universities

PARUSSAYA KIATKHEEREE

SUMMARY Being an English as a Foreign Language (EFL) lecturer in a Thai university might not be difficult, but the way to maintain and advance the professional standing of those in this teaching profession *might* not be easy. Having experience as an EFL lecturer at two Thai universities for more than ten years enables the author to study and discuss the field with many lecturers in the field of English language. The author started her career as a lecturer in teaching English at a university in northern Thailand, where she gained insights into students, staff and faculties within a university where the focus was on being a leading educational institution in the field of technology. At present, the author is a lecturer teaching English in the Faculty of Education and also serving as the director of the Association of Southeast Asian Nations (ASEAN) Studies and Development Centre in her university, which is located in the southern part of Thailand. Here, the author has the opportunity to work with other scholars and extend her insights into the EFL teaching profession. The main focus of her present university is on teaching education within the ASEAN community. This chapter combines discussion of her experience as an EFL lecturer with insights from her study on the research involvement of EFL academic staff in the Thai tertiary context. The data were collected using a qualitative case-study approach. Semi-structured interviews, observations and a focus group were conducted with lecturers teaching English in Thai universities. Document analysis was also carried out to provide background to the study.

Introduction

English plays a crucial role in Thai higher education. It is also a working language of the Association of Southeast Asian Nations (ASEAN), which has increased the demand for improving the quality of English language teaching in Thailand. The emergence of ASEAN has also raised the status of Thai English language lecturers to a higher level than lecturers teaching other foreign languages. This supports previous literature that English is accorded the highest status and value in Thai education (Boonkit, 2002). However, EFL lecturers in Thailand may face a lot of changes as a result of the ASEAN developments, particularly with regard to balancing their various academic duties in order to maintain and advance their academic profession.

The Ministry of Education in Thailand (MOE, 2008) recently introduced a plan to develop the teaching profession to ensure that lecturers will be assessed and promoted in accordance with their teaching and academic performance. Lecturers are required to meet criteria across the three academic duties of teaching, research, and community service. Research, however, is considered to be the core value in advancing their academic profession to gain status as an assistant professor, associate professor or professor. Governments and institutions worldwide have raised the importance of research. It is considered that research activity is a key university mission in order to enhance both national and international reputation (Boyer, 1990; MOE, 2005; Marginson, 2006; Tynan & Garbett, 2007 Holligan et al, 2011). Thai lecturers teaching English are not exempt from this requirement despite the fact that they are often not ready to produce research. My research has shown that Thai teaching staff have a high teaching workload, which reduces the time they have available to get involved in the research process (Kiatkheeree, 2015). The literature also confirms that teaching as well as administrative workloads affect both mental and physical energy in lecturers' research involvement (Tynan & Garbett, 2007). It can be stated that the more time they spend on teaching, the less time they can devote to research, and this situation ultimately disrupts their career path.

While lecturers teaching English in Thai tertiary institutions are well respected and have gained the advantages of speaking English, their efforts seem to fade away with regard to advancing their academic status through research. The level of research publication by Thai university staff is considered to be low when compared with other countries (Sangnapaboworn, 2003). A study by Jaroongkhongdach et al (2012) revealed that, in the period from 2000 to 2010, Thai lecturers teaching English have produced very small numbers of research publications, with a total of 578 articles, of which only 28 articles have been published in international journals, while 550 articles have been published in either local journals or conference proceedings. This situation suggests the need for immediate action to increase the number of publications by EFL lecturers in Thai higher education institutions.

The Role of Research and its Influence on the EFL Teaching Profession

Very little was found in the literature on the position of EFL lecturers in relation to research in a Thai tertiary context even though there is an awareness of the need to increase the quality of teaching in Thai higher education through research. However, academic staff have been encouraged to improve and enhance their teaching capacity through research since the early 1970s, when research and publications were first counted as the criteria for academic promotion (Suwanwela, 2008; OHEC, 2010b); and the latest policy from the Thai Ministry of Education (MOE, 2013) also indicates the importance of research to increase the body of knowledge in the field of education. This policy is intended to promote an institute on the basis of its curriculum research and pedagogy development, and also implies that lecturers in all fields, including the field of teaching English, are required to produce research. The literature indicates that recent EFL research trends focus on communication skills by using technology tools (Winitchaikun et al, 2002; Darasawang, 2007; Sukamolson, 2010). However, the current data demonstrate that there are few research publications in the field of English language teaching by Thai lecturers which address issues related to their teaching profession within higher education institutions. The lack of research publications in this area can be seen as the result of several factors, including lack of English proficiency, institutional priorities, a lack of professional development in research skills, other workload pressures, a preference for teaching, the low quality of research undertaken, impacts of internationalisation, limited research funding and unstable national policy. These factors will now be elaborated on in more detail.

English Proficiency as an Obstacle

English plays a critical role as a language for communication between nations as well as being a compulsory subject within Thai higher education institutions. It has been shown that EFL scholars are required to serve national demands for increased English skill, including promoting and enhancing students' proficiency to survive in the ASEAN community. However, even though EFL lecturers hold a privileged position in using English language, the scores of Thai people in international tests of English proficiency are the third lowest in the Asian region (Educational Testing Service, 2015). This may imply that Thai lecturers teaching English might not be fluent in English. This assumption is supported by the finding that research projects conducted by Thai lecturers teaching English are written in Thai. This subsequently limits their chances of publishing their findings in international journals, in which English is the language for publication (Marginson, 2007).

Institutional Priorities

Moreover, my findings reveal that the participating universities did not consider research in the area of language as their primary focus, which may explain the low level of EFL research publications by Thai scholars. In addition, the lecturers involved in the study appear to have limited research knowledge as well as limited English proficiency in terms of English for publication. The present findings seem to be consistent with a study by Syananondh and Wannaruk (1990) which found that Thai EFL lecturers had little research experience; therefore, they could not produce research publications, particularly at the international level.

Professional Development of Research Skills

Limited proficiency in English is not the only factor that seems to prevent EFL lecturers from producing research and publications. A further possible explanation for limited output in this area is that faculty staff in the area of English language teaching appear to lack ongoing professional development to develop their research skills. In addition, in many Thai universities, lecturers teaching English do not have a variety of courses to teach, which may also affect their capacity for contributing new knowledge. Contrary to expectations, the current study revealed that the participating EFL lecturers also tended to overlook the importance of professional development programmes, in particular with regard to research knowledge. These development programmes, as well as consulting with research mentors, attending research seminars, and teaching in specific research-informed programmes, are regarded as essential factors in enhancing research skills (Tynan & Garbett, 2007). Participating EFL lecturers mentioned that they had never attended research seminars, consulted with research mentors, or used the university research database. Some mentioned that they did not even know the university research database existed. This can explain why they produced just small numbers of research publications, and why none of the EFL lecturers involved in this study had published research that met international standards.

Workload Pressures

Another possible explanation for the lack of research publication by EFL lecturers is that these lecturers would need to neglect other academic duties if they focused on research. In general, research is counted as 30% of the total academic duties. However, the current study found that EFL lecturers avoided conducting research, or tended to undertake low-quality research. This situation seems to occur across universities in Thailand. The reason EFL lecturers gave for avoiding undertaking research was that it was due to their heavy teaching workload. They reported being frustrated by the lack of time for research when they also needed to fulfil their teaching and service responsibilities. Participating EFL lecturers stated that they had teaching workloads ranging between 21 and 31 hours per week. They mentioned that they would like to have a lighter teaching workload, between 12 and 15 hours per week, so that they could spend more time undertaking research. To prove that a light teaching workload will facilitate EFL lecturers to produce research, additional observations and interviews were undertaken with EFL lecturers who had a lighter teaching workload of 12-15 hours per week. However, it appeared that they also avoided conducting research for the same reason – no time. Therefore, it is possible to say that teaching workload might not be the main factor affecting their involvement in research. This finding differs from that of a study by Pratt et al (1999) which indicated that reducing teaching workload or increasing time for research, such as providing a research day, might increase research productivity. There are, however, other possible explanations why EFL lecturers may not have a positive attitude towards research activity, or do not complete a PhD qualification.

Preference for Teaching

Some findings indicated that EFL lecturers tended to devote their time to teaching, and considered themselves to be teachers, not lecturers. Furthermore, they seemed to be against getting involved in the research process, and some even viewed research as an 'unpleasant job'. This view may be the result of their lack of experience in producing quality research. It seems possible that these gaps in research experience and quality research outputs may be due to the lack of PhD qualification among participants. In fact, all participating lecturers held a master's degree in the field of English. This supports previous studies that indicate that the lack of a PhD qualification may prevent academic staff from producing high-quality research (MOE, 2005).

Research Quality

Finally, the data revealed that EFL lecturers participating in the study did actually produce a small quantity of research, approximately one to two research projects per person. However, that research was not of good quality. Some EFL lecturers mentioned short one-month research projects which aimed to increase the Key Performance Indicators of the university. However, these kinds of projects cannot be used to promote their academic profession. As one participating EFL lecturer mentioned, 'there is nothing in this project'. Therefore academic advancement is disrupted and EFL lecturers often fail to meet the expectation as academics who are required to be producers of new knowledge.

Impacts of Internationalisation

Despite the obstacles identified, the current study also found that the research system of Thai higher education institutions is positively influenced by the wider internationalisation movement, in which research is considered as an integral part of nation building. This focus is in line with the literature showing that universities worldwide seem to privilege research over teaching, and research publications are major criteria for academic promotion (Teichler, 2004; Healey, 2005; Marginson, 2006; Hemmings & Kay, 2009; Houston et al, 2010). In addition, the Ministry of Education, in accordance with the Office of the Higher Education Commission (OHEC) in Thailand, has shown an increased interest in improving and promoting research capacities of Thai lecturers in different areas of study to meet business, economic and technology needs at both national and international levels (MOE, 2008, 2009a; OHEC, 2008).

Limited Research Funding

The increased interest in research is having a significant effect on the status of Thai lecturers teaching English. Despite the fact that English is regarded as the working language in the ASEAN community (which has raised the status of lecturers teaching English in Thai universities), EFL lecturers are still threatened by limited research funding and support. The current study demonstrates that EFL lecturers could apply for only the internal research funding provided by the university research centre. The amount of internal research funding in each higher education institution was varied, but mostly did not exceed 100,000 baht (approximately NZ$4,000). Furthermore, it appears that EFL lecturers have lower academic status as their field of study is not the focus of either the university or the country. It is likely therefore that lecturers in the field of teaching English gained less opportunity to be rewarded and promoted through professional advancement compared with other lecturers in the fields of science, technology and innovation. EFL lecturers received less research funding as the priority is placed on research in the science and technology fields (OHEC, 2010a). In addition, participating lecturers indicated that the University Research Centre had reduced the amount of the research funding that they could apply for. The situation of having insufficient financial support affected their motivation, resulting in them being less enthusiastic about conducting research.

That the Thai government tends to grant more funds in the field of science and technology rather than for research in the field of English can be seen in the investment plan under the Second Stimulus Package of Economic Reform (2010-2012). In this plan, the government has invested more of its budget on education and learning in general science and mathematics, and also emphasised, and allocated more budget on, research in the development of innovations and technologies (MOE, 2009b, 2013). Participating EFL lecturers in the study, in addition, asserted that their professional status was limited, particularly in terms of applying for external research funding, which appeared to be reserved for faculty members in the field of science and technology. According to the Office of the National Research Council of Thailand (NRCT, 2014), the major proportion of government research funding was granted to research in the area of economic development, as well as in science and technology. The findings of this current study are interestingly consistent with others internationally; for example, Boyer (1990) as well as Mohrman et al (2008) found that research funding is limited for those who work in the non-science field. This demonstrates that research trends and funding support available for Thai scholars are similar to what scholars find in other international contexts, and that EFL lecturers receive less support for undertaking research.

The impact of internationalisation therefore not only affects the amount of research funding available to certain groups, but also the status of EFL lecturers. According to the Thai higher education reform, academic staff are encouraged to be active in both teaching and research (Suwanwela, 2005; Nonkukhetkhong et al, 2006; OHEC, 2010b). It seems, however, that the low level of research publications by Thai EFL lecturers reduces the level of their profession. Recently, Thai higher education institutions have introduced many English-taught courses to attract more international students during the era of internationalisation. The variety of English-taught courses also means that Thai lecturers teaching English are not the only group of academics who *can* teach English. Even though there is a shortage of EFL lecturers in Thai higher education institutions (MOE, 2012), it seems that internationalisation effects will definitely affect the position of EFL lecturers. This downward slide may also be further impacted by the effect of the forthcoming ASEAN community policy, which allows universities to employ academics from other ASEAN countries more freely. As a result, it is argued that Thai lecturers teaching English need to take steps to improve their profession. This situation requires immediate changes in order to maintain and advance EFL lecturers' professional standing, and this can be mainly informed by conducting research.

National Policy

Currently, there is an attempt to promote a national research system that will improve the amount of budget available for both basic and comprehensive research (MOE, 2008). Also, the National Research Council of Thailand (NRCT) has been set up as a means to serve national research policy, as guided and directed by the government (NRCT, 2015). However, that same national policy may also have serious implications for the position of EFL lecturers. It appears that the Thai national policy on higher education is not being progressively developed due to the disruption by ongoing political issues. EFL lecturers can be said to be victims of unstable policy and implementation since the political crisis in Thailand started in 2001. Thai higher education is now undergoing radical change due to these political issues. The uncertainty of Thai higher education policy and implementation is reflected in the large number of ministers who have led the Ministry of Education in the last 15 years (16 ministers from 2001 to the present). The frequent change of ministers affects the policies on higher education and the directions for each institution, in terms of responding to the country's needs.

It appears that the country's main focus is on technology and innovation, as mentioned earlier. However, there is no measurement in terms of research activity of lecturers, and there is no national research excellence framework. It is possible that Thai lecturers undertake research, the quality of which has only a vague measurement, and that EFL lecturers in particular are struggling in finding ways to advance their status through publishing research at either national or international levels.

There has been an attempt to improve research quality and increase research publications. Academic staff are now required to publish their findings in at least one national journal approved by the Thai-Journal Citation Index Centre (TCI). At present, there are 256 journals in the humanities and social sciences approved by TCI (TCI, 2015). However, there is no clear assessment or strategy to promote research productivity of lecturers in the field of English. The current study found that the participating universities did not have a policy on publishing research as part of an academic duty. Therefore, EFL lecturers involved in the study did not disseminate research findings in any journals. This can also be seen in the delays in implementing a National Language Policy. The draft of the National Language Policy has been signed since 2010 with the expectation of finalising and implementing this by 2015 (UNESCO, 2015). This late implementation affects EFL lecturers' academic status as such a policy is likely to direct and inform the status of English language and research.

There is also a discussion emerging to promote a teaching professorship as a new position in Thai higher education institutions. It is expected that this new professorship may increase the numbers of staff with academic status across faculties. The nature of EFL lecturers' employment in Thai universities may fit with this new position, as they can be promoted based on their achievements in teaching rather than in research. However, the literature appears to indicate that a teaching professor may have a lower status compared with a research professor. Also, the introduction of a teaching professorship may cause EFL lecturers in Thai universities to be less motivated in undertaking research. A study by Macfarlane (2011) indicated that a *teaching* professor may still struggle to join research activity as they do not work in depth in this area or make an effort to develop their skills as researchers. However, it is possibly too early to state how this new professorship will positively or negatively affect the academic status of EFL lecturers as it is still in the drafting process.

Looking Forward

The controversy about the level of publication and the academic status of EFL lecturers has been an issue in most Thai higher education institutions, and the current research results are also not encouraging in this regard. At best, it can be said that the position of EFL lecturers is unstable. As research is an integral part of teaching it is unavoidable that EFL lecturers will be required to undertake research and disseminate their research findings, in addition to teaching and community service, in order to gain academic status. However, the current study showed that EFL lecturers involved in this study encountered crucial problems in relation to research and that this significantly affected their academic status. Limited English proficiency for publication, the impact of internationalisation on research trends, and the unstable national policy were found to threaten the academic life of EFL lecturers in Thai universities. EFL lecturers were found to be less active in research and their teaching position was found to be lower than lecturers in the fields of science and technology. This finding has important implications for developing the research capacity of EFL lecturers and enhancing their academic and professional status.

As it appears that EFL lecturers have limited English proficiency, particularly affecting their ability to achieve international publication, it is recommended that they need to increase their English proficiency as well as devoting more time to research activity and attending research programmes provided by their institution. It is important that they are provided with the necessary support to conduct quality research. Advancing their degree to doctoral level would be another possible way to gain better understanding about conducting quality research. In addition, EFL lecturers need to ensure that their research is published at the very least in national journals.

There is evidence from the study showing that the level of support provided for research was consistently and strongly predictive of staff research efficacy. While EFL teaching staff are required to enhance their English as well as their research skills, the Thai government and the university need to reconsider the strategy and policy for advancing the academic position of lecturers in non-science fields. This implies that systematic strategies and significant resources will need to be allocated for staff training and support (Deem & Lucas, 2007; Lawn et al, 2010; Hardré et al, 2011; Hanover Research, 2014). Also it is important that the universities provide continual development courses in relation to research activity, in a way that suits the needs of EFL lecturers. For example, it would be useful to provide a research programme in writing English for publication.

The current study also appears to indicate that the lack of policies within the university and the country with regard to supporting EFL lecturers to publish research and advance their academic status may be negatively impacted by the internationalisation movement. The impact of internationalisation on research influences the amount of research publication by Thai EFL scholars since the country's and the universities' research priorities are focused on science and technology. However, research into the field of English cannot be neglected as language is a key tool for the transfer of knowledge globally. Therefore, it is recommended that the universities and the Thai government provide more support and funding for research in EFL. The most important aspect, however, is that EFL lecturers themselves will need to perceive the value of producing more quality research. Without that they will continue to be respected only as a 'teacher' who can speak English, not as a 'lecturer' who can contribute knowledge in the educational field.

References

Boonkit, K. (2002) Listening Strategies with Television Texts: a study of Thai university students of English as a Foreign Language. Unpublished PhD thesis, University of Tasmania.

Boyer, E.L. (1990) *Scholarship Reconsidered: priorities of the professoriate*. New York: Carnegie Foundation for the Advancement of Teaching.

Darasawang, P. (2007) English Language Teaching and Education in Thailand: a decade of change, in D. Prescott (Ed.) *English in Southeast Asia: varieties, literacies and literatures*, pp. 187-204. Cambridge: Cambridge Scholars Publishing.

Deem, R. & Lucas, L. (2007) Research and Teaching Cultures in Two Contrasting UK Policy Contexts: academic life in education departments in five English and Scottish universities, *Higher Education*, 54(1), 115-133. http://dx.doi.org/10.1007/s10734-006-9010-z

Educational Testing Service (2015) Test and Score Data Summary for TOEFL Internet-based and Paper-based Tests between January–December 2014. https://www.ets.org/s/toefl/pdf/94227_unlweb.pdf

Hanover Research (2014) *Building a Culture of Research: recommended practices*, pp. 1-33. May. http://www.hanoverresearch.com/media/Building-a-Culture-of-Research-Recommended-Practices.pdf

Hardré, P.L., Beesley, A.D., Miller, R.L. & Pace, T.M. (2011) Faculty Motivation to Do Research: across disciplines in research-extensive universities, *Journal of the Professoriate*, 5(1), 35-69.

Healey, M. (2005) Linking Research and Teaching to Benefit Student Learning, *Journal of Geography in Higher Education*, 29(2), 183-201. http://dx.doi.org/10.1080/03098260500130387

Hemmings, B. & Kay, R. (2009) Lecturer Self-efficacy, Research Skills, and Publication Output. http://www.aare.edu.au/08pap/hem08131.pdf (accessed 3 September 2011).

Holligan, C., Wilson, M. & Humes, W. (2011) Research Cultures in English and Scottish University Education Departments: an exploratory study of academic staff perceptions, *British Educational Research Journal*, 37(4), 713-734. http://dx.doi.org/10.1080/01411926.2010.489146

Houston, N., Ross, H., Robinson, J. & Malcolm, H. (2010) Inside Research, Inside Ourselves: teacher educators take stock of their research practice, *Educational*

Action Research, 18(4), 555-569.
http://dx.doi.org/10.1080/09650792.2010.525017

Jaroongkhongdach, W., Todd, R.W., Keyuravong, S. & Hall, D. (2012) Differences in Quality between Thai and International Research Articles in ELT, *Journal of English for Academic Purposes*, 11, 194-209.
http://dx.doi.org/10.1016/j.jeap.2012.04.006

Kiatkheeree, P. (2015) Nurturing the Research Culture in an EFL Context. Paper presented at the 9th International Technology, Education and Development Conference, in Madrid, Spain.

Lawn, M., Deary, I.J., Bartholomew, D.J. & Brett, C. (2010) Embedding the New Science of Research: the organised culture of Scottish educational research in the mid-twentieth century, *Paedagogica Historica*, 46(3), 357-381.
http://dx.doi.org/10.1080/00309230903396480

Macfarlane, B. (2011) Prizes, Pedagogic Research and Teaching Professors: lowering the status of teaching and learning through bifurcation, *Teaching in Higher Education*, 16(1), 127-130. http://dx.doi.org/10.1080/13562517.2011.530756

Marginson, S. (2006) Dynamics of National and Global Competition in Higher Education, *Higher Education*, 52(1), 1-39.
http://dx.doi.org/10.1007/s10734-004-7649-x

Marginson, S. (2007) Global Position and Position Taking: the case of Australia, *Journal of Studies in International Education*, 11(1), 5-32.
http://dx.doi.org/10.1177/1028315306287530

Ministry of Education (MOE) (2005) Wisdom Thailand 2015.
http://www.powershow.com/view/92a3f-NWVhM/Wisdom_Thailand_2015_for_KnowledgeBased_Society_powerpoint_ppt_presentation (accessed on 21 April 2011).

Ministry of Education (MOE) (2008) Policy Statement of the Council of Ministers. Bangkok: Ministry of Education.

Ministry of Education (MOE) (2009a) Focus on Quality Improvements in Education in 2009. Bangkok: Ministry of Education.

Ministry of Education (MOE) (2009b) Investment Plans under the 2nd Stimulus Package of Economic Reform (2010-2012). Bangkok: Ministry of Education.

Ministry of Education (MOE) (2012) New Directions of Ministry of Education. Bangkok: Ministry of Education.

Ministry of Education (MOE) (2013) *Excerpt from the Minister of Education's policy*. Bangkok: Ministry of Education.

Mohrman, K., Ma, W. & Baker, D. (2008) The Research University in Transition: the emerging global model, *Higher Education Policy*, 21, 5-27.

National Research Council of Thailand (NRCT) (2014) National Policies on Research. http://en.nrct.go.th/en/RDindexofThailand.aspx (accessed 15 May 2015).

National Research Council of Thailand (NRCT) (2015) http://www.nrct.go.th/

Nonkukhetkhong, K., Baldauf Jr, R.B. & Moni, K. (2006) Learner-centredness in Teaching English as a Foreign Language. Paper presented at the 26th Thai TESOL International Conference, in Chiang Mai, Thailand.

Office of the Higher Education Commission (OHEC) (2008) Executive Report Framework of the Second 15-Year Long Range Plan on Higher Education of Thailand. Bangkok: Ministry of Education, Commission on Higher Education.

Office of the Higher Education Commission (OHEC) (2010a) Report and Statistics. http://www.mua.go.th/pr_web/content_3.html (accessed on 21 April 2011).

Office of the Higher Education Commission (OHEC) (2010b) Thai Higher Education: policy & issue. http://inter.mua.go.th/?cat=13

Pratt, M., Margaritis, D. & Coy, D. (1999) Developing a Research Culture in a University Faculty, *Journal of Higher Education Policy and Management*, 21(1), 43-55. http://dx.doi.org/10.1080/1360080990210104

Sangnapaboworn, W. (2003) Higher Education Reform in Thailand: towards quality improvement and university autonomy. Paper presented at the Shizuoka Forum on Approaches to Higher Education, Intellectual Creativity, Cultivation of Human Resources Seen in Asian Countries, in Shizuoka, Japan.

Sukamolson, S. (2010) English Research Trends. http://www.culi.chula.ac.th/research/webboard/forum (accessed on 27 June 2012).

Suwanwela, C. (2005) Higher Education Reform in Thailand. http://www.international.ac.uk/resources/Higher%20Education%20Reform%20-%20Thailand.pdf (accessed on 10 December 2011).

Suwanwela, C. (2008) The Political and Social Contribution of Research. http://www.slideshare.net/guni_rmies/social-contribution-of-research-in-developing-countries-charas-suwanwela (accessed on 19 April 2009).

Syananondh, K. & Wannaruk, A. (1990) An Investigation of Literacy, Attitudes, and Motivations Concerning Methodology and Statistics among EFL Instructors in State Universities in Thailand, *PASAA*, 20, 41-54.

Teichler, U. (2004) The Changing Debate on Internationalisation of Higher Education, *Higher Education*, 48, 5-26. http://dx.doi.org/10.1023/B:HIGH.0000033771.69078.41

Thai-Journal Citation Index Centre (TCI) (2015) http://www.kmutt.ac.th/jif/public_html/Evaluation/2558/Announced/News.html

Tynan, B.R. & Garbett, D.L. (2007) Negotiating the University Research Culture: collaborative voices of new academics, *Higher Education Research and Development*, 26(4), 411-424. http://dx.doi.org/10.1080/07294360701658617

United Nations Educational, Scientific and Cultural Organization (UNESCO) (2015) Having Their Say: state of mother-tongue based education in region. http://www.unescobkk.org/news/article/having-their-say-state-of-mother-tongue-based-education-in-region/ (accessed on 25 May 2015).

Winitchaikun, K., Wiriyachitra, A. & Chaikitmongkol, W. (2002) *Appropriate Approaches to English Language Teaching and Learning in the General Education Curriculum in Chiang Mai University*. Chiang Mai: Chiang Mai University.

CHAPTER 15

Economy Class? Lived Experiences and Career Trajectories of Private-sector English-language School Teachers in Australia

PHIONA STANLEY

SUMMARY 'If I worked in a nice restaurant I'd make more money than I do here ... But I love my job', says a teacher interviewed for this research project. This chapter asks: 'what does it feel like to work in a teaching job that pays less than waitressing? What kinds of teachers are drawn to, and stick around in, commercial English Language Teaching (ELT)? What are the effects on teaching, and on students?' The study was conducted among teachers, students, and directors of studies in 11 language schools in four cities in Australia. This chapter considers the various 'types' of teachers in this sector and their different career trajectories. Also discussed are the effects of teachers' lived experiences in the sector on the ELT profession more widely, in particular on the well-documented low status of the profession. This chapter therefore has relevance for all English language teachers, regardless of the sector in which they work. Might all teachers' professionalism be tainted by association, and if so, how might a case be made for 'upgrading' ELT from 'economy class'?

Introduction and Contextualizing Literature

'If I worked in a nice restaurant ... I'd make more money than I do here ... but I love my job,' says a teacher whom I interview for this study. I wonder: what does it *feel* like to work in a teaching job that pays less than waitressing? What kinds of teachers are drawn to, and stick around in, commercial English Language Teaching (ELT)? What are the effects on teachers' morale and identity and on the sector more broadly? These questions motivated this ethnographic study, which was conducted among teachers, students and directors of studies in eleven language schools in four cities in Australia.

A few articles have appeared in the past 25 years lamenting the dubious professional status of the ELT 'profession' or 'industry' (Maley, 1992). Some focus on the teach-and-travel phenomenon, which arguably taints the ELT profession by association with untrained western 'teachers' teaching English as they travel the world (Thornbury, 2001; Stanley, 2013). Others have considered the problematic privilege of native speaker teachers, arguing that if native-ness is a more important criterion than professional preparation, the profession's professionalism has a long way to go (e.g. Kabel, 2008; Kirkpatrick, 2006; Kubota & Lin, 2006, 2009; Phan, 2008). And still others have pointed to the 'second-class' earning status of English language teachers in academic institutions (Pennington, 1992). In Australian universities, for example, English language teachers earn less, on separate pay scales, than teachers in other academic disciplines. As a result, Matei and Medgyes (2003, p. 74) write that ELT is 'held in low esteem in most parts of the world', arguing that 'it is very doubtful whether, without adequate financial means, teachers can command the respect of contemporary society and maintain a level of self-esteem required to pursue this profession'. Teachers' salaries, then, perhaps reflect English language teachers' limited professional prestige internationally.

To some extent, the 'economy-class' problem is well documented in the literature. However, the articles cited here are written by and from the perspective of old hands, and in addition many of the key articles on this topic are now rather dated; for the old hands, this is old hat. But while many readers of this chapter, including the author, doubtless enjoy the security of 'proper' (academic? management? teacher education?) jobs and salaries, not everyone working in our industry enjoys these conditions. Therefore the voices missing from this conversation about professional identity are those of precariously hired, minimally qualified, low-waged teachers at the chalk face of language school ELT. The case study discussed here is Australia, but it could just as easily be Canada, or the USA, or the UK, or elsewhere. These teachers are part of 'centre' ELT, perhaps seen by students and others as somehow 'better' than ELT in the 'periphery'. But is it really? To address this, and to give voice to ordinary teachers getting by on short contracts and low pay, this chapter explores our professional identity narrative and the less desirable realities that we may prefer to hide.

I have written elsewhere about the 'soft underbelly' of ELT, where teachers and institutions of limited legitimacy may operate without censure in Asia and elsewhere (Stanley, 2013, p. 2). But this chapter describes a different, though related, problem. All the language schools in this study *are* accredited, which in Australia requires teachers to be university graduates with qualifications akin to the Cambridge CELTA (Certificate in English Language Teaching to Adults). This is therefore not what Thornbury (2001) calls 'the unbearable lightness of EFL', in which unqualified 'natives' may reinvent themselves, problematically, as 'teachers' by dint of buying a plane ticket. Instead, these *are* teachers. But they are, I argue, effectively volunteering at least part of their time because their pay and conditions do not reflect the complexity of the technically skilled and emotionally challenging roles they perform. So I ask: how does this phenomenon contribute more widely to the well-documented low status of ELT? This chapter therefore has relevance for *all* English language teachers. Might our *own* professionalism be tainted by these issues and, if so, how might we 'upgrade' the ELT profession from its 'economy-class' status?

At its core, this is a problem of low salaries. Beginning teachers in Australian English language schools earn much less than newly qualified high school teachers. In 2013, for instance, full-time, newly qualified language school teachers earned AUD$45,000 a year, while newly qualified NSW public-school-sector schoolteachers made AUD$60,000 a year (Fair Work Commission, 2010; NSW Department of Education and Communities, 2014). However, many language school teachers are casual employees hired on hourly rates, which are therefore a more useful measure of teachers' actual income. Beginning graduate language school teachers in 2013 (Fair Work Commission, 2013) earned AUD$41.40 per teaching hour, while the 2015 rate is AUD$44.87. Lesson preparation and marking, while expected of teachers, are not paid separately. So if, for example, an hour-long lesson takes a beginning teacher an hour to prepare, and if every classroom hour results in half an hour of marking and other administration after class, this 'hourly' rate is actually for *two and a half* hours' work, paid at about AUD$16/hour of real time. However, in my experience of training students on University of Cambridge CELTA courses, beginning teachers may spend much longer than this on lesson preparation. Teachers therefore earn below the national minimum wage, which is almost AUD$17 per hour. Although this may sound substantial to readers in lower-income/cost countries, some perspective can be found in comparisons. For example, a $45,000 language school teacher's full-time salary equates to, or is less than, the salaries of tram drivers, bakers or real-estate salespeople, none of whom require degree-level qualifications and all of whom can increase their base salary through overtime, commissions and/or penalty rates (Open Universities Australia, 2015a,b,c). Further, as a standard language school teaching day is four hours' classroom time, teachers can expect to earn only about AUD$900/week if they are lucky enough to find full-time work. After 20-30% tax, this does not leave much to live on. In Sydney, for example, which is where the majority of English colleges are located, a one-bedroom flat costs AUD$400-500/week to rent.

Nevertheless, language schools manage to find staff. Teachers, it seems, are not driven primarily by money or job security. Instead, most of those interviewed for this study said they appreciate the flexibility of short contracts and seasonal work, not least as many had 'portfolio careers' encompassing diverse income streams. Interviewees included professional musicians and massage therapists, among myriad other non-teaching roles. In addition, most participants said they appreciated their diverse, interesting and sometimes well-travelled students and colleagues. These factors speak of an industry in which staff motivation may be wonderfully intrinsic, but one in which teacher recruitment and retention may be limited to those with independent means. Many participants spoke of private incomes and/or wealthy spouses. These issues of teacher motivations, demographics and identities are explored through participants' contributions in this chapter.

Research Method and Context

In common with all qualitative research, my objective in this study was not to survey *all* teachers or to 'prove' that these participants' experiences are representative of all teachers in conceptually comparable contexts. Instead, this was an exploratory study whose objective was to illuminate this issue so as to spark discussion. The data for this chapter come from interviews conducted with 28 teachers and 13 directors of studies and directors at eleven language schools in four Australian cities in 2012 and 2013. Most of the interviews were conducted individually, although two teachers and two directors of studies were interviewed in pairs at their own request. The interviews were conducted in private in spare offices/classrooms in participants' places of work. Interview duration ranged from 40 to 90 minutes, averaging 55 minutes per interview. All recordings were professionally transcribed and checked against the originals. The data were then inductively coded, and the themes that emerged highlighted participants' priorities and concerns. The study was funded by a UNSW Australia School of Education research grant and was approved by the UNSW Human Research Ethics Advisory ethics panel. All participants' names are pseudonyms.

The data set discussed in this chapter comes from a larger study that investigated students' expectations and experiences at language schools where English is bundled with home-stay, cultural immersion and tourism (Stanley, 2015). The language schools were of different 'types': university-attached, international chain accredited, and independent and privately operated. Most were members of English Australia, the industry peak body, and all were accredited ELICOS providers (this acronym stands for English-Language Intensive Courses for Overseas Students). Accreditation in Australia means that schools can accept students on ELICOS visas and ensures that certain teacher qualification and other standards are maintained.

Schools provide teacher support in the form of master's-in-ELT-qualified directors of studies and ongoing professional development. Most teachers were teaching general English, including examination preparation classes, and a few taught academic or business English. Most of the teachers interviewed had less than five years' teaching experience, although some directors of studies with up to thirty years' experience in the industry reflected on their teaching experiences and the experiences of teachers they supervised, so the data set represents a range of teacher-experience durations from a few months to thirty years. Some of the directors of studies were also CELTA trainers, and they also related information based on their teacher training experiences.

Findings and Discussion

The findings are discussed in terms of teachers' motivations, salaries, promotion steps, and the extent of their roles.

Teachers' Motivations

Why teach English in a language school? What motivates teachers? The following quotations are illustrative rather than necessarily representative from sample to population, and provide insights as to what motivates these teachers:

> [What I enjoy most about the job] it's the people. The students ... [are] really keen to learn. ... You feel a great sense of need. You're helping them and you feel you can do things to help them on their journey. The staff are very interesting, too. You get such interesting conversations. So it's a very stimulating place to work ... It's amazing the places people have been and experiences they've had ... It's certainly one of the best jobs I've had. I mean, I've had some really well paid jobs in the past ... but I think this is the job I enjoy the most. (James, private language school teacher, two years' teaching experience, 2012)

> I like meeting people from other countries. I can't travel as much as I would like to any more so I feel, in a way, I'm travelling every day. I've got 30 Brazilians [in my class at the moment] and I'm interested [in them] ... When teachers move away from the classroom, they move into management ... I just think that they get further away from what teaching's about. For some people, I'm sure that's fine. For me, I really have no ambition to lose contact with students. It's something that I really enjoy. (Matt, university language centre teacher, twelve years' teaching experience, 2013)

> I've got one [teacher] who lives on his boat ... He goes up to the Whitsundays for three or four months ... and then he comes back when it gets busy. Because May, June, July is really quiet. We don't have enough work. He says, 'okay, I'll be in touch from the yacht'. Then he comes back when it gets busy ... He's also a dive-master and he can just do other things. (Lena, chain language school director of studies, 2012)

These quotes draw out areas of language school teaching that appeal to teachers and that came up frequently in the data set. Teachers enjoy feeling needed by students. They enjoy interesting conversations with colleagues, the multicultural milieu of international students, and the flexibility of seasonal work that offers a chance to take unpaid leave while returning to the same job in the high season.

Teachers' Salaries

For all that teachers described the enjoyment and fulfilment they experience in their workplaces, many were quick to note that the low pay was a major issue for them. In addition, the 'stepped' pay scale, in which teachers earn more as they gain experience and further qualifications, meant that, paradoxically, more experienced teachers felt under-valued. The following quotes, taken from one dyad interview and three individual interviews, illustrate these points:

> *Cecilia*: [Salaries are] one of our biggest discussions. It's like, 'why is there such a big difference between what high school teachers get paid and what we get paid?' We're teaching. We go through all of the stress and pressure but we're ... getting the same [pay], or less, than a secretary or a receptionist.
> *Louise*: Yeah, if I worked in a nice restaurant ... where I got tips, I'd make more money than I do here.
> *Phiona*: So how do you feel about that?
> *Cecilia*: I love the job. Right now I want to stay in this industry ... So it doesn't bother me that much, but I do think it's really unfair ... You have to have a bachelor's degree and CELTA. So we're paying back all this money for education, although we don't have to pay it back because we never earn enough to have to pay it back. [In Australia, the earning threshold for repaying student loans is $53,000 p.a.; both Cecilia and Louise make less than this.] But I love teaching and it's something I want to continue.
> Louise: I'm single, I live at home [with my parents], and I don't have a lot of expenses and so this job pays for what I need it to pay for. But I know a lot of people who are teachers and their partner has a really well-paying job or they're like semi-retired and they teach just because they like it. So they don't need the money.
> (Chain language school teachers, less than two years' experience, 2012)

> The pay is really demoralising for somebody who has just gone and spent $3000 on a CELTA ... It's not a huge return on investment. It seems really quite cruel ... It's factory-like, there's a conveyor belt of people coming into [CELTA] training programs ... It's a conveyor belt of [teachers] coming in[to schools], and

190

there's a conveyor belt of [teachers] leaving at the other end ... Some people go, 'this isn't for me, this is ridiculous, I'm going to train to be something completely different'. I think a lot of people try it out because they like the idea of it and then realise, 'God, this is really hard work ... and I get paid bugger all for it.' (Anna, freelance CELTA trainer, 20+ years' experience, 2012)

Because of my background [as an accountant] I've had the opportunity to earn a decent salary and had permanency and so on. So it's given me a financial cushioning that's enabled me to work in [ELT] ... But I look at my colleagues and think, 'they don't have the opportunities I had'. Like, I've paid off my mortgage, [but] they can't even get a car loan because they're casual ... I have to admit when I first joined, I knew it was low pay so I made sure that I was financially comfortable before I transitioned [from accountancy]. But now I'm just like, 'this is really not okay'. (Jane, chain language school teacher, three years' teaching experience, 2013)

I have one-third of my [teaching] staff who are of flexible economic means but who love doing what they're doing here ... They're not working for the money. They're not after a career path. They're all in their 50s or 60s ... There's that calmness that they bring to a staffroom ... It's got to be the right kind of person ... They're hard to find. I will never get rid of those [teachers] because they're economically flexible. [One teacher] says, 'I just love working here. I love the interaction with young people ... But I'll be flexible. If you can only give me two hours a day only or just three weeks here but not for the next seven weeks that's okay.' Those people are like gold. Don't get rid of those. Because they're your little moveable parts that enable the machine to keep going. (Lena, chain language school, director of studies, 2012)

Salient in these quotes is the volunteer-like nature of language school teaching alluded to by Cecilia and Jane. Both acknowledge that their love of teaching trumps its low remuneration, although both express concern about just how low the pay actually is and how unfair they feel it is, considering the complexity of the work they do. While Louise and Jane describe strategies for managing the low-pay issue, including prior earnings to provide a financial cushion, living in low-cost or no-cost accommodation, and teaching at a stage of life when earning is not of primary importance, Anna goes deeper into her perception of the adverse effect this has on the profession more generally, noting high rates of teacher attrition and the sense that teachers come and go and therefore may be regarded as interchangeable.

In addition, there is the issue raised by Lena: the ELT industry is highly seasonal, with significant lean times in the year during which student numbers (and therefore teacher employment) drop off. Having teachers 'of flexible economic means' allows schools to offer casual work at certain times of the year only, although this further entrenches the problem of attrition, particularly among those teachers who rely on a year-round salary to stay afloat. Indeed, the numbers support this analysis of teacher attrition in ELT. While around 10,000 candidates worldwide undertake CELTA annually, far fewer undertake higher qualifications in ELT (Cambridge DELTA or Masters in ELT, for instance), which suggests that there is a steep drop-off in numbers between entry-level and long-term ELT teachers across the industry (Green, 2005; Cambridge ESOL, 2009).

Priced Out of the Market?

Another important part of the Australian language school 'story' is the pay agreement, which divides teachers' salaries into 'steps' that recognise teachers' experience and qualifications: as teachers gain classroom experience they move up the step system and their pay increases. (That said, even highest-step language school teachers, with many years' teaching and higher qualifications in ELT, earn only $65,000 per year; this is just over the *starting* salary of a schoolteacher. While language school pay may be low at the *entry* level, it is arguably lower, proportionate to expertise, at the *upper* end of the spectrum!) Although well intentioned as a way to recognise and reward expertise, the step system, I contend, in fact does more harm than good. It must be noted, also, that not all schools adhere to the same pay scale. In particular, teachers at the university language centres are better paid, either on a separate step system or on a flat hourly rate. But newly qualified teachers are less frequently hired by the university centres, and the private and chain language schools are much more numerous and they hire many more teachers. So the step system has an important, and I think very damaging, impact on the ELT industry. The following quotes provide an insight into how the system affects teacher-hiring decisions:

> My budget [for teacher salaries] is to be an average of a step seven [teacher] ... That means if you've got someone who's got a degree and a CELTA they come in at step two ... But you've got these great teachers, you're hanging on to them, and they're slipping up the steps every year ... Then I have to sacrifice somewhere. So at the moment I look for any step two [teacher] and throw them into the mix so I can keep my step 12 [teacher] ... But then [a step two teacher] becomes a step three very quickly, and then a step four. Your average slips up ... So I'm constantly keeping an eye on it ... There's always a turnaround. So, for instance, I'm about to lose [one of the teachers], who's a step eight. When I lose him, regardless of what I find [in terms of new teacher hires], it's got to be a step two to come in to replace that step eight, to average it out. (Lena, chain language school, director of studies, 2012)

We do hire a lot of very good teachers ... but we lose them when they become too expensive for the school. It's not that they want to leave; there are many people I know who would have loved to have stayed, but they weren't given more work because they'd reached that part of the [salary] award where they became an expensive teacher, and there's somebody cheaper who could do the job ... [In ELT] you have a shelf life, and when you become too expensive [you lose your job] ... We've definitely kept not-so-good, inexpensive teachers and we've let expensive, very good teachers go ... How can this be a serious industry when the price of a teacher matters more than their experience? It's very disheartening ... When you talk to other teachers, many people think oh, 'I don't know how long I'm going to be in this industry.' People say to me, 'Oh you're studying your master's [degree in ELT], why? What are you going to do with that? What other school's going to hire you? You're going to have this [step] level and your master's, where on earth are you going to find a job?' (Amy, chain language school senior teacher, five years' experience, 2012)

It seems incredibly paradoxical that teachers become *less* employable as they gain skills, qualifications and experience. But in language school ELT, it is so. Indeed, in the research for this project and in ten years of involvement with the ELICOS sector I have distressingly often heard of teachers whose pay step has risen beyond a level their school can afford who are negotiating their own salaries *down*, so as to keep their jobs. Obviously, at an industry level, this is problematic, conspiring to reward and value inexperience and lack of professional expertise; as Amy says, 'how can this be a serious industry when the price of a teacher matters more than the experience?' She is right.

But the 'price' of teachers' salaries *does* matter to the small private language schools and to the chain-school operations. It matters enormously. These are very lean business operations with little money to spare. This is because the ELT industry is beholden to diverse stakeholders, each of whom takes a sizeable slice from the students' fees. These include facilities and equipment costs and the salaries of ancillary staff (e.g. cleaners and receptionists, but also directors of studies, accountants and marketing staff). But, perhaps most significantly, schools bear the cost of agents' fees and agent discounting. The phenomenon of education agents is akin to that of travel agents in the tourism industry. Despite the Internet, many students approach education agents to navigate the complexity of overseas courses, and even students on-shore in Australia often book through agents rather than directly with institutions. Agents market to students and are often engaged as problem-solving middlemen. This role of agents was explained by almost all the participants who were directors of studies. But agents, and discounts, account for a large proportion of school income, which is one reason that teacher salaries are low compared with student fees. It is not (just) that most schools are for-profit businesses with sizeable overheads. It is also that many hands are reaching for a share of the spoils.

Going the Extra Mile

But is it not the case, murmur the sceptics, that English teaching is easy (Thornbury, 2001)? Isn't language school teachers' pay low because any reasonably proficient user of English can do the job? Sadly, this view permeates in the Australian social imaginary, in which many people have heard of, or even undertaken, 'teach-and-travel' ELT work during extended overseas sojourns. This is the 'soft underbelly' problem I referred to in the introduction. Against a background of discourse that constructs ELT as an easy way for young backpackers to make money on the road (Stanley, 2013, pp. 26-30), teachers' perceptions of low pay may originate, in part, from comparing the complexity of (the reality of) the job with the meagre salary it attracts. The following quotes speak to this complexity and the high expectations of teachers that students, and schools, may have:

> This job, it's lots of fun but also at the same time it is really difficult because you work with people five or six hours a day ... You're 'on', you have to be 'on', all that time ... I spend more time with [the students] than with my husband. So it can be really hard work. (Natasha, private language school teacher, six months' teaching experience, 2012)

> You need teachers who notice the moods of the students and who actually say, 'are you okay? You look a bit quiet today.' They might say 'I'm just – I'm not feeling that well.' So, 'make sure if you're sick go and see a doctor, we can help organise that' ... These are 22-, 23-year-old [students]. They're away from home ... You don't want to bring in [a teacher] who will say, 'I'm just here to teach' ... [Part of the job] is that caring for students as individuals. Sometimes being prepared to give that little bit of extra time, that one to one with students as they need it. Just being a real, like a surrogate family ... [the teachers] have got to understand that, that it's part of their role. (Lena, chain language school, director of studies, 2012)

> Some language schools won't look at [higher step teachers] so it's hard for them to find work ... You can't afford to have probably more than one or two step 12s. But you want them, you need them, they're important ... Somebody who's a step 10, 11, 12 has to be much more than just experienced ... Maybe they're happy to run PD [professional development] sessions [for other teachers].

Be a bit of a leader and a mentor, not just come in [to school] and go, 'I'm just here for four hours.' They might be the grammar guru or whatever [in the staffroom], and also they can teach anything that you need them to teach. If you say, 'well can you go and teach [Cambridge Proficiency; a very high level class]?' [They'll say], 'yep, no problem.' (Chris, private language school, director of studies, 2012)

I'm a history buff, I could bore you for hours [laughs]. The first day we went to [a historical site]. So I spent half a day [taking] them around [the area] and explained about the hotel, it's got a tunnel underneath where they used to shanghai the sailors ... The other day we went to [another historical site] ... Then last week we went to the market and they were interested in the cheese, this array of cheese. So I bought them some blue cheese and we had it, it was really quite good actually. Every second week we go somewhere on excursion. (Serena, chain language school teacher, two years' teaching experience, 2013)

[Teaching in a language school, as a newly qualified teacher] is actually not much less stress than the CELTA course, and [the teachers] get paid bugger all for it. [They feel,] 'I give, give, give' ... and, you know, once you've started getting feedback, you get feedback on everything. Stand in the corner with your hands in your pockets, and some DOS [director of studies] will come in the room and say, 'what are you doing standing in the corner with your hands in your pockets?' There's always feedback, there's like constant feedback. I think that's really tiring ... [There are] such high expectations, such low rewards. (Anna, freelance CELTA trainer, 20+ years' experience, 2012)

I have selected a large number of quotes here because, together, they construct the teacher role as multi-faceted and highly complex. Within the written and, perhaps more importantly, unwritten language school job description, the importance of 'going the extra mile' is obvious for teachers hoping to keep their (mostly casual, usually seasonal) jobs. Natasha highlights the emotional labour of many hours of face time, while Lena emphasises the pastoral-care role of teachers (to reiterate: most of whom are hourly paid and not contracted to work beyond their classroom contact hours). Chris's extra mile is staffroom peer support by being the grammar guru or running professional development sessions, while for Serena the extra mile is the extra skills and dedication her historical expertise and passion bring to her role (as well as buying cheese!). Anna's text, perhaps more nuanced, concerns the burden on teachers of surveillance. The extreme casualisation and implicit daily re-interviewing for one's own continuing employment mean that every action is under constant scrutiny, and teachers cannot afford to let their guard down for a moment.

Matt also described an expectation on teachers to 'go the extra mile', in this case in pursuit of stable year-round contracted employment. Having worked as a casual teacher, on five-week contracts and often only during peak periods, in the same language institute since 2005, he says:

> At the end of the year, all the teachers apply for [annual] contracts [as opposed to five-week agreements that a majority of teachers are on] ... Quite a big part of [the selection criteria] is developing materials; how much work you put into that. That's tricky, though, because, as a casual I'm expected to be there for six hours a day; four hours teaching, a couple of hours prep. To develop materials on top of that, they're pushing it to get that from us ... The other [criterion] is professional development days and training courses, so if you go on those they're unpaid. They used to be [paid] but now they're not ... So if you're a casual that develops a lot of materials, goes on all the professional development days, that would put you in better stead for a contract ... But it's beyond me so far. I've got a daughter in school, so it's complex. (Matt, university language centre teacher, twelve years' teaching experience, 2013)

I have separated out Matt's contribution from the excerpts above as it also illustrates a point I raised in the introduction, and want to revisit – that much of the conversation in the literature on the issue of ELT and low status/low pay is written by people who are safely ensconced, themselves, in much more secure and fairly paid jobs. This is also my story. Although I worked in language schools from 1994 to 2006, in a range of roles, a variety of countries, and a series of somewhat precarious contractual situations and sometimes low pay, I am now much more secure in a 'proper' academic job with a reliable income, a transparent and merit-based career structure, and a sense that I am fairly remunerated for my work. So while I still respond viscerally and emotionally as much as intellectually to the central ideas in this chapter, my own normativities have changed. I was shocked by Matt's point that teachers were expected to attend unpaid professional development sessions. When I expressed my surprise and checked I had understood Matt's intended meaning: yes, these sessions are unpaid. For Matt, this is the natural way of things; for me, it seems unusual. Therefore, while researchers, like me, are more likely to be writing chapters like this one, we must still strive to listen to, and *to hear*, teachers at all levels of ELT.

The excerpts discussed in this section reveal a world of unwritten expectations and subtle and not-so-subtle demands made of teachers. While social imaginaries, in part born of the 'teach-and-travel' phenomenon, may construct ELT as easy, these teachers' testimonies speak to a complexity and emotional labour that may be relentless, thankless and exhausting. While plenty of teachers certainly enjoy their work, minimal pay and low-status perceptions are a high price to pay given the attendant complexity of succeeding in the role itself, particularly given its many demands for going the 'extra mile' in areas such as out-of-class pastoral care for students, materials preparation, peer mentoring/troubleshooting, attending unpaid meetings, drawing on teachers' other areas of expertise, and submitting to constant surveillance.

Conclusion

Teachers' low pay, the problematic salary step system, insecure working conditions, and unwritten 'extra mile' expectations do not appear to actually hinder teacher recruitment to the extent that schools find it impossible to recruit teachers. Perhaps if they did, things would change. If school owners and directors (whose status, stake and longevity in the industry make them much more influential than most teachers) were to experience teachers' working conditions as an operational problem, they might push for a salary system that values and recognises good teachers above cheap ones and that pays graduate teachers more than bakers, tram drivers and real-estate sales agents. Such a change would be good for teacher recruitment, morale and retention, and would create a sense that language school teaching is a viable career option rather than a semi-volunteer, pocket-money-earning hobby to be enjoyed by those who do not need the money or whose stage of life allows them to live cheaply.

Individual teachers' experiences of the ELT industry also matter in and of themselves, beyond the more obvious effects on the industry of teacher recruitment, morale and retention. Bearing in mind the 'conveyor belt' through CELTA and language schools, and teachers' subsequent disillusionment, as Anna described above, there are many, many people for whom ELT is something with which they experimented before moving on to pastures new. This means that for most people who have first-hand experience of ELT, the experience is likely to be fun but ultimately not viable as a career for any of the reasons discussed above. A small minority go the distance. These majority early experiences then contribute to the social imaginary of ELT as low status; it is not just the 'teach-and-travel' discourses that construct the idea that ELT is, as Thornbury puts it, a 'low status, even slightly disreputable thing to do' (2001, p. 391). So by attending to beginning teachers' experiences, and to their constructions about the industry, we are attending to the industry itself both at an operational level, as in the previous paragraph, and at a reputational level, as discussed in this paragraph.

There is a final point to be made that is perhaps the most important point of all. The issues discussed here are, I feel, quite simply unfair at a human level. Novice teachers' enthusiasm, expertise, flexibility, care for the students, and goodwill are being exploited and squandered through ever higher expectations of minimally paid and marginally employed teachers. While the ELT industry offers some job satisfaction and a chance to work in an interesting and international milieu, it also seems to result in teachers struggling with the difficulty of getting and keeping ongoing work that provides a living wage. But *they* have not failed; the industry has failed them. This is the depressing reality of 'economy-class' ELT.

References

Cambridge ESOL (2009) Certificate in English Language Teaching to Adults (CELTA). 13 November. http://www.cambridgeesol.org/exams/teaching-awards/celta.html

Fair Work Commission (2010) College of English (Teachers) Agreement. https://www.fwc.gov.au/documents/documents/agreements/fwa/AE878120.pdf (accessed on 18 January 2015).

Fair Work Commission (2013) College of English (Teachers) Agreement. http://m.ieu.asn.au/media/49867sydney_college_of_english_pty_ltd__teachers__a greement_2013.pdf (accessed on 18 January 2015).

Green, T. (2005) Staying in Touch: tracking the career paths of CELTA graduates, *University of Cambridge ESOL Research Notes*, 19, 7-11.

Kabel, A. (2008) Native-speakerism, Stereotyping and the Collusion of Applied Linguistics, *System*, 37, 12-22. http://dx.doi.org/10.1016/j.system.2008.09.004

Kirkpatrick, A. (2006) Which Model of English: native speaker, nativised or lingua franca?, in M. Saraceni & R. Rubdy (Eds) *English in the World: global rules, global roles*, pp. 71-83. London: Continuum.

Kubota, R. & Lin, A. (2006) Race and TESOL: introduction to concepts and theories, *TESOL Quarterly*, 40, 471-493. http://dx.doi.org/10.2307/40264540

Kubota, R. & Lin, A. (Eds) (2009) *Race, Culture, and Identities in Second Language Education*. New York: Routledge.

Maley, A. (1992) An Open Letter to 'the Profession', *ELT Journal*, 46(1), 96-99. http://dx.doi.org/10.1093/elt/46.1.96

Matei, G. & Medgyes, P. (2003) Teaching English is a Political Act: a non-PC dialogue, in P. Radai (Ed.) *The Status of Language Educators*, pp. 69-77. Strasbourg: European Centre for Modern Languages, Council of Europe Publishing.

NSW Department of Education and Communities (2014) Employment Conditions and Benefits. http://www.teach.nsw.edu.au/grp/orientation/cb-salary_growth.htm (accessed on 22 November 2014).

Open Universities Australia (2015a) Careers: bakers. http://www.open.edu.au/careers/tourism/bakers-pastrycooks (accessed on 21 January 2015).

Open Universities Australia (2015b) Careers: real estate. http://www.open.edu.au/careers/real-estate-property/real-estate-sales-agents (accessed on 21 January 2015).

Open Universities Australia (2015c) Careers: transport. http://www.open.edu.au/careers/transport/train-tram-drivers (accessed on 21 January 2015).

Pennington, M.C. (1992) Second Class or Economy? The Status of the English Language Teaching Profession in Tertiary Education, *Prospect*, 7(3), 7-19.

Phan, L.H. (2008) *Teaching English as an International Language: identity, resistance and negotiation*. Clevedon: Multilingual Matters.

Stanley, P. (2013) *A Critical Ethnography of 'Westerners' Teaching English in China: Shanghaied in Shanghai*. Abingdon: Routledge.

Stanley, P. (2015) Language-learner Tourists in Australia: problematizing the 'known' and its impact on interculturality, in D.J. Rivers (Ed.) *Resistance to the Known: counter-conduct in language education*, pp. 23-46. Basingstoke: Palgrave Macmillan.

Thornbury, S. (2001) The Unbearable Lightness of EFL, *ELT Journal*, 55(4), 391-396. http://dx.doi.org/10.1093/elt/55.4.391

CHAPTER 16

English Language Teachers in Greece: building professional identities

STAVROULA KALDI, EMMANUEL KONSOLAS & IOANNA SYRIOU

SUMMARY The research presented in this chapter focuses on the professional development of English language teachers in Greece. More specifically our study attempts to identify the key factors affecting the professional development of Greek teachers who specialized to teach English as a Foreign Language (EFL), to highlight positive and negative landmarks during their career experiences and investigate contextual factors affecting their professional trajectories and identities. A qualitative methodological paradigm is applied based on life histories research. Biographical interviews are used in order to explore career experiences, including the use of metaphors. Six Greek teachers, graduates of university courses specializing in teaching EFL, representing a range of age, prior experience, education, current professional post and responsibilities, participated in this study. The main findings indicate the differences between the public and the private sector of education and between primary and secondary education. Implications for educational policy are also discussed.

Introduction

The demand for teachers who can meet the requirements for higher student achievement in the twenty-first century has provoked discussions among researchers and educational authorities on teachers' professional learning and the way they build their professional identities. It is strongly argued that student achievement can be improved 'only by building the capacity of teachers to improve their instructional practice and the capacity of school systems to advance teacher learning' (Chung Wei et al, 2009).

Professional development is viewed as a learning process which aims to improve teachers' knowledge, skills and practice throughout their teaching career, resulting in the enhancement of their status (Day, 1999; Evans, 2008). Such a process engages educators' creative and reflective capacities in ways that strengthen their practice (Bredeson, 2002). Kelchtermans (2004) relates teachers' professional development to their professional context, both in time and in space. Within this professional context, teachers' professional identity is believed to be a complex and dynamic process (Volkmann & Anderson, 1998) which involves a non-linear, unstable development through 'which an individual confirms or problematizes who she/he is/becomes' (Zembylas, 2003, p. 221). 'It represents the process by which the person seeks to integrate his various statuses and roles, as well as his diverse experiences, into a coherent image of self' (Epstein, 1978, p. 101).

The relationship between professional development and English as a second language teacher identity has previously been studied by exploring teachers' personal experiences through either life history research or narrative and reflexive inquiry. In addition, the use of metaphor in examining aspects of teachers' identity is an approach that has started to be used to provide insight into ways in which teachers conceptualize their experience. It has been shown that learning and functioning in a second language are important factors in the development of language teachers' identity. According to Kiernan (2010), the identity of foreign language teachers reaches across the borders of language into foreign cultures and their professional life is intrinsically involved with linguistic identity.

In Greece, English as a Foreign Language (EFL) was first introduced in private primary schools in 1940 and in Gymnasiums [1] in 1945. Teachers are either graduates of a four-year university course, who can teach English in public or private primary and secondary schools, as well in frontisteria [2], or holders of the Cambridge or Michigan Proficiency Certificate [3], who can only teach in frontisteria or private tuition, addressing mainly the needs of learners who need to acquire English language competence and certification.

English teachers' professional development in Greece is the responsibility of regional training centres, universities, higher technological institutions, the Training School of Employees in Vocational and Technical Education, and the Institute of Educational Policy. These institutions organize and implement induction training programmes for newly appointed teachers, annual training for teachers who have completed at least five years of service, and short periodic training. Additionally, legislation provides for teacher training programmes organized by schools. Participation in these programmes is voluntary, except for induction training programmes of newly appointed teachers. However, the existing teacher training programmes have been accused of failing to meet the actual needs of the teaching staff, ignoring diversity among trainees regarding professional experience and background knowledge, which limits the promotion of lifelong education in Greece (Papastamatis et al, 2009).

The purpose of this chapter is to identify the key factors affecting the professional development of Greek teachers who have specialized in teaching EFL, to highlight positive and negative landmarks during their career experiences and investigate contextual factors affecting their professional learning and identities.

Teachers' Professional Identities

Teachers' professional identity is a research area that emerged in the last decade of the twentieth century. The idea originated in the concepts of the 'self' and 'identity', often used interchangeably in the social sciences and philosophy, although it remains unclear how exactly these concepts are related (Beijaard et al, 2004). From a social perspective, Mead (1934) first discriminated between personal and social aspects of identity, arguing that the 'self' is a reflexive process of social experience and activity and 'develops in the given individual as a result of his relations to that process as a whole and to other individuals within that process' (p. 135). Later, Erikson (1968), from a psychology perspective, argued that the individual must establish 'a sense of personal identity' through interaction with significant others and sustained individual effort.

Goodson and Cole (1994) define teachers' professional identity in terms of professional realities whose construction is 'an ongoing process of personal and contextual interpretation' (p. 88). The development of teachers' professional identity is 'an ongoing and dynamic process which entails the making sense and (re)interpretation of one's own values and experiences' that may be influenced by personal, social and cognitive factors (Flores & Day, 2006, p. 220). Bromme (1991) argues that teachers' professional identity originates from the image they have of themselves as 'subject matter experts', 'pedagogical experts' and 'didactical experts'. Similarly, Beijaard (1995) defines identity on the basis of three distinctive categories: the subject one teaches, the teacher's relationship with students, and the teacher's role or role conception.

In their literature review on teachers' professional identity, Beijaard et al (2004) reported the way researchers conceive professional identity. Professional identity consists of 'sub-identities' and is 'an ongoing process' which includes the notion of 'agency' and implies both 'person and context' (p. 122). Identity is contextual, relational and emotional. It is 'dependent upon and formed within multiple contexts which bring social, cultural, political, and historical forces to bear upon that formation' and it 'is formed in relationship with others and involves emotions' (Rodgers & Scott, 2008, p. 733). Additionally, it is shifting, unstable and multiple, and involves the construction and reconstruction of meaning through stories over time (Rodgers & Scott, 2008, p. 733). Cooper and Olson (1996) claim that identity formation is an ongoing process during which 'multiple I's of teacher identity' develop over time and through interaction with others (p. 80). In their study on experienced secondary school teachers' perceptions of their professional identity, Beijaard et al (2000) claim that the factors that influence a teacher's perceptions of his or her professional identity are: the teaching context, their teaching experience, and the biography of the teacher. Kozminsky (2011) adds 'time context' to these factors and explains that it includes 'periods of educational changes and reforms, and it can serve as a platform for reconstruction of professional identity in teaching' (Kozminsky, 2011, p. 14).

During their professional life teachers develop 'a professional self, a personal conception of oneself as a teacher and a subjective educational theory, a personal system of knowledge and beliefs about their job' (Kelchtermans, 1993, p. 444). The current literature shows that understanding the development of teacher identity requires exploring teachers' life experiences not only in the context of the personal self but in the context of the professional self as well. Envisioning the self as a professional is a crucial stage in the development of an effective teacher identity as self encompasses not only notions of 'who am I?', but also of 'who am I as a teacher?' (Thomas & Beauchamp, 2011).

Method

The aim of this study was to investigate career experiences of EFL teachers in the Greek education system and to identify stages and landmarks while developing their professional identity. A qualitative methodological paradigm based on life histories research (Cohen et al, 2007) and metaphors (Thomas & Beauchamp, 2011) was used. Semi-structured biographical interviews (Merill & West, 2009) were used to explore career experiences which have formed the professional identity.

EFL teachers were also asked to use metaphors to describe themselves as novice professionals at the beginning of their career and as more experienced teachers now. Metaphor is a Greek word used in research to refer to 'an implied analogy which imaginatively identifies one object with another' (Holman, 1980, p. 264). It can be highly reflective of personal interpretations, and 'is employed when one wants to explore and understand something esoteric, abstract, novel or highly speculative' (Yob, 2003, p. 134). Researchers (i.e. Leavy et al, 2007; Saban et al, 2007; Thomas & Beauchamp, 2011) have used metaphors to investigate in-service and pre-service teachers' views and experiences about teaching. However, metaphors were not fully explored in the present study, as this was not our main objective.

The demographics of the six Greek teachers teaching EFL in the Greek education system who participated in this study are presented in Table I. Anonymity is secured as pseudonyms are used.[4]

The research questions were:

1. What are the main landmarks in English language teachers' professional life in the Greek context?
2. What are the main barriers that English language teachers in Greece encounter in developing their professional identities?

Name	Type of current education post	Years of teaching experience	Type of teaching experience	Studies
Chrysothemis	Teacher in a private school	10	Frontisterio, private primary schools and public primary and secondary schools	BA[a]
Nafsika	Teacher in a public primary school	16	Frontisterio, public lower, upper and vocational secondary school and public primary schools	BA
Galateia	Teacher in a public primary school and deputy head	24	Frontisterio and public primary schools	BA & MA
Galene	Teacher in a public upper-secondary school (Lyceum)	20	Frontisterio and public lower-, upper- and vocational secondary schools	BA
Ifigeneia	Teacher in a public upper-secondary school and head (Lyceum)	24	Frontisterio, public lower-, upper- and vocational secondary schools	BA & MA
Kreon	Owner of a frontisterio and a teacher there	30	Frontisterio	BA & MA

[a]BA is the degree of Bachelor of Arts obtained from a four-year university course. The participants of this study have graduated from a Greek university and are qualified as EFL teachers.

Table I. Demographic information about the participants of the present study.

Findings

The main themes that emerged from the data related to: (a) issues concerning public versus private education which came up from the participants' teaching and work experience; (b) primary versus secondary schooling in the public sector of education; (c) English language teachers' development from novice to an 'expert' teacher; and (d) current targets and future plans.

Public versus Private Education

All participants in the study had experience gained in the private sector, teaching in either private afternoon foreign language schools, private tutorials or private schools. Almost all of them indicated that private education lessons differed from lessons provided in the public sector. The differences focused on the following points:

(1) Frontisteria and private schools provide rich material and audio-visual means of supporting teaching and learning, and students are assigned to groups according to their level of English:

> In the private schools I have worked there was updated technical
> infrastructure (i.e. interactive boards, digital projectors, endless
> photocopies) whereas in the public schools I could hardly make a
> few photocopies. (Chrysothemis)

(2) Teachers in the private sector feel more insecure regarding their job because the owner of a private school or a frontisterio can replace teachers more easily and employ those with minor qualifications, such as foreign language certificates, in order to reduce the cost. The frontisterio is thought to be a business where employers aim to make a profit, while at the same time they mainly provide children and young people with the skills needed to acquire foreign language certificates rather than contributing to students' cognitive and social development:

> In frontisterio there is always at the back of your head that you
> work in a business rather than in a school and the target basically
> is on students to acquire language certificates. (Nafsika)

(3) Private education serves as a way to earn a living rather than as a workplace where EFL teachers can experience self-development at their own pace. Teachers in public education feel satisfied with their work environment, in which they aim to develop collaborative relationships both with colleagues and with students.

(4) Parents have great demands and expectations for English language learning from frontisteria, whereas in the public school they do not expect their children to learn English at a proficient level:

> Parents [of children who attend frontisteria seem to want their
> children to have mastered English via obtaining the highest
> certificate before even getting into senior secondary school [which
> is at the age of 15]. (Kreon)

> I am disappointed by the fact that in the public school learning
> English in general is not considered to be a productive task as it

does not lead into an English language certificate and children
spend more of their time in afternoon frontisteria than in their
play. We, as EFL teachers experience the deterioration of the
English language subject in the public sector of education.
(Nafsika)

Even after the introduction of EFL teaching in public primary schools,
parents have lost trust in public schools as a vehicle for learning foreign
languages and have assigned the responsibility for foreign language teaching
to frontisteria. This has affected students' views about EFL at school; they
consider it a play time since they attend the frontisterio courses in the
afternoon. The preparation of children for success in foreign language since
the age of six when starting primary school and the demand for children to
acquire language certificates early in their life are very dominant themes in
the education culture of every Greek family, which has led to the popularity
of the frontisterio. Moreover, the Greek state has reinforced these trends with
laws about frontisteria:

The state has obliged all frontisteria to have an official sign in
front of the building saying: 'the consumer has the right not to pay
unless he receives a receipt'. Thus the relationship between
students and teachers is similar to a trader and a consumer, so
there is devaluation of knowledge throughout the recent years.
This is another reason why parents and students do not respect
learning as it is offered. (Kreon)

Primary versus Secondary Schooling in the Public Sector of Education

The EFL teachers of this study have gained experience teaching in both
public primary and public secondary schools. They appear to agree that
primary education offers more opportunities for contributing to students'
cognitive and social growth than secondary schools:

In primary school the overarching framework is pedagogy-centred
and students have not yet developed entrenched ideas about how
to study or learn and the teacher has further chances to intervene
and influence them considering that they are still 'flexible'.
(Nafsika)

This is also in line with the view that teachers in secondary schools hold
about the student profile and how this affects their confidence as teachers.
They state that in many cases students in secondary schools can be ill-
mannered and unwilling to learn. Moreover, children's transition from
primary to secondary school seems to have effects on their attitude towards
learning and their behaviour towards adults. Adolescence is a difficult
transition period in one's life and vast changes do happen: 'the latest
generations of students are getting more and more difficult and teachers need

to be equipped with knowledge of psychology to cope with them' (Galene). Nevertheless, this transition does not necessarily mean that teenagers have acquired the cognitive skills expected by adults. Teenagers attending frontisteria appear to be anxious about exams for obtaining English language certificates:

> Secondary school students' interest in English and learning in general deteriorates and we get many problems to attract their attention and they do not appear to study the language. ...
> Children are not interested in real knowledge and they do not seem to have ambitions. They want to get the certificate as a qualification which will be needed for a job later. ... Many parents send their children in summer intensive courses to cover a year class and children often cannot follow, therefore children have got gaps in learning. Children often do not have the level to correspond to such exams at young ages but adults do not seem to understand this. (Kreon)

In addition, the teacher-centred approach, which is applied by many class teachers, and the demands adults have of children in the Greek school system do not seem to provide an encouraging classroom environment for effective learning. Children in senior classes of primary schools are expected to do a lot of homework in the afternoon, which largely increases in secondary schools:

> Students are not motivated to learning. This may be due to the rote learning imposed in the Greek school still; children have to learn useless information by heart without analyzing it and using critical thinking. They do not have time to play, to grow in a natural way and they are bored in the school. ... They do not respect teachers as in the past. They do not respect the whole educational system let alone English. (Kreon)

Developing from a Novice to an 'Expert'

The English language teachers of the present study admitted that the major difficulties they faced at the threshold of their career were the lack of teaching experience and the lack of knowledge about the school structure. These difficulties were overcome through a friendly working climate, the support of the senior and more experienced teachers, thorough preparation of each lesson and careful observation of all events in the school environment, and via self-determination, engaging with in-service training.

Most of the EFL teachers of this study have changed their initial 'theory' about teaching English. This shift has been influenced by personal experiences which include parenthood, teacher status and adjustment to new working environments and teaching methodologies. The ideas which have altered in the course of time include the following:

(a) Students' study time: the belief that students must spend a lot of time studying at home in order to learn has changed to the idea that learning occurs mainly in the class and heavy homework must be limited, after watching their children struggling to cope with studying or doing exercises at home after school for hours.

(b) Teaching methodology: teachers argued that responding to students' needs and interests should be recognized, and their teaching was adjusted to those needs:

> When I started teaching I followed methods and techniques I had experienced as a student..., I used to teach English following the instructions given in teachers' books without questioning their effectiveness. ... After 24 years of teaching, I have surely changed my views regarding teaching and I am using more student-centred activities (problem-solving in teams) and innovations in my teaching such as ICT which make the lessons more attractive to the students. (Ifigeneia)

The participants' development from novice to expert teachers is depicted in the metaphors they used to describe themselves at the beginning of their career and at the time of this study. The metaphors were influenced by the experiences they had in teaching and the situations they had been exposed to regarding teaching and school environments. The majority described themselves at the beginning of their career as naïve, insecure, helpless and lacking knowledge of the reality, and only in two cases did they claim to be confident from the beginning. With regard to their current beliefs about their 'self', they stated that they felt secure, confident and mature – feelings which usually come along with experience, lifelong learning and accepting the reality of the 'teacher world' as well as their 'own world'. The metaphors used by the participants are presented in Table II.

Name	At the beginning of the career	Currently
Chrysothemis	Full of dreams	A Don Quixote still tilting at windmills in education
Nafsika	Tightrope walker	'Happy' plasticine
Galateia	The suspended step of the stork	I stand well on my feet
Galene	I have the world at my feet	I feel the weight of the world on my shoulders
Ifigeneia	A newbie in the wilderness	Lifelong learner
Kreon	A great lover of teaching	Prisoner in teaching

Table II. Metaphors used by the participants.

Current Targets and Future Plans

The EFL teachers in the study used expressions which indicate their expectations (a) to support students to be inclined to learn foreign languages and about other cultures; (b) to build students' and parents' trust regarding EFL in the public school; (c) to improve students' skills via integrated learning corresponding to their needs; and (d) to contribute to students' emotional growth and positive stance toward life. All the views mentioned above are expected to lead to self-realization and satisfaction from their professional life.

The participants' future plans include teaching and experiencing a stable working environment in a public school (this even applies to Chrysothemis, who has mainly worked in the private sector of education), either teaching or acting as a head/director or a school advisor (in cases where the participants have carried out postgraduate studies). Only Kreon, who is the owner of a frontisterio, plans to keep working in the private sector, offering tutorials and choosing the students to teach.

Conclusion and Discussion

The present study investigated the career experiences of EFL teachers in the Greek context and the contextual factors affecting their professional trajectories and identities. In this research EFL teachers were university graduates who have had significant teaching and professional experience and built noteworthy professional identities in their careers so far. University graduate EFL teachers have been trained and educated in higher education institutions not only to teach vocabulary and grammar but to communicate the English culture as well.

The research findings indicate contextual differences between the public and the private sector for EFL learning. Job security in the public school (due to a stable salary as a permanent civil worker) versus job insecurity in the private sector of education where the EFL teacher is perceived as an entrepreneurial professional rather than as an activist professional (Sachs, 2001, pp. 155-159) is an example of these differences. The entrepreneurial identity of the EFL teacher in the private sector is based on the efficient operation of the market (an efficient, active and reliable educator who complies with the market rules) and is promoted via institutional mechanisms and indexes for academic performance ending in competition rather than cooperation.

On the contrary, the activist identity (Sachs, 2001, pp. 155-159), which can be identified in the Greek public school EFL teacher, is founded on the teacher belief about the importance of teaching and education in general as imparting wider social values and ideals. Moreover, it is evident that EFL teachers in the private afternoon foreign language institutions (frontisteria) experience teaching as subject-matter experts who should aim to teach students in order for them to master the English language and acquire the relevant certificate. On the other side, public school EFL teachers perceive themselves as pedagogical and didactical experts on top of being subject-matter experts; they are more inclined to humanistic approaches as they attempt to educate students holistically (a pedagogical caring for students). This view of EFL teacher self-perception in the Greek context is also supported in the literature about the threefold identities (as subject-matter, pedagogical and didactical experts) that teachers ascribe to themselves (Beijaard et al, 2000; Day et al, 2006).

Another contextual aspect concerns the amount of resources and teaching aids used on the two sides of the coin. In the private sector of the Greek education system there is a variety of teaching aids/materials and resources available to support the teaching process, whereas in the public school the resources are minimal and in many cases the student textbooks – which are prescribed centrally by the Ministry of Education – are not appropriate for the syllabus to be taught. It may be a fact that the Greek Ministry has not treated English as a taught subject in public schools as efficiently as it has been treated by the private sector of education. However, the public sector in the Greek education system generally suffers from budgetary cuts and resources are poor. Many public school teachers struggle to find extra teaching materials and they show occupational commitment from the beginning of their career. These efforts are also part of their growth into the profession.

Moreover, in the present study it was shown that the level of education in which the Greek EFL teachers work can affect the way they face their professional life. Primary education differs from secondary in terms of the student academic and social behaviour. In general it seems that students' attitude toward learning English is not positive. In the public schools, students perceive learning English as 'a playtime in the classroom' as long as they can learn the language in the frontisteria, which they attend under their parents' pressure to acquire foreign language certificates. Children are not interested in learning environments provided in the formal educational context – an issue which should be the concern of the Greek educational policy.

Children's limited interest in learning EFL is regarded by the participants as one of the most frustrating situations in their professional life. The teacher–student relationship is considered to be an important factor in the teacher's development of professional identity. Beijaard (1995) illustrates that students' behaviour affects teachers' self-concept, which can be positive only through students' projection of a positive stance. Moreover, parents appear to have lost their trust in the public education system and tend to spend a significant amount of their monthly budget on frontisteria, not only for foreign languages but also for supporting their children's learning outside the formal school system. All these can be said to have put pressure on the teachers' side, and the latter appear to find themselves involved in 'emotional labour' and 'emotional work' (Flores & Day, 2006, p. 221). The 'emotional labour' refers to the teacher's efforts to manage his/her emotions and relationships with students, colleagues and other adults, such as parents, while the 'emotional work' refers to the teacher's attempts to manage challenges caused during the teaching and learning process. A smooth relationship between teachers and the students alongside their families could act positively on the teachers' professional development (Beijaard, 1995; Day et al, 2006).

Another finding is that the EFL teachers in this study expressed their professional identity as it has been reshaped over the course of time. They started their professional career with a hidden sense of insecurity which emanates from the lack of experience, but at the same time with dreams, affection for teaching, energy, willingness for changes and the tendency that young professionals exhibit for the notion of social contribution. Most of them have changed their initial ideas about teaching and tended to put a strong emphasis on the social appreciation of their profession rather than on the evaluation of their subject matter itself, which is in accordance with literature on how new professionals view themselves and their profession (Beijaard, 1995).

The EFL teachers in this study feel like they are experts not simply on subject matter or on pedagogical/didactical matter – even though many of them claimed that they do not feel confident about their pedagogical knowledge – but also on life knowledge, which comes with exposure to various social and learning situations. Teachers' growth is imprinted in the three stages suggested by Lacey (1977): 'the honeymoon at the threshold, the crisis and the failure of getting by or the continuation'. After they have passed through the honeymoon and whichever crisis they experienced via discovery and survival, they have managed to cope with teaching. They seem to have accomplished self-awareness through the inner-self conflict about understanding and changing oneself as a teacher (Featherstone, 1993), but all by themselves via networking or personal efforts.

The present study showed that Greek EFL teachers develop their professional identity in relation to their experiences and interaction with their professional context, which is in accordance with the general view about the influences on teachers' development of professional identity (Beijaard et al, 2000; Flores & Day, 2006). EFL teachers appear to perceive and interpret their professional characteristics according to their interaction with social situations and the negotiation of their multiple 'selves and roles' within the experienced context as this has been also reported by Cooper and Olson (1996) and Beijaard et al (2000). Nevertheless, the EFL teachers in this study seem to have connected their professional commitment to their self-efficacy as this has been reported earlier by Day (2004), and pay attention to seeking solutions and making efforts to improve the quality of EFL teaching without the support of the state.

Although there is a limitation when interpreting the findings of this study, which is due to the small number of participants, it should be acknowledged that the results of this study could be very helpful concerning the provision of EFL teaching in the public sector. The state and/or educational institutions should enhance EFL provision in public schools in order to regain stakeholders' trust. Regarding language certification awarded by public schools, the Ministry of Education should make arrangements so that public schools provide foreign language certificates linking foreign language learning to the National Foreign Language Exam System. Going further, induction training programmes for newly appointed teachers should be reinforced with other forms of training. This study showed that communication with peers and peer appraisal in the school context are factors related to successful teacher development. More experienced teachers serving as mentors for newly appointed teachers could be an alternative to English language teachers' professional training.

Postscript

We dedicate this chapter to the people in Greece and all over the world who share our concern for the current economic and political situation in Greece. The research and writing of this chapter took place during the five months from January to June 2015, and its completion coincided with one of the most crucial and dramatic moments in modern Greek history. Because of the country's geopolitical position, people in Greece have experienced misfortunes for over 180 years due to foreign countries' external interference on the one hand and Greek politicians' perseverance on certain political issues on the other. Greek people have been feeling loneliness, disappointment, betrayal and fear about their future. However, they love and have invested in this country. For this reason, we feel we should express our wish for unity across the country and we expect that politicians in Europe and Greece will realize these feelings and contribute to the development and sustainability of the country in peace.

Notes

[1] The Gymnasium covers the three final years of compulsory education and constitutes the lower level of secondary education.

[2] Frontisteria are private English language institutes run either by university-degree-holding English language teachers or by holders of the Cambridge or Michigan Proficiency Certificate.

[3] The recently elected leftist government has proposed that this practice should be abolished unless holders of the Cambridge or Michigan Proficiency Certificate have passed the equivalent exams in the last two years of their job application.

[4] Pseudonyms are all Ancient Greek names.

References

Beijaard, D. (1995) Teachers' Prior Experiences and Actual Perceptions of Professional Identity, *Teachers and Teaching*, 1(2), 281-294.

Beijaard, D., Meijer C.P. & Verloop N. (2004) Reconsidering Research on Teachers' Professional Identity, *Teaching and Teacher Education*, 20, 107-128. http://dx.doi.org/10.1016/j.tate.2003.07.001

Beijaard, D., Verloop, N. & Vermunt, J.D. (2000) Teachers' Perceptions of Professional Identity: an exploratory study from a personal knowledge perspective, *Teaching and Teacher Education*, 16, 749-764. http://dx.doi.org/10.1016/S0742-051X(00)00023-8

Bredeson, P.V. (2002) *Designs for Learning: a new architecture for professional development in school.* Thousand Oaks, CA: Corwin Press.

Bromme, R. (1991) Wissenstypen und professionelles Selbstverstandniss [Types of knowledge and professional self-concept], *Zeitschrift fur Padagogik*, 37, 769-785.

Chung Wei, R., Darling-Hammond, L., Andree, A., Richardson, N. & Orphanos, S. (2009) *Professional Learning in the Learning Profession: a status report on teacher development in the United States and abroad.* Dallas, TX: National Staff Development Council. http://learningforward.org/docs/pdf/nsdcstudytechnicalreport2009.pdf ?sfvrsn=0 (accessed on 14 June 2015).

Cohen, L., Manion, L. & Morrison, K. (2007) *Research Methods in Education*, 6th edn. London: RoutledgeFalmer.

Cooper, K. & Olson, M.R. (1996) The Multiple I's of Teacher Identity, in M. Kompf, W.R. Bond, D. Dworet & R.T. Boak (Eds) *Changing Research and Practice: teachers' professionalism, identities and knowledge*, pp. 78-89. London: Falmer Press.

Day, C. (1999) *Developing Teachers: the challenges of lifelong learning.* London: Falmer Press.

Day, C. (2004) Change Agendas: the roles of teacher educators, *Teaching Education*, 15(2), 145-158. http://dx.doi.org/10.1080/1047621042000213584

Day, C., Kington, A., Stobart, G. & Sammons, P. (2006) The Personal and Professional Selves of Teachers: stable and unstable identities, *British Educational Research Journal*, 32(4), 601-616. http://dx.doi.org/10.1080/01411920600775316

Epstein, A. (1978) *Ethos and Identity*. London: Tavistock.

Erikson, E.H. (1968) *Identity, Youth and Crisis.* New York: W.W. Norton.

Evans, L. (2008) Professionalism, Professionality and the Development of Education Professionals, *British Journal of Educational Studies*, 56(1), 20-38. http://dx.doi.org/10.1111/j.1467-8527.2007.00392.x

Featherstone, H. (1993) Learning from the First Years of Classroom Teaching: the journey in, the journey out, *Teachers College Record*, 95(1), 93-112.

Flores, M.A. & Day, C. (2006) Contexts Which Shape and Reshape New Teachers' Identities: a multi-perspective study, *Teaching and Teacher Education*, 22(2), 219-232. http://dx.doi.org/10.1016/j.tate.2005.09.002

Goodson, I.F. & Cole, A.L. (1994) Exploring the Teacher's Professional Knowledge: constructing identity and community, *Teacher Education Quarterly*, 21(1), 85-105.

Holman, C.H. (1980) *A Handbook to Literature*, 4th edn. Indianapolis, IN: Bobbs-Merrill.

Kelchtermans, G. (1993) Getting the Story, Understanding the Lives: from career stories to teachers' professional development, *Teaching and Teacher Education*, 9, 443-456. http://dx.doi.org/10.1016/0742-051X(93)90029-G

Kelchtermans, G. (2004) CPD for Professional Renewal: moving beyond knowledge for practice, in C. Day & J. Sachs (Eds) *International Handbook on the Continuing Professional Development of Teachers*, pp 217-237. Maidenhead: Open University Press.

Kiernan, P. (2010) *Narrative Identity in English Language Teaching: exploring teacher interviews in Japanese and English*. Basingstoke: Palgrave Macmillan.

Kozminsky, L. (2011) Professional Identity of Teachers and Teacher Educators in a Changing Reality, in I. Žogla & L. Rutka (Eds) *Teachers' Life-cycle from Initial Teacher Education to Experienced Professional (Proceedings of the ATEE 36th Annual Conference, Riga, 2011)*, pp. 12-19.

Lacey, C. (1977) *The Socialization of Teachers*. London: Methuen.

Leavy, A.M., McSorley, F.A. & Boté, L.A. (2007) An Examination of What Metaphor Construction Reveals about the Evolution of Pre-service Teachers' Beliefs about Teaching and Learning, *Teaching and Teacher Education*, 23, 1217-1233. http://dx.doi.org/10.1016/j.tate.2006.07.016

Mead, G.H. (1934) *Mind, Self and Society*. Chicago: University of Chicago Press.

Merrill, B. & West, L. (2009) *Using Biographical Methods in Social Research*. London: SAGE.

Papastamatis, A., Panitsidou, E., Giavrimis P. & Papanis, E. (2009) Facilitating teachers' and educators' effective professional development, *Review of European Studies*, 83. http://www.ccsenet.org/journal/index.php/res/article/view/4044/3912 (accessed on 14 June 2015).

Rodgers, C.R. & Scott, K.H. (2008) The Development of the Personal Self and Professional Identity in Learning to Teach, in M. Cochran-Smith, S. Feiman Nemser, D.J. McIntyre & K.E. Demers (Eds) *Handbook of Research on Teacher Education: enduring questions in changing contexts*, 3rd edn. New York: Routledge, Taylor & Francis Group/Association of Teacher Educators.

Saban, A., Kocbeker, B.N. & Saban, A. (2007) Prospective Teachers' Conceptions of Teaching and Learning Revealed through Metaphor Analysis, *Learning and Instruction*, 17, 123-139. http://dx.doi.org/10.1016/j.learninstruc.2007.01.003

Sachs, J. (2001) Teacher Professional Identity: competing discourses, competing outcomes, *Journal of Education Policy*, 16(2), 149-161. http://dx.doi.org/10.1080/02680930116819

Thomas, L. & Beauchamp, C. (2011) Understanding New Teachers' Professional Identities through Metaphor, *Teaching and Teacher Education*, 27, 762-769. http://dx.doi.org/10.1016/j.tate.2010.12.007

Volkmann, M.J. & Anderson, M.A. (1998) Creating Professional Identity: dilemmas and metaphors of a first-year chemistry teacher, *Science Education*, 82(3), 293-310. http://dx.doi.org/10.1002/(SICI)1098-237X(199806)82:3%3C293::AID-SCE1%3E3.0.CO;2-7

Yob, I.M. (2003) Thinking Constructively with Metaphors, *Studies in Philosophy and Education*, 22, 127-138. http://dx.doi.org/10.1023/A:1022289113443

Zembylas, M. (2003) Emotions and Teacher Identity: a poststructural perspective, *Teachers and Teaching*, 9(3), 213-238. http://dx.doi.org/10.1080/13540600309378

CHAPTER 17

'In Between' English and Spanish Teaching: the story of a linguistically diverse student becoming a teacher

LESLIE GAUNA

SUMMARY This chapter recounts a novice bilingual/English as a Second Language (ESL) teacher's story transitioning from being a student teacher to a hired teacher. The narratives come from a Mexican-descent young adult male, who had been born and raised in the United States speaking Spanish while receiving a majority-in-English education. His narrative provides an opportunity to understand the challenges, sources of support and negotiations experienced while becoming a teacher of non-English-background children. His story tells of a loss in his naïve status after multiple attempts at securing a teacher position and then the challenge of not passing the Spanish proficiency test required for bilingual certification. This event aligned him with the many children who have been left without knowledge of the standardized version of their native language of Spanish. Paradoxically, as an ESL teacher, he affirms the value of his Spanish language as a source for teaching and connecting with Hispanic students and parents. Surprisingly, it is not languages – Spanish or English per se – that he emphasized as his most valuable resource when relating with Hispanic and Black students, but urban culture. Oscar's narratives help to understand students raised with a language other than English and envision them as learners with multiple resources and unique paths.

Introduction

For nearly a decade, I have been working as a teacher educator at the University of Houston with candidates preparing to become bilingual teachers. I teach all of the courses required for students who are seeking certification as bilingual teachers, and which are designed to support them in teaching at linguistically diverse settings as well as prepare them to pass the state-mandated bilingual teacher certification exam. Prior to this I was a bilingual elementary teacher in a local school district. I have been raised speaking Spanish in Argentina; I studied English as a Foreign Language (EFL) since the age of twelve and I became an exchange student in New Jersey at seventeen. In addition, after Houston became my home, my husband and I purposefully raised our three children speaking Spanish.

Living and working in one of the most diverse universities in one of the most diverse cities in the United States, I am continually confronted by the intersections and impact of issues related to languages and education. My students arrive as juniors and seniors, eager to complete their education coursework and student teaching to become bilingual teachers of children who have been raised in linguistically diverse households, often with a wide range of English proficiency. When I listen to stories of the students' experiences, I simultaneously worry about and admire how they have dealt with being persistently defined by labels that reflect deficit thinking. My research seeks to illuminate and address the challenges students raised in a language other than English in the United States encounter in their unique trajectories as bilingual speakers and educators. From it, I offer possibilities as to how we, as teacher educators, teacher education programs, educational institutions and policy makers, can support them in their journeys as bilingual educators working to serve diverse students and communities.

This chapter shares insights from an ongoing longitudinal inquiry into the experiences of bilingual teacher candidates as they transition from student teaching into practicing educators. It focuses on one participant from this inquiry, Oscar (a pseudonym), whose stories reflect his experiences of being 'in between' languages, English and Spanish, in his trajectory of teaching as both a teacher and a learner, in ways that resonate with the experiences that many of my students express when becoming a bilingual teacher, but about which little is found in literature on novice teachers (Soto, 2010). The idea of *in between* does not echo deficit-rooted notions of students being left without a language, as soundly rejected by Cummins (2007) and recently by May (2014). On the contrary, the notion of being *in between* is reclaimed as an empowering state where the bi/multilingual speaker is driving an all-terrain vehicle at the center of the language act, making decisions for his/her own benefit on how to best overcome obstacles along the journey (García 2009).

The sharing of Oscar's experiences is presented in three parts. The first story revolves around what he calls the loss of his naivety in thinking that it would be easy to attain a bilingual teaching position and that he was guaranteed a job after graduating. Oscar recounted his multiple failed attempts in securing a position as a teacher, and how he persistently and skillfully 'built' his school family after taking a substitute teaching position. The second of Oscar's stories recounts how, in the midst of losing his bilingual placement as a result of failing his Spanish proficiency exam, he embraces his multicultural and multilingual identity as an English as a Second Language (ESL) teacher. He affirms the value of his Spanish language as a source for teaching and connecting with Hispanic students and parents while, simultaneously, his familiarity and comfort with urban African American English variety and culture emerges as a resource when relating with Black students. With both groups, he 'knew how to speak their language' (interview excerpt). The third of Oscar's stories offers his reflections upon his complex ongoing relationship with the Spanish language. His story resonates with many students who have become monolingual English adult speakers, losing their native Spanish, after experiencing what has been referred to as *subtractive bilingualism* (García, 2009). Subtractive bilingualism is understood as the process 'where the politics of a country favors the replacement of the home language by the majority language (e.g. Spanish being replaced by English in US)' (Baker, 2011, p. 4).

Guided by a narrative approach (Connelly & Clandinin, 1990), this inquiry focuses on Oscar's storied experiences of becoming a bilingual teacher. For more than four years, I have journeyed alongside Oscar and other participants on their paths to becoming bilingual educators. Throughout the inquiry process of gathering field texts and composing research texts (Clandinin & Connelly, 2000), I taught them in courses, followed their student teaching, witnessed their graduation, spent time in their new classrooms, met administrators and co-workers, and visited them in their neighborhoods and even in their homes, all with the goal of listening to and recording their stories. Through listening and telling, storying and restorying, and relistening and retelling (Connelly & Clandinin, 1990; Clandinin & Connelly, 2000) Oscar's experiences, this inquiry illuminates the challenges and successes of one participant's journey to becoming a bilingual English/Spanish educator. It acknowledges that 'a life as led is inseparable from a life as told – or more bluntly, a life is not "how it was" but how it is interpreted and reinterpreted, told and retold' (Bruner, 2004, p. 708). By sharing Oscar's stories of becoming a bilingual teacher, this inquiry seeks to break with prescribed deficit notions of *ways of being* for linguistically diverse students and their teachers. Through this inquiry, I hope to continue and contribute to the dialogue surrounding linguistic diversity and bilingual education in ways that promote new understandings and possibilities.

Restorying the Trajectory of a Novice Bi/Multilingual Teacher

Oscar is a young Hispanic male in his mid-twenties who was raised in a Spanish-speaking household with parents employed in the service sector and two older bilingual siblings. He attended instruction in a bilingual program where native language support is used to transition into English until the middle of first grade. Then he attended schools where language instruction was primarily in English. I met Oscar as part of a close-knit trio with two other classmates with whom he had much in common. All three had been raised in Spanish-speaking Mexican families. They also had all completed their student teaching and went on to become teachers in the same local urban school district that they had attended themselves as children. The demographics in this district are composed of a 75% majority of Hispanic students, 25% of African American students, and with Asian and White students representing less than 2% (Aldine Independent School District, 2013).

Overcoming Naivety: building his school family

Oscar begins one of our conversations by telling of a time when he had almost given up on his goal of becoming a teacher. 'From the very beginning, we were naïve,' he reflected. 'Oh! Maybe she [the principal] will give us a chance to work here [the student-teaching placement]' (Interview excerpt). Time proved Oscar wrong: he witnessed how his principal entered and exited student teachers, including him, through a revolving door. 'I felt horrible ... depressed, ... angry, [and] frustrated' (interview excerpt). As a teacher candidate seeking a position as a bilingual teacher in an area 'considered of critical shortage' (Sass et al, 2012, p. 4), Oscar assumed that he was guaranteed a job once he graduated. However, this was not the case, as Oscar went to multiple interviews without receiving an offer. His realization resonates with what is called the 'struggle to survive, and loss of idealism' (Feiman-Nemser, 2003, p. 27).

Oscar made sense of the first rejection by affirming that he was not the kind of teacher who could be easily controlled like the ones the principal at his student teaching placement had hired:

> Yo no me dejo más ... [la directora] no... iba a poder controlarme
> a mí (I don't let myself ... [the principal] was not ... going to be
> able to control me).

Oscar's words, of not wanting to be controlled, echoed testimonies of novice and minority teachers leaving the profession. The non-access to decision making in the schools and lack of autonomy in the classroom are documented reasons for new and minority teachers' desertion (Ingersoll, 2014). Minority teachers like Oscar are successfully being recruited into the profession but there is a problem in keeping them (Ingersoll, 2014). By the time Oscar went on his fifth interview, he was ready to give up:

> No quiero ir. No, no me van a dar el trabajo ... ya me vale (I don't
> want to go. No, they are not going to give me the job ... I don't
> care).

Oscar went expecting one more failure while simultaneously being surprisingly 'relaxed', 'calmer', and 'not even nervous' (interview excerpt). During this final attempt, he was 'talking the talk' of a teaching professional (interview excerpt). Oscar transformed the 'hour-and-a-half interview' into an extended trial period when he offered to be a substitute teacher (interview excerpt). During this time, Oscar gained confidence as a teacher, demonstrating student-centered practices to what he had learned are the 'ever-observing-administrators' (interview excerpt). He became comfortable in the building and assisted other teachers moving in and out of classrooms; he built alliances and generated trust. He crafted a real *'chanza'* (an opportunity), at his new school, unlike at his student teaching placement, where the principal had promised one but did not deliver (interview excerpt). Oscar built his own *'familia escolar'* (school family) (interview excerpt).

Overcoming Isolation: speaking the same language

In order for Oscar to secure a *bilingual* teaching position he needed to overcome one final obstacle: pass the state-mandated Spanish proficiency exam, the Bilingual Target Language Proficiency Test (BTLPT). In Texas, in order to become a bilingual teacher, the candidate has to pass four certification exams, compared with only two required for other certifications. Having failed the BTLPT nine times, Oscar found himself again at the brink of giving up: '*Ya me vale* ... this is the last try' (interview excerpt). Oscar was being tested on something he had lost: his Spanish.

> Me da pena hablar enfrente de ... como 20 gentes alrededor de mí hablando ... me podían oir y ... empecé a ponerme rojo (I was embarrassed to speak in front of twenty people who were also speaking ... they could hear me... I began to turn red).

Oscar, to his surprise, was not fired as a result of his failure to pass the BTLPT, but temporarily placed as a teacher in an ESL program. Being an ESL teacher meant that most of Oscar's students spoke something other than standard English at home and that Oscar had to teach only in English. Once teaching, however, Oscar would switch to Spanish as needed for clarifying a concept: 'You don't get it? Oh! *Así es* [It's like this].' He also used his Spanish with the Spanish-speaking parents to strengthen his connection with them. With African American students, Oscar found himself speaking as he would have done with his neighbors and high school friends where he grew up; 'the children would understand me and begin laughing. I found the way to speak with them. I grew up in the area, therefore ... I knew that they speak like that' (interview excerpt).

By using a Black English variety and a Spanish language not privileged in the schools Oscar joins multicultural and bi/multilingual scholars debunking deficit views of bi/multilinguals. Oscar reclaims his languages as his identity markers, and works from there to build a teaching relationship with his students. His words resonate with views that contest that causes of Hispanic and African American underachievement are intrinsic, or due to 'pathological lifestyles that hindered [children of color's] ability to benefit

221

from schooling' (Ladson-Billings, 2006, p. 4). Multicultural and bilingual scholars place the cause of students' underachievement not on the student, but instead on the schools for not valuing the socio-cultural and linguistic resources of diverse background.

In fact, the fault lies not with a child and his or her culture, but with the manner in which the school and the pedagogy that is used address culture and language (Banks 1993; Nieto, 1996, 2002; Cummins, 2007; Gándara 2009; Gay, 2010). The teaching relationship either reaffirms the historical devaluation of language-minority students, or values 'students' language, culture, intellect and imagination, with a curriculum and instruction based on empowerment, understood as the collaborative creation of power' (Cummins, 2001, p. 653). Oscar, in using his linguistically and culturally diverse knowledge and experiences, aligns with what multicultural and bilingual scholars have persistently affirmed. Students coming to the classroom bring a wealth of resources with their culture and language that should be an integral part of the shared generation of knowledge.

Overcoming the Set Road to Monolingualism: '*Niños Como Yo*'

No matter whether they are placed in the bilingual or the ESL classroom, Oscar's concern was that Spanish-speaking children are pressured by the teachers – who are pressured by the principals – to be moved into English monolingual classes as quickly as possible.

> Va a salir una generación de niños como yo ... que no pueden ni hablar los dos idiomas (What is going to come out is a generation of children like me ... who cannot speak either of the two languages).

Oscar's parents worked until very late at night. He had an older sister whom he remembers mostly in her room, an older brother being in the streets and a TV set that acted as his 'babysitter' (interview excerpt). Even though Spanish was his first language, and he attended half of first grade in a bilingual classroom, by eighth grade, Oscar recalls the moment he realized he had turned into a monolingual English speaker. He had asked his mother for permission to stay at school overnight in a 'lock-in' for band practice. Oscar's mother had to call his older brother to translate for the two of them. 'Since when I cannot speak with my mom?' Oscar wondered (interview excerpt). Following this realization, Oscar requested to be enrolled in Spanish classes. In tenth grade, after testing out of the beginner's Spanish level class, he was hoping to learn the Spanish that could help him communicate with his parents. Remembering his teacher, he explained:

> He put you down a lot, he was very condescending ... towards non-native speakers, non-Spanish speakers ... Whenever that started, you know what? I'm not going to pay attention, I was trying to learn the language and then he would throw it in my

face, you know what? I don't want to learn Spanish anyway ...
There is going to be nothing but English, nothing but English. I
didn't do no homework, I didn't participate, nothing. I had him
for two years, I barely passed, barely. (Interview excerpt)

Oscar continued to explain his relationship with his lost Spanish. He told
about meeting his fiancée Marlene, who was raised speaking Spanish in
Mexico, and how his interactions with her family helped him learn not only
Spanish but also the Mexican culture that he felt he had not experienced
growing up. When students raised in Spanish-speaking families, like Oscar,
are schooled in the United States, they learn English as a Second Language
(ESL). Such labels emphasize the learners' non-access to English as a first
language and therefore their non-native status. The learners are labeled as
limited English proficiency students (LEP). The LEP label is an acronym that
highlights the learner's limitations (Palmer & Martínez, 2013). To move
away from deficit-perspective labels, scholars have coined some alternative
labels that focus on what the learners are doing and possess. Such constructs
are *emergent bilinguals* (García et al, 2008), *linguistically diverse students* or
students of different background than English (Valdés et al, 2014). the case of
oscar, who was initially labeled as LEP, and was later faced with his lack of
spanish proficiency, highlights the inadequacy of classifications and labels.

Both his experiences in a school system that push him into becoming a
monolingual English speaker, and the Spanish teacher humiliating him
because of his lack of native-like pronunciation, portray what critical applied
linguists have labeled the *monolingual bias* (May, 2014; Ortega, 2014). Such
bias views the bilingual person from a monolingual perspective, as two
monolingual people living in one body (García, 2009). A bilingual person has
to demonstrate proficiency in two different languages, measured at the level
of monolingual speakers. Students who learn a language later in life are seen
as 'aspiring monolinguals of the new language ... characterized by deficit by
being less than a full language user' (Ortega, 2014, p. 36). Oscar's complex
story of feeling *in between* languages is an example of having been schooled by
the school system to show proficiency as a monolingual of either english or
spanish, and then tested and failed by it.

Conclusion

As a teacher educator and researcher, Oscar's narratives reflect the rich and
complex histories of students arriving in my classroom aspiring to become
bilingual teachers. Oscar's loss of naivety, when he was not given a real
opportunity to stay at his student teaching placement, questioned his
assumption that graduating from college would automatically grant him a
teaching job. If the obstacle he faced was not getting a job offer, building
towards that first job offer by demonstrating his capabilities as a substitute
teacher offers a unique path to overcoming that obstacle. Teacher education
institutions can learn from this experience to provide narratives of multiple

possibilities for teacher candidates transitioning from student teaching into practicing educators. This may avoid college teacher graduates prematurely giving up on their chosen career path.

Oscar's story about losing his hard-sought bilingual position and getting a temporary one as an ESL teacher suggests the value of rooting the student–teacher connection in what the teacher and the students bring to the classroom in terms of their linguistic and cultural resources. Oscar, conscious of his own schooling, characterized by navigating both the bilingual and the monolingual instruction classrooms, rejects mandates requiring strict separation of languages and uses his multicultural and multilingual upbringing as a teaching tool. His use of a Black variety of English and Spanish in a classroom where standardized English is the *only* approved language of instruction challenges a narrative of monolingualism as the norm. It also tells students, through his example, that their language practices are legitimized. If the obstacle Oscar faced was to be labeled as a non-academic Spanish-proficient teacher, how he challenged this label was by embracing his multilingual practices, showing once more a unique path to overcoming that obstacle.

Finally, in the context of *restrictive* (Ovando, 2003) language policies that push students towards English monolingualism, Oscar's story is about grappling with language loss and reclamation in his journey as a learner and a teacher. His connection with his own cultural and linguistic experiences is reflected in the way he faced the challenge to pass the BTLPT:

> Pero ¿cómo yo puedo exigir tanto de ellos si yo no voy a esforzarme para practicar y tomar el mismo examen? ... Voy a seguirle, no importa, aunque ni quiera ser de maestro bilingüe lo voy a ser porque yo quiera, porque yo quiero mejorar y por eso tuve ánimo para tomarlo otra vez y otra vez ... Si yo quiero mejorar ellos van a querer mejorar también y practicamos ... y los dos ... ellos me estaban enseñando a mi (How can I ask so much from them if I cannot push myself into practicing and taking the exam? ... I'll keep going, it doesn't matter, even if I would not want to be a bilingual teacher, I'm going to do it because I want to improve and that's how I got courage to take it one time after another ... If I want to improve they would want to improve also and so we practice ... and we both ... they were teaching me).
>
> They taught me, I guess, not to give up. They knew I was taking a test: 'It's OK guys I didn't pass my test either, but you know what I'm going to do? I'm going to keep trying, 'cause that's all I can do, I can't give up.'
>
> Ellos me enseñaban y yo les enseñaba también (They were teaching me and I was teaching them too).

Oscar's resonance with his students' experiences in their own struggles to pass the state-mandated standardized tests simultaneously situates him as a teacher and as a learner. After passing the Spanish proficiency exam that would rightfully place him in a bilingual classroom, today Oscar can choose between teaching in a bilingual classroom, providing Spanish instruction, and teaching in an ESL classroom using his Spanish at his own discretion. He admits that as someone who finds himself 'thinking it all in English' he feels more comfortable in the ESL classroom (interview excerpt). If the obstacle he faced was symbolized by not passing the BTLPT, the story behind that was his long, treacherous road into reconnecting with the language of his mother that he had lost. As he said, it was not about the bilingual placement but about living the example of not giving up.

From my experiences listening to the linguistically diverse students who are wanting to become teachers I don't think persistence is unique only to Oscar. Nevertheless, I wonder about those downhearted left behind in their attempt to become a certified bilingual teacher. Educational institutions can learn from Oscar's narratives to look at students raised by speakers of other languages than English and not think of them as aspiring English monolinguals or as two deficient monolinguals in one person, but see them as learners with multiple resources and unique paths. This may help avoid the linguistically and culturally diverse student prematurely giving up or being left *in between*.

References

Aldine Independent School District (2013) Fast Facts. Aldine Independent School District. 2 December. http://www.aldine.k12.tx.us/sections/about/fast_facts.cfm

Baker, C. (2011) *Foundations of Bilingual Education*, 5th edn. Tonowanda: Multilingual Matters.

Banks, J.A. (1993) Multicultural Education: historical development, dimensions and practice, *Review of Research in Education*, 19, 3-49.

Bruner, J. (2004) Life as Narrative, *Social Research*, 71(3), 691-711.

Clandinin, D.J. & Connelly, F.M. (2000) *Narrative Inquiry: experience and story in qualitative research*. San Francisco: John Wiley.

Connelly, F.M. & Clandinin, D.J. (1990) Stories of Experience and Narrative Inquiry, *Educational Researcher*, 19(5), 2-14. http://dx.doi.org/10.3102/0013189X019005002

Cummins, J. (2001) Empowering Minority Students: a framework for intervention, *Harvard Educational Review*, 71, 656-675.

Cummins, J. (2007) Language Interactions in the Classroom: from coercive to collaborative relations of power, in O. García & C. Baker, *Bilingualism: an introductory reader*, p. 187. Toronto: Multilingual Matters.

Feiman-Nemser, S. (2003) What New Teachers Need to Know, *Educational Leadership*, 60(8), 25-29.

García, O. (2009) *Bilingual Education in the 21st Century: a global perspective*. Chichester: Wiley-Blackwell.

García, O., Kleifgen, J.A. & Falchi, L. (2008) *Equity in Education of Emergent Bilinguals: the case of English language learners. Campaign for Educational Equity Research Review*, Series 1. New York: Teachers College. http://files.eric.ed.gov/fulltext/ED524002.pdf

Gay, G. (2010) *Culturally Responsive Teaching: theory, research, and practice*. New York: Teachers College Press.

Ingersoll, R.M. (2014) *Seven Trends: the transformation of the teaching force*. Updated April 2014. CPRE Report #RR-80. Philadelphia: Consortium for Policy Research in Education, University of Pennsylvania. http://www.cpre.org/sites/default/files/workingpapers/1506_7trendsapril2014.pdf

Ladson-Billings, G. (2006) From the Achievement Gap to the Education Debt: understanding achievement in US schools, *Educational Researcher*, 35(7), 3-12. http://dx.doi.org/10.3102/0013189X035007003

May, S. (2014) *The Multilingual Turn: implications for SLA, TESOL, and bilingual education*. New York: Routledge.

Nieto, S. (1996) *Affirming Diversity: the sociopolitical context of multicultural education*. 2nd edn. White Plains, NY: Longman.

Nieto, S. (2002) *Language, Culture and Teaching: critical perspectives for a new century*. Mahwah, NJ: Lawrence Erlbaum Associates.

Ortega, L. (2014) Ways Forward for a Bi/Multilingual Turn in SLA, in S. May (Ed.) *The Multilingual Turn*, pp. 32-53. New York: Routledge.

Ovando, C.J. (2003) Bilingual Education in the United States: historical development and current issues, *Bilingual Research Journal*, 27(1), 1-24. http://dx.doi.org/10.1080/15235882.2003.10162589

Palmer, D. & Martínez, R.A. (2013) Teacher Agency in Bilingual Spaces: a fresh look at preparing teachers to educate Latina/o bilingual children, *Review of Research in Education*, 37, 269-297. http://dx.doi.org/10.3102/0091732X12463556

Sass, D.F., Flores, B.B., Claeys, L. & Pérez, B. (2012) Identifying Personal and Contextual Factors that Contribute to Attrition Rates for Texas Public School Teachers, *Education Policy Analysis Archives*. http://epaa.asu.edu/ojs/article/view/967 (accessed 7 March 2014).

Soto, L.D. (2010) *Teaching Bilingual/Bicultural Children: teachers talk about language and learning*. New York: Peter Lang.

Valdez, V.E., Freire, J.A. & Delavan, G. (2014) *Market-ability Overshadowing Equity: How Utah Print Media Positions the Value of Dual Language Education Policy*. Paper presented at the annual meeting of the American Educational Research Association (AERA), Philadelphia, PA, April.

CHAPTER 18

Self-determination in Career Trajectories of English Language Teachers

PENNY HAWORTH

SUMMARY While becoming an English language teacher may not be initially perceived as a destination, career trajectories in this field in fact often follow an evolutionary process, with individual teachers taking unique routes along the way. This chapter describes how the career trajectories of two English language teachers were initiated by a significant experience that increased awareness of their role within the wider global community. In particular, the journeys of these two teachers were found to be inspired by a sense of *relatedness*, which is identified as one of the three key motivational factors in self-determination theory. My own story and that of Suzie, who recently began working as an English language teacher in a New Zealand primary school, illustrate how *relatedness* is linked to *autonomy* and *competence*, the other key factors in self-determination theory. Their journeys show how the interaction of these three key factors not only serves to reinforce a sense of purpose, but can also support teachers in identifying strategic steps in achieving their career goals. This chapter therefore challenges notions about the lower status of English language teaching, which are based on a perception that such positions have often been attained solely on the basis of being a native speaker of English. Instead, it is suggested that this may be merely the initial stage of what can potentially develop into a more creditable career trajectory.

Introduction

This chapter opens by describing my career trajectory as an English language teacher and teacher educator, which I characterize as an ongoing search for answers in meeting diverse student needs. I then move to examining the journey of another English language teacher who is at an earlier stage of her career trajectory. These data are drawn from a more extensive study of English language teacher trajectories, which draws on a *rivers of life* approach, depicting teachers' life journeys as a series of bends in a river (Denicolo & Pope, 2001; Ingvarsdottir, 2014, p. 97). My conversation with Suzie (a pseudonym) began with a question about how she had first come into

English language teaching, and moved on to discuss where that was taking her, and exploring the factors that sustained her motivation in this field. In this chapter I reflect on our different yet intersecting journeys through the lens of the three intrinsic motivation factors identified in *self-determination theory*: competence, autonomy and relatedness (Deci & Ryan, 1985; Ryan & Deci, 2000).

Thirty-five Years in English Language Teaching

The first six years of my career were spent teaching Year 7-8 students. I had taken languages at secondary school and had specialized in English in my teacher education course, but had not thought about teaching English as an additional language, maybe because this was not a viewed as a possible career option back in the 1970s in New Zealand. However, while I was home with my two pre-school children in the early 1980s, an article in the local newspaper called for volunteers to assist with teaching English to refugees from Cambodia and Vietnam (sometimes referred to as 'boat people'). Years before, I had been moved by seeing television news clips of children fleeing down a road from scenes of conflict in Vietnam, and somehow felt connected to their plight. Besides, it might also provide a remedy for my 'baby brain'. May Needham, the founder of the voluntary home tutor group in my city, answered my phone call, and asked me what skills I thought I might be able to bring to this task. I replied that I was a qualified teacher, and I therefore knew a lot about how to teach reading and writing. The silence on the other end of the phone indicated my answer had missed something important; but fortunately May decided to give me a chance.

I enrolled in the voluntary home tutor training programme and subsequently began teaching English to a young Vietnamese mother with young children about the same age as mine. She taught me how to knit jerseys for my children, and I taught her English. However, in reality she taught me far more as a novice home tutor than I could ever teach her. That first one-hour meeting each week grew into an evening per week, reading and talking together, Vietnamese cooking lessons, cultural exchanges, until finally her little daughter would fall asleep over the kitchen table and another family member would quietly enter the room and carry her off to bed. As an immigrant myself, with no extended family in New Zealand, this was a privileged experience that had a sense of wider 'relatedness' for me, and set my feet on a pathway that led to a career in English language teaching spanning the next thirty-five years.

At this time, teaching English was very much *learning-on-the-job*. As my journey developed, I taught Saturday morning classes, and a group of fellow voluntary tutors and myself set up full-time work skills classes for new migrants, funded by the Department of Labour. I later taught English to military personnel from various Pacific Islands who were studying trades courses in New Zealand. Over this period I worked with an amazing group of tutors who became part of my community of practice (Lave & Wenger, 1991). Looking back, a binding factor in the strong sense of *relatedness* we built was perhaps our shared sense of social justice. As in Sheldon and Elliot's (1999) self-concordance model, there is consistency between goals and the individual's values and interests.

The term *tutor*, rather than *teacher*, was fitting as we were constantly co-constructing and reconstructing understandings with our learners. One morning, as I began teaching a unit on renting and buying houses in New Zealand, I asked the students to draw me a picture of a house, intending to develop related vocabulary. This led to insights into the students' cultures beyond anything I had anticipated. A Vietnamese student drew a house on stilts with a long set of steps leading up to the top floor; a Samoan student drew an open-sided house with a wide, overhanging roof; but no images resembled the stereotypical western house with a roof, a chimney, two windows and a door. The pictures were displayed in the classroom and led to much interesting discussion on the differences in houses in New Zealand. One student from Hungary told me she felt unsafe in a New Zealand house as it had no shutters on the windows, and it lacked thick stone walls for insulation against the cold.

In response to a need, a local college provided a venue for an advanced evening class in English for adults. However, some students were dissatisfied with *just an English language course*. In search of answers, I enrolled for a postgraduate diploma in second language teaching. Massey University had recently set up a course locally that was available part time and by distance, so there was no longer a need to attend full-time internal study in Wellington. At the first on-campus course I was amazed to find around a hundred students from all over the country and knew a really good qualification would be needed to build a career in this area.

The need to build competence in new contexts continued to challenge me to fill gaps in my professional knowledge. While completing the final paper in my postgraduate diploma, I was offered the opportunity to be the Acting Coordinator for New Settler and Multicultural Education, providing advice to teachers throughout the central North Island of New Zealand. I quickly discovered that teachers had no prior input on teaching English to students from non-English-speaking backgrounds. In one session I co-opted teachers who were doing interesting and/or valuable things to share these ideas with the group. Teachers were thirsty for knowledge, and enthusiastic about having an opportunity to hear what others were doing.

Although better equipped by now, I was even more aware of the gaps in my knowledge. Teachers in New Zealand classrooms needed more than the knowledge from my postgraduate course. At the end of the year, I applied for and won a position in a Japanese-owned college. At that college, I had an opportunity to teach on an academic English course with Fiona Hyland. Finally, I began to find answers that were missing pieces in the pedagogical jigsaw puzzle I was struggling to complete.

I moved into teacher education and completed my master's thesis, and a much clearer picture was emerging of how to meet learners' needs in different contexts. My later PhD study (Haworth, 2004) confirmed the findings of an earlier Ministry of Education–funded study which identified that class teachers tended to use a trial-and-error process in developing working theories for teaching English language learners (Kennedy & Dewar, 1997), but also revealed the care and concern class teachers felt for these children. Teachers also had conflicting feelings about their roles with English language learners due to their identification as *class teachers*. Including just a few English language learners in the class who did not easily fit into the existing instructional groups in the class challenged traditional New Zealand values for equality, and revealed a lack of commitment to equity (Haworth, 2009).

Building a Career Trajectory as an English Language Teacher

This year I have been talking to English language teachers in New Zealand primary and secondary schools about their career trajectories. In this chapter I share the story of one teacher, Suzie.

Suzie was originally from the UK, and had travelled and worked overseas before eventually settling in New Zealand. When we talked, she was working as a part-time English language teacher in a primary school located in the South Island of New Zealand. However, she felt it was more difficult to develop a career as an English language teacher in this location: 'If we were to go to ... a much bigger centre, then I think it would be more worthwhile. ... at our school we only have twenty-two students on our ESOL register.'

Suzie had been a full-time teacher in the same school prior to being an English language teacher: 'Three years ago I worked full time at the same school and I just found it unmanageable with young children. I survived the year, but that's what I feel it was – a survival. ... At that school it is very high achieving, and the principal is very driven. I think that's what burnt me out in the year that I was full time there ... I had to address the work–life balance; so for the last two years I have been part time, and for both of these two years I have done a day and a half.' English language teaching provided a more flexible career choice: 'I don't see that I will ever go back to full-time teaching. I feel like my days of that are over. The part-time work and relieving [substitute teaching] as well ... it is just a much better balance.'

Suzie's trajectory is now discussed in terms of the three motivating factors in self-determination theory: competence, relatedness and autonomy.

Competence

Being an English language teacher was something Suzie had considered: 'I had always toyed [with the idea of being an English language teacher] ...

Before I left [the UK], I was interested in doing one of those qualifications [in teaching English as a Foreign Language], you know, those short six-week programmes. Anyway, it never happened.'

Travel was an initial source of competence for Suzie. Originally from the UK, she had 'done a lot of travelling ... [including] Kathmandu in Nepal. We [my husband and I] have done a lot of backpacking and been to a lot of different countries. I have always had an interest in other countries and other cultures.'

Working as an English language teacher in a school had encouraged Suzie to apply for a Ministry of Education scholarship, and this funded her study in Teaching English as an Additional Language. She noted: 'I guess it is just a genuine interest from my part', but it also reflected her commitment to developing as a teacher: 'I don't want to stay stagnant. ... I am really enjoying the learning.' Her career pathway was an evolving phenomenon: 'You know, you need to safeguard your future. I don't know that I will be in [this city] for ever ... so I think it would be a good skill to have.'

At this early stage, however, she lacked confidence about her skills:

I don't want to call myself a specialist because I think that sounds a bit self-indulgent ... I guess it is the British personality – you don't blow your trumpet sort of thing. It is basically what I want to do but ... At the moment, I don't have those skills so that's what I aspire to do. Maybe when I have got those skills I will feel less self-indulgent about it and more worthy of it. I don't know.

However, being a qualified teacher did provide Suzie with some assurance in her role: 'It is probably more my confidence of being able to do that, because I can see it from ... a teaching perspective.'

Although part time, Suzie was viewed as the lead ESOL (English for Speakers of Other Languages) teacher, and she felt that this 'raised awareness within the school ... even the way that I sign off an email. ... Whereas last year I think it just said ... part-time teacher ... this year it says "ESOL Lead Teacher". So I think ... every time I meet staff ... just seeing those words in their face helps.'

Suzie also shared her developing knowledge with other teachers: 'Anything that is useful [on the Primary ESOL email list] ... I will flick through to all the staff. So, they're just resource ideas ...a few things like that I discover, I share that with the staff. Most of them are grateful for that.'

Relatedness

Suzie's early travel experiences were strongly linked to her sense of social justice, as seen in her description of her travel to Uganda in Africa, where she lived for six weeks:

I got an award and worked over there as a teacher. There were about twenty of us [who] went to Uganda, because ... their education went free, overnight. So some of these poor teachers – from having had like six students whose parent could afford to pay – suddenly they were inundated with one hundred students turning up the following day. So we went over to give them some professional development – just ideas ... to support their teachers there. So that was ... you know, a really amazing experience.

As a result of that experience, Suzie actively worked on creating in her students a sense of relatedness to the wider world:

The school that I was at, we then linked with the African school. We fundraised and ... sent the money over, which could have been used for building more classrooms or providing more desks or what the school saw fit ... Part of the purpose of that whole project was to build those bridges between the two countries. ... the children there could write to our kids and send pictures and vice versa ... it was building [for] the kids in our school – their awareness of life outside Bristol ... You know, there is more to life than that. ... I came to New Zealand shortly after that ... I am sort of hoping that over the next course of the next couple of years I can start making the children here more aware of life outside of this beautiful bubble we live in. It's different.

Being an immigrant herself, Suzie had a sense of affinity with English language learners, a connection that she felt some other teachers did not feel:

Sometimes teachers see these ESOL kids as a bit of an inconvenience to them in their class because they can't quite read and write properly in English, so they therefore need extra work, rather than embracing the fact that in the long run these kids are going to be so much better off than us, because they will be able to communicate beautifully in two or more languages, and I don't think that a lot of the teachers see it that way. They see it as a bit of an extra thorn in their side that they have to prepare extra work for and differentiate for.

Autonomy

A core feature of growth goals in relation to self-determination (Deci & Ryan, 1985; Ryan & Deci, 2000), is that these goals are *determined by individuals, about themselves and for themselves.* This perspective on autonomy can be seen in how Suzie was actively seeking ways to extend her role, while maintaining her part-time status:

Another brand new school that is just being built ... opened their doors in February ... I would quite like to approach them ... I was thinking I might wait till next term and say, 'Hey, as you start to get more ESOL students on your roll, if you would like to employ

me I would be more than happy to help oversee it. ... It might be
that they don't want to employ me on a permanent basis for half a
day a week. [However] if, when funding rounds are due, if they
could employ me to help them through the process of working
with the teachers, and filling out the forms, and collecting the data
... Employing me ... nearly like a consultant, you know, that
comes in for a short time [to] help them out, set them up.

However, autonomy is not just motivated by an inward focus on self-
advancement. It can also be outward-facing in terms of the benefits for
learners. In this view, autonomy reflects a sense of altruism that can be
intrinsically linked to the work of English language teachers. An example of
this can be seen in how Suzie also sought to develop opportunities for
students and parents within her own school. She explained: 'I have got a big
long list that I shared with the principal at the start of the year of the things
that I would like to do.' One particular plan emerged from a discussion with
a Year 3 class:

I just said, 'Wouldn't it be interesting to find out what other
languages are spoken at school?' This little very bright girl ... came
up with, 'Can children who speak one language teach it to other
children who don't speak that language?' ... and that's what we are
in the middle of investigating. So, we have collected our data, and
there's twenty different languages spoken, and there're 377
students, which is 67% of our population, who want to learn
another language. ... [I was] somewhat overwhelmed ... So, that's
in progress. ... We will start with year threes and we will work up
from there. So we are going to find out from our year threes next
week what language they would like to speak, and then we are
going to find out from within the whole school ... who would like
to teach that language. But the main thing that I was really
wanting to do was getting our ESOL kids sitting together at lunch
to speak their first language ... and also to see if their families
might like to come in and join them. ... Because I'm only there on
a Tuesday, every Tuesday we could invite their parents to come
and join us for lunch, at school, bring their own lunch; so, we
could have a global cultural kids' group, where they sit together
and speak their first languages. Because, ... [what] we are finding
– particularly with a couple of our students, is that their parents
are speaking to them with a mixture of English and Portuguese at
home; so ... they don't have a strong base – [for] their thinking, or
for their general sort of academic approach ... Whereas, with our
students who speak their first language only at home, we are
finding that they're academically much more capable. So, I just
thought that might be one way to encourage, and also to make the

other children aware of who in our [overseas partner] school can speak other languages, to embrace that rather than hide it.

Having passion for what you do, allied to a sense of altruism, was strongly motivating for Suzie, and led her to work hard for her learners and the English language learner (ELL) community:

> Your pay is only a notional indication of the number of hours you actually put in. I love having the flexibility for that ESOL, because the deputy [principal], at one point, was wanting me to have like a fixed time; but it just doesn't work like that, so having that flexibility is really good. But the 0.1 [position] doesn't even scratch the surface of the number of hours I do, because that only amounts to two and a half hours a week and I do a whole lot more than two and a half hours a week for that.

Self-determination in English Language Teachers

The three motivating factors in self-determination theory are clearly evident in these stories. English language teachers *autonomously* build *competence*, not only for themselves but also for their students, their wider school community and other teachers. *Relatedness* appears to be a motivating factor that provides a sense of affinity with English language learners early in English language teachers' career trajectory journey.

Building a career in this field is not just motivated by teachers' selfish ambition; rather it seems to involve a more embracing concept that includes identification with a wider global community of practice. Although interest in and value for languages and cultures seems to be intrinsic to getting into and staying in the field, there is more of a sense of *being* an English language teacher than of *becoming* an English language teacher. Once entry is gained, however, there appears to be a strong motivation to acquire the necessary skills and knowledge that contribute to relevant competence. In building their careers, English language teachers also seem to take advantage of serendipity rather than consciously undertaking long-term career planning. In my early career that was also the case. Having formed close connections, I simply took the opportunities that arose from those.

Competence, autonomy and relatedness are often referred to as discrete aspects of self-determination. However, in the two English language teacher career trajectories illustrated in this chapter, motivating factors are embedded and interconnected in an early career stage, even before the idea of becoming an English language teacher emerged as a clear trajectory. It is that sense of inter-relatedness that led to autonomy and developing competence, and it seems to be that sort of life-changing experience that sets the path travelled by English language teachers apart from many other career trajectories.

In New Zealand schools, while English is needed for academic achievement, teachers need a closer connection to the wider global community. It has been argued that the unbearable lightness of English language teaching (Thornbury, 2001) does not constitute a career in this field, but nonetheless when such experiences create a sense of relatedness they may provide a legitimate introduction to the field of English language teaching and perhaps draw a teacher towards setting a foot more firmly on a longer career trajectory. As the individual identity of an English language teacher evolves it is progressively constructed, co-constructed and reconstructed. This process is facilitated when the three key motivating factors linked to self-determination (relatedness, competence, autonomy) combine. Finally, and most importantly, positive movement along the English language teacher career trajectory is motivated and made more meaningful when it is interwoven with the lives and learning trajectories of the English language learners with whom teachers work.

References

Deci, E.L. & Ryan, R.M. (1985) *Intrinsic Motivation and Self-determination in Human Behaviour*. New York: Plenum. http://dx.doi.org/10.1007/978-1-4899-2271-7

Denicolo, P. & Pope, M. (2001) *Transformative Professional Practice: personal construct approaches to education and research*. London: Whurr.

Haworth, P. (2004) Developing Praxis for a Few Non-English Speaking Background Children in the Class. Unpublished PhD thesis, Massey University.

Haworth, P. (2009) The Quest for a Mainstream EAL Pedagogy, *Teachers College Record*, 111(9) (September), 2179-2208.

Ingvarsdottir, H. (2014) Reflection and Work Context in Teacher Learning, in L. Orland-Barak & C. Craig (Eds) *International Teacher Education: promising pedagogies*, Part A, pp. 91-112. *Advances in Research in Teaching*, vol. 22. Bingley: Emerald Group.

Kennedy, S. & Dewar, S. (1997) *Non-English Speaking Background Students*. Wellington, NZ: Research and International Section, Ministry of Education.

Lave, J. & Wenger, E. (1991) *Situated Learning: legitimate partial peripheral participation*. Cambridge: Cambridge University Press. http://dx.doi.org/10.1017/CBO9780511815355

Ryan, R.M. & Deci, E.L. (2000) Self-determination Theory and the Facilitation of Intrinsic Motivation, Social Development, and Well-being, *American Psychologist*, 55(1), 68-78. http://dx.doi.org/10.1037/0003-066X.55.1.68

Sheldon, K.M. & Elliot, A.J. (1999) Goal Striving, Need Satisfaction, and Longitudinal Well-being: the self-concordance model, *Journal of Personality and Social Psychology*, 76, 482-497. http://dx.doi.org/10.1037/0022-3514.76.3.482

Thornbury, S. (2001) The Unbearable Lightness of EFL, *ELT Journal*, 55(4), 391-396. http://dx.doi.org/10.1093/elt/55.4.391

Oxford Studies in Comparative Education

Series Editor: David Phillips

Most recent volumes....

Teaching Comparative Education: trends and issues informing practice, Patricia K. Kubow & Allison H. Blosser (eds), 2015

The Global Testing Culture: shaping education policy, perceptions, and practice, William C. Smith (ed.), 2015

Students, Markets and Social Justice: higher education fee and student support policies in Western Europe and beyond, Hubert Ertl & Claire Dupuy (eds), 2014

Transnational Policy Flows in European Education: the making and governing of knowledge in the education policy field, Andreas Nordin & Daniel Sundberg (eds), 2014

Internationalisation of Higher Education and Global Mobility, Bernhard Streitwieser (ed.), 2014

PISA, Power, and Policy: the emergence of global educational governance, Heinz-Dieter Meyer & Aaron Benavot (eds.), 2013

Higher Education and the State: changing relationships in Europe and East Asia, Roger Goodman, Takehiki Kariya & John Taylor (eds.), 2013

Education in South-East Asia, Colin Brock & Lorraine Pe Symaco (eds.), 2011

Reimagining Japanese Education: borders, transfers, circulations and the comparative, David Blake Willis & Jeremy Rappleye (eds), 2011

Further details of all volumes in this series can be found at
www.symposium-books.co.uk
and can be ordered there, or from
Symposium Books, PO Box 204, Didcot,
Oxford OX11 9ZQ, United Kingdom
orders@symposium-books.co.uk

CONCLUSION

Reflecting on the Changing Nature of English Language Teaching Internationally, the Status of the Profession, and Future Visions for Teacher Education

CHERYL CRAIG & PENNY HAWORTH

The contributors to this book bring a breadth and depth of practical teaching and research experience to bear on the wider discussion about English language teachers' career trajectories. The various chapters are located in seventeen different countries, so collectively they provide a unique overview of the range of different contexts for English language teachers and teacher educators internationally. The resulting insights into the perceived benefits and pitfalls of the profession are useful not only for those who wish to enter English language teaching but for other researchers currently working in this field and for those involved in providing teacher education programmes.

Many of the themes that emerge within this book are common across a number of chapters. For example, the theme of travel and interest in diverse cultures permeates the work of several authors. Some chapters highlight socio-political issues that influence teachers of English language in their particular contexts. Others uncover liminal spaces that exist between geographical, cultural and linguistic worlds, bringing in elements of self-reflection as well as the role of critical friends, dialogic partnerships and communities of knowing. A number of authors have taken a 'rivers of life' approach to illustrating the changes in direction in English language teachers' career trajectories and the personal, professional and contextual influences on these. Finally, chapters provide an understanding of the identity of the good teacher of English language, an awareness of the teacher's role as a curriculum maker rather than just a curriculum implementer, and a view of how the journey to find an English language teacher's best-loved self is often driven by a sense of social justice.

World Travelling

McKeown's Chapter 1 exemplifies the geographical world travelling often associated with English language teaching. McKeown's career, for example, began in Canada, included an exchange teacher trip to Scotland, and then became increasingly international as he accepted English language teaching posts in Angola, Turkey and Bahrain. Along the way, McKeown, who began as a fully certified teacher (not as a backpacker!), further increased his teaching credentials, eventually obtaining a doctoral degree.

A teach-and-travel motif is later illustrated by Stanley in Chapter 15, with travel being a key motivating factor for several English language teachers in her study. Haworth also identifies travel as an English teaching career precursor in her case study of 'Suzie' in Chapter 18. Travel, teaching and study are also intertwined in Badiozaman's career (in Chapter 4). In addition, the global mobility aspect of English teacher travelling is a strong theme in Gimenez et al's Chapter 13, in which all five authors document how their careers have spanned multiple nations and continents.

However, McKeown and Gimenez et al, along with other chapter contributors, also discuss world travelling in quite a different sense: the ability to view others' worlds by vicariously experiencing them through insider lenses (Lugones, 1987). This second type of world travelling involves the letting go of cultural/linguistic imperialism and the 'arrogant perception' that frequently accompanies it. It means 'lovingly accepting' others in their efforts to become bi/multilingual and multicultural. This quality is especially present in Boone et al's Chapter 3, when Boone as an English language teacher imagines her Hispanic student's despair about his family's possible expulsion from the United States due to his mother's undocumented worker status. A similar theme is also evident in Ratnam's Chapter 5 when she awakened to the fact that her students were 'victim[s] of [her] teaching'.

Numerous other examples of world travelling can also be explicated. They, like the Boone and Ratnam chapters, do not involve travel to international locales. In fact, Brown's Chapter 8 revolves around Australian student teachers' metaphorical and lived world travel from urban to rural communities while simultaneously moving from 'have' to 'have-not' environments. In Brown's work, one teacher took up the challenge and embraced world travel to others' realities. The other teacher in her study, for a variety of reasons, not all of her making, is unable to adapt to remote community living in either a lived or a vicarious sense. She becomes disheartened and isolated because 'everything [she] knows [from her urban world] ... won't work'.

Socio-political Context

There are also challenges in the contexts for English language teachers. For example, the broader socio-political context emerges as a major influence on English teachers' career trajectories. For instance, Kaldi et al (Chapter 16) present novice and expert teacher views to highlight the contrasting conditions for English language teachers in private and public schools, showing how teachers can be faced with a choice between having less desirable working conditions but greater job security in public schools as opposed to better learning environments and greater parental trust, yet less job security in private schools. Similarly, Kiatkheeree (Chapter 14) reveals how English language teachers in university settings hold less status than their colleagues in areas such as science and technology and therefore gain less funded support for research. While many university teachers are faced with the need to balance research and teaching, the dilemma for these English language teachers is further compounded by the need to decide whether to teach more hours for more pay, or to do research for less pay while enhancing their longer-term promotion prospects. Stanley (Chapter 15) also refers to *economy-class teachers* in private English language schools, whom she describes as 'precariously hired, minimally qualified, [and] low-waged'. Nonetheless, it is revealing that these teachers still choose to stay in these jobs, which they say they love. These insights illustrate some of the personal and professional dilemmas involved in English language teachers' decisions about their career trajectories.

It is not always the case that teachers can purposely navigate the bends in their rivers of life ahead of time. McKeown (in Chapter 1) relates how the crisis he faced in Bahrain led to a crucial change in his career trajectory. The economic crisis in Greece also served as backdrop for the chapter by Kaldi et al (in Chapter 16). Yet, there is still strength in the teachers to carry on. McKeown highlights that there is also a sense of adventure in navigating new waters and in gaining the skills needed to do so along the way. Experience gained in travel is part of most English language teachers' journeys. Sometimes travel is linked to adventure, and sometimes it generates empathy through earlier personal experiences as a migrant (e.g. Haworth in Chapter 18), or teachers may be challenged through travelling to less familiar territory within their own country, as noted in Brown (Chapter 8).

The chapters by Yang (Chapter 6) and Minaříková et al (Chapter 10) illustrate how external factors, such as a nation's wider educational policies, can influence the course of individual rivers of life. For example, Yang explains how teachers of English language needed to reconstruct themselves as intercultural educators but were still required to meet the existing assessment priorities. On the other hand, Minaříková et al explain how the impact of globalization on the position of English language has resulted in English now being regarded on a continuum between first and second language.

Gauna (Chapter 17) also illustrates how language policies can have a wide-reaching impact on teachers' career trajectories. She describes a young teacher education graduate trained as a bilingual teacher, an area in which there was a high demand for qualified teachers. However, he failed to find work since an external assessment deemed that his first language (which had been de-emphasized in his English-medium education) was not sufficiently proficient. He finally gained work as an English language teacher but went against the flow by implementing an effective, although not officially condoned, bilingual approach in his work with Hispanic students.

The context for English language teaching can also be challenging, as described by Brown (in Chapter 8), who presents two cases of English language teachers in remote community schools in Australia. This shows how English language teachers often need a high level of resilience to overcome the challenges of isolation in very culturally different communities. The desire for travel and adventure does not always turn out as expected, and being resilient in their own setting is no guarantee that teachers will be able to transfer that quality to surviving in settings where there is little professional or personal support. To overcome these challenges, resilience needs to be linked to a sense of connection, a desire to make a difference in these communities. A similar theme is echoed in both Suzie's and Penny's stories (in Haworth, Chapter 18), which relate how a sense of connectedness arose from a critical incident that ignited empathy for the community of learners for whom they worked. That initial inspiration directed their first steps into this career choice. It is also clear that this has sustained Wendy (in Brown, Chapter 8) over a significant number of years. However, as Haworth (in Chapter 18) points out, there are three intertwined motivational factors in self-determination: autonomy, relatedness and competence. The teachers whom Brown describes were in many ways ill prepared for the culture shock, and for the pedagogical expectations of the new community, which were unfamiliar and not necessarily subscribed to by an English-speaking teacher. A willingness to consider how to construct one's identity as a teacher, as well as having the support to know how to do so, are key factors in being successful as an English language teacher in the setting described by Brown. Haworth (Chapter 18) also refers to constructing, reconstructing and co-constructing identity as an English language teacher.

Liminal Spaces

Closely associated with metaphorical world travel is the anthropological term *liminal spaces*. Liminal spaces are spaces where one finds oneself between worlds – whether those worlds are geographical, cultural, linguistic and/or transitional in nature. Two chapters in this volume explicitly refer to in-between spaces – liminal spaces – in their titles. McKeown's Chapter 1, 'From Canada to Turkey with Places in Between', documents the author's geographical world travelling and how it morphed into metaphorical world travel across many global contexts. He asserts that this made him a 'knowmadic' (Hokanson & Karlson, 2013), a person who lives in an embodied sense *in* the land, not *on* it (Said, 1994). Gauna's Chapter 17, 'In Between English and Spanish Teaching', similarly characterizes the linguistic and cultural in-between-ness that occurs when Spanish-speaking Americans become part of English-dominant society and experience loss of their home language.

Wei (in Chapter 2) features a different kind of liminal space: a liminal space that resulted from her having taught in an EFL (English as a Foreign Language) context in China and in an ESL (English as a Second Language) context in the United States. Wei consequently is able to make distinctions between learning a language and learning *about* a language. Brown, in Chapter 8, likewise traverses rural and urban living in Australia, showing what occurred when her preservice students attempted to bridge two disparate worlds. Meanwhile, Kaldi et al in Chapter 16 find themselves lodged in a liminal space in Greece where they are able to look backward with certainty on their country's cradle-of-civilization heritage while cautiously looking forward to the continued unity of Europe and the sustainability of Greece as a member of the European Union.

Self-reflection

The critical importance of self-reflection is stated in two chapter titles and forms a central theme that threads throughout the book. Athanases et al, in Chapter 9, centre on 'self-reflexive inquiry in teacher education for diversity'. For that author team, self-reflection opens the gate to understanding culture, language and identity. Later, Zheng and Yin, in their Chapter 12 title, focus on reflective knowing as embedded in action. This orientation also resulted in their preservice teachers understanding the English language in a lived sense instead of them simply stockpiling linguistic knowledge.

Many other chapters favour reflection as well. Wei, for example, in Chapter 2, quotes Samura (2011, p. 203), who stated that 'when teachers cease to be inquisitive about their practices, their practices cease to be professional'. Other authors, such as Ingvarsdóttir (Chapter 7), Gauna (Chapter 17) and Haworth (Chapter 18), also place a premium on reflectivity in their contributions. In addition, McKeown (in Chapter 1) attributes his linguistic and cultural engagement over his quarter-century career to 'the power of reflection'.

Critical Friends, Dialogic Partners and Communities of Knowing

Throughout the volume, critical friends and knowledge communities (Craig, 1995a, b, 2007) are frequently mentioned. Critical friendship and communities of practice are important sources of support, storytelling and sustenance for McKeown in Chapter 1. Boone, in Chapter 3, also reflects on her priorities as an English language learner in the United States in the flesh-and-blood company of critical friends/fellow knowledge community members/co-authors Cutri and Pinnegar. In addition, Zheng and Ying, in Chapter 12, assert the vital importance of knowledge community members

241

and critical friends in coming to know as English language teachers. The same is true for Gimenez et al, in Chapter 13, who connect their found international community of knowing to the need for them to individually overcome isolationist tendencies in Brazil, Mexico, Kuwait, the United Arab Emirates and the United Kingdom. In this author team's case, an international research project plays a pivotal role in bringing them and others together.

Conversely, Wei, in Chapter 2, admits that her absence of native English critical friends and communities of knowing has interfered with her growth as an English language learner/teacher. Like Wei, Brown, in Chapter 8, bemoans the absence of active communities of knowing for teachers in the Australian Outback. The notion of dialogic partners is also raised in Ratnam's Chapter 5, and is visible too in Haworth's accounts of her own construction, co-construction and reconstruction of pedagogic and world knowledge with her students.

Rivers of Life

The *journey to becoming English language teachers* has some commonalities as well as some differences. All English language teachers' journeys mention encounters with other cultures and the ways in which these encounters create connections, challenges and new directions. This is reflected in the *rivers of life* and/or *life history* approaches taken in many chapters (e.g. those by McKeown, Yang, Wei, and Haworth). Taking a *rivers of life* approach allows life journeys to be depicted as a series of bends in a river (Pope & Denicolo, 2001; Ingvarsdóttir, 2014, p. 97), as changes in direction occur along the way. Teachers' careers have also been described as tending to progress in a zigzag fashion (Bateson, 1994), a feature which appears to be more prominent in English language teachers' trajectories than in many other teaching journeys.

Haworth, in Chapter 18, suggests that a sense of relatedness as well as autonomy or agency can lead teachers to acquire and grow competence. Hence, during the rivers of life, smaller and larger streams flow into each other and influence trajectories. Increased competence can also bring rewards of leadership, as noted in Suzie's case study in Haworth (Chapter 18), and changes in roles can provide further incentives for developing new skills. As highlighted in McKeown (Chapter 1) these rewards can also build confidence for navigating future more turbulent waters. However, new challenges can also initiate growth in professional competence, as in Ratnam (Chapter 5). As the course of the river changes, the territory can move from easy plains and at times turn into cascading gorges due to critical events. The teacher has to constantly accommodate these changes while also, as Wei notes (in Chapter 2), endeavouring to be true to themselves. However, as Wei as well as Yang (Chapter 6) and Zheng and Ying (Chapter 12) also point out, it can be difficult to join the main direction of a policy change when the new practices do not align well with existing priorities. For example, Wei highlights how assessment continues to focus on language-as-a-subject rather than refocusing on the new direction of enhancing intercultural skills.

For other teachers, however, their pathways can evolve in a more coherent way, as the result of being true to themselves as individuals and professionals. For example, Suzie's case (described by Haworth in Chapter 18) demonstrates that undertaking part-time work as an English language teacher can be a personal decision to balance life–work priorities. In other contexts, untenured positions can result in teachers being expected to accept low pay for more work, as described in Chapter 15 by Stanley, who refers to *economy-class teachers* who have resigned themselves to lesser conditions because they love the job, the students, or the stretch of water and the challenges they are currently navigating. Haworth points out that while such career stages could be perceived as Thornbury's notion of the 'lightness of English teaching', these less frenetic periods can also create the initial steps that may lead to a longer career trajectory.

Images of Self

Teachers' images of themselves are revealed as we move through the various chapters in the book. These images often show English language teachers to be curriculum makers, as well as uncovering ideals around the notion of a good English language teacher, which are inextricably linked to endeavours to achieve individual perceptions of their best-loved selves, a vision that is frequently marked by a strong sense of social justice.

English Teachers as Curriculum Makers

The theme of teachers as curriculum makers is highlighted in two chapters: Wei's Chapter 2 and Zheng and Ying's Chapter 12. Wei contrasts the image of teacher-as-curriculum-implementer (doing what one is told to teach) with the image of teacher-as-curriculum-maker (becoming one's best-loved self). Zheng and Ying likewise assert the primacy of the teacher-as-curriculum-maker image in teacher 'formation'. The latter two authors applaud the ability of teachers to 'weave themselves, students and subject areas together' in self-directed ways.

Other chapters also spotlight the image of teachers-as-curriculum-makers, without directly using the term. In Chapter 7, Ingvarsdóttir's participant teacher, Birna, likens low-level talk to 'crap' and advocates for a 'more flexible syllabus'. Birna champions teachers who do 'something worthwhile and interesting with students' rather than those who make them work in with 'those uninspiring textbooks'. In Birna's words, the teacher-as-curriculum-maker image emerged in an unnamed way. A second example is Abrahams and Ríos who, in Chapter 11, specifically address how teacher education became part of technical institutions (with teachers becoming technicians or implementers) when military juntas controlled Chile's political system. However, when a democratic form of government was returned to the country, the professional role of teachers and the critical importance of their pedagogies also were restored. So, too, was the preference for teachers-as-curriculum-makers re-introduced and the desire for such teachers to be 'the agents of change Chile needs'. A third example is Minaříková and her colleagues (in Chapter 10), who hint that a similar change may be under way in the Czech Republic in the aftermath of Soviet rule. Yet another example of a curriculum maker is found in Gauna (Chapter 17) with regard to the young man who fails to gain a bilingual teaching position, but then creates his own form of bilingual pedagogy as an English language teacher working with Hispanic students.

Badiozaman, in Chapter 4, forms a fifth example. She suggests that Malaysian teachers and professors enacting the teacher-as-curriculum-implementer image 'produced a new breed of students and graduates who [could] do well in examinations but [who had] limited competency in using English' (Shakir, 2009). Badiozaman recognizes her personal need to be a curriculum maker who is 'aware that the type of support [her] student teachers need transcends ... [mere] pedagogical resources'. In Badiozaman's words, such teachers also need to 'value inclusivity and diversity' and to exude 'a positive sense of self' as 'teachers and members of the teaching community' – a notion that transitions us effectively to a discussion of the 'good' EL teacher.

The 'Good' English Language Teacher

Throughout the many chapters in this volume, the notion of the good teacher of English language learners (ELLs) arises in both articulated and unarticulated ways. Ratnam's Chapter 5 from India specifically wrestles with what it means to be a good EL teacher. Ratnam admits that she 'struggle[s] with others' thoughts' about who the good teacher is. The views of those in authority particularly confront her. Brown, in Chapter 8, seeds the thought that the good ELL teacher in an urban context may not be the same as a good ELL teacher in a rural context, suggesting that context has a major role to play in teacher success. Stanley, in Chapter 15, vicariously describes the good EL teacher as the 'one who goes the extra mile'. She adds that such a person is able to deal with the emotional burdens of teaching, among other key attributes. Stanley sadly concludes that the demand for English language teachers in Australia is often satisfied by 'cheap teachers', who are not necessarily 'good teachers', but this is perhaps an outsider view because the teachers themselves state that they love their jobs. As for Yang, in Chapter 6, she discusses how Chinese language education policies have shifted over time in ways that have not always allowed the teaching force to 'digest changes' and concurrently adapt their visions of good teaching.

Some chapters, such as the one authored by Minaříková et al (Chapter 10), associate particular practices with good teaching and quality career development. For the Czech Republic author team (in Chapter 10), the use of video in English language teacher development would be advisable. American authors Athanases et al (in Chapter 9) recommend self-reflexive inquiries that surface issues of language, power and authority as resources to inform language teachers' career trajectories in productive ways. As for Abrahams and Ríos from Chile (Chapter 11), they present an integrated curriculum for meaningful English learning that presumably should result in quality beginning EL teaching and produce 'good teachers'. New Zealander Haworth, in Chapter 18, concludes that the interwoven nature of students' and teachers' lives gives rise to a sense of relatedness which she associates with 'positive movement along the EL teacher career trajectory' and which presumably is linked to the pursuit of the good teacher and quality teaching.

Teachers' 'Best-loved Self'

A further notion, the best-loved self of teachers (Craig, 2013), is traced to Schwab's scholarship (Schwab, 1954/1978), and emerges in a stated sense in Wei's Chapter 2. Wei connects the best-loved-self conceptualization to passionate teaching by ELL teachers, in a manner that suits their identities (without the study of themselves becoming the curriculum). For her, this teacher image stands in stark opposition to the image of teacher implementer where the teacher only implements the dictates of the state.

While Badiozaman in Chapter 4 does not explicitly use the term *best-loved self* in her chapter contribution, her focus on lifelong learning and her desire to deal productively with educational change leads her to defend teachers using pedagogies most suited to their beliefs and ways of being. It also includes her blending of her research identity with her best-loved self in her workplace despite the challenges presented by such a union.

A further example of the best-loved self is found in Gimenez et al's Chapter 13. In that transnational work (Brazil, Mexico, Kuwait, United Arab Emirates, United Kingdom), it is apparent that the community of knowing (Craig, 2007) that the English language teachers/researchers have formed is essential to their best-loved selves as professors. Their shared knowledge community addresses significant isolation problems they experience in their countries of residence. In Yang's Chapter 6 as well, teacher/professor participant Huiwen strives to integrate her research identity with her best-loved self despite the Chinese policy environment being less accepting of that merger. Similarly, Kaldi and her Greek collaborators (Chapter 16) are well versed in what their best-loved selves need to experience personal and career satisfaction, perhaps even more so given their current feelings of 'loneliness, disappointment, betrayal and fear ... [for] the future' in the throes of Greece's financial crisis.

Social Justice

In Ratnam's Chapter 5, from India, the theme of social justice rings through loudly. She characterizes her career trajectory from beginning as a novice English as a Second Language teacher and then progressing to become a 'more mature social justice educator'. The author's connecting of her miseducative (Dewey, 1938) teaching with multiple students' failures lays the groundwork for her transformation from being a language teacher 'oppressor' to being a 'dialogic partner', learning and teaching alongside her disadvantaged students.

Brown, in Chapter 8, similarly identifies herself as an educator consciously embracing and enacting 'social justice and equity' principles in remote Australia. This allows her to interrogate discrepancies in the education of mainstream and marginalized Australians within the context of her institution's teacher education programme. Suzie, the teacher in Haworth's Chapter 18, also articulates a social justice agenda and displays altruistic tendencies in a manner similar to Haworth herself.

Athanases and his chapter collaborators, in Chapter 9, directly confront the sociopolitical hegemonies of the US system that complicate English language learning situations. This author team circumvents highly problematic issues that potentially could emerge. In Chapter 17, Gauna, like Athanases et al, deplores the 'subtractive bilingualism' of the US melting pot. Kaldi et al (in Chapter 16) take a critical stance toward private language learning in Greece, highlighting the importance of an activist identity in a manner somewhat like Athanases and his colleagues' call for teacher agency. Kiatkheeree (in Chapter 14) also places teacher agency at the forefront. Finally, Stanley in Chapter 15 equates English language teaching with economy-class teaching in her Australian setting, and Zheng and Ying (in Chapter 12) term their English language teaching practices in China 'emancipatory'.

Final Words

Within a volume such as this one, there are many stories of, overlapping themes about, and insights into the career trajectories of English language teachers. While the contexts of English language teaching vary widely, the teacher trajectories portrayed in this book intersect with individual beliefs about the best-loved self as a teacher, with a prevailing interest in the diversity of cultures, and in meeting with resilience the changing challenges of enhancing English language learners' experiences, wherever they may be. Like the different sides of a diamond, light reflects unique views. Collectively, though, these chapters come together to offer more holistic insights into the lives and careers of English language teachers internationally.

References

Bateson, M.C. (1994) *Peripheral Visions: learning along the way*. New York: HarperCollins.

Craig, C. (1995a) Dilemmas in Crossing the Boundaries in the Professional Knowledge Landscape, in D.J. Clandinin & F.M. Connelly (Eds) *Teachers' Professional Knowledge Landscapes*, pp. 16-24. New York: Teachers College Press.

Craig, C. (1995b) Knowledge Communities: a way of making sense of how beginning teachers come to know, *Curriculum Inquiry*, 25(2), 151-172. http://dx.doi.org/10.1080/03626784.1995.11076175

Craig, C. (2007) Illuminating Qualities of Knowledge Communities in a Portfolio-making Context, *Teachers and Teaching: theory and practice*, 13(6), 617-636.

Craig, C. (2013) Teacher Education and the Best-loved Self, *Asia Pacific Journal of Education*, 33(3), 261-272. http://dx.doi.org/10.1080/02188791.2013.788476

Dewey, J. (1938) *Experience and Education*. New York: Basic Books.

Hokanson, B. & Karlson, R.W. (2013) Borderlands: developing character strengths for a knowmadic world, *On the Horizon*, 21(2) 107-113. http://dx.doi.org/10.1108/10748121311323003

Ingvarsdóttir, H. (2014) Reflection and Work Context in Teacher Learning: two case studies from Iceland, in C.J. Craig & L. Orland-Barak (Eds) *International Teacher Education: promising pedagogies*, Part A, vol. 22. *Advances in Research on Teaching*. Bingley: Emerald Group.

Lugones, M. (1987) Playfulness, 'World'-travelling, and Loving Perception, *Hypatia*, 2, 3-19. http://dx.doi.org/10.1111/j.1527-2001.1987.tb01062.x

Pope, M. & Denicolo, P. (2001) *Transformative Education: personal construct approaches to education and research*. London: Whurr.

Said, E. (1994) *Representations of the Intellectual*. New York: Random House.

Schwab, J.J. (1954/1978) Eros and Education: a discussion of one aspect of discussion, in I. Westbury & N. Wilkof (Eds) *Science, Curriculum and Liberal Education: selected essays*. Chicago: University of Chicago Press.

Shakir, R. (2009) Soft Skills at the Malaysian Institutes of Higher Learning, *Asia Pacific Education Review*, 10(3), 309-315. http://dx.doi.org/10.1007/s12564-009-9038-8

Notes on Contributors

Mary Jane Abrahams, teacher of English, MA in Education, has taught at university level for over 35 years. Her main interest is teacher education. She has been involved in training mentor trainers and then mentors for schools in Chile, working very closely with the Ministry of Education. She was a member of the team who wrote the standards for initial teacher education in English. She was involved in the new curriculum design for UAH. She is the head of the English Department at the School of Education in Universidad Alberto Hurtado, the Jesuit University in Chile. She is also the president of TESOL Chile, a post she has held for the last ten years. *Correspondence*: mabraham@uahurtado.cl

Steven Z. Athanases (PhD, Stanford University) is a professor in the School of Education, University of California, Davis. He studies diversity and equity in the teaching and learning of English and in teacher education. He co-edited *Mentors in the Making: developing new leaders for new teachers* (Teachers College Press) and participated in curriculum working groups for the first teachers' college in Ecuador. His articles on language teaching and English language learners appear in the *Journal of Teacher Education*, *The New Educator*, and the *Bilingual Research Journal* and in relevant book chapters in *Teacher Preparation for Linguistically Diverse Classrooms* (ed. T. Lucas) and *L2 Writing in Secondary Classrooms* (ed. L.C. de Oliveira & T. Silva). A former high school English teacher, he is the recipient of numerous teaching honors, Spencer and McDonnell Foundation postdoctoral fellowships, and research awards from the Association of Teacher Educators and the National Council of Teachers of English. *Correspondence*: szathanases@ucdavis.edu

Ida Fatimawati bt Adi Badiozaman graduated from the University of Malaya (UM), Malaysia with a Bachelor of Education Honours degree, majoring in TESL, in 2002. After spending two years teaching English and English literature in a residential school in Kuching, she went on to pursue her MA TESOL degree at Victoria University in Wellington, New Zealand. She then obtained her PhD in Education (TESOL) from Massey University, New Zealand in 2012. While undertaking her PhD, she worked at two tertiary institutions, International Pacific College and Professional and Continuing Education (PaCE) in Massey University. She was also a tutor for the Licentiate Diploma and Certificate in TESOL (Trinity College London), specializing in academic writing papers. She is now the MA TESOL Coordinator and Associate Dean of Academic Operations in the Faculty of Language and Communication in Swinburne University of Technology Sarawak Campus. *Correspondence*: ifabadiozaman@swinburne.edu.my

Leslie C. Banes (MA, Education) is a doctoral candidate and associate instructor in the School of Education, University of California, Davis. She draws on five years as a bilingual classroom teacher in the United States and Spain and two years working with bilingual pre-schoolers and their parents in a math intervention program, and has experience teaching English as a second language and math in Spanish to bilingual adults. Her research interests include equity in mathematics education and the relationship between mathematics and language learning/literacy. Her recent work involves the effect of classroom mathematical discussion on emergent bilinguals, formative assessment in mathematics, and supporting linguistically diverse elementary students in writing mathematical explanations. She is currently involved in professional development programs with STEM teachers in California and Beijing and recently published an article on prospective bilingual teachers in the *Bilingual Research Journal.* *Correspondence*: lcbanes@ucdavis.edu

Johanna Boone is an elementary school teacher in a Title I school in Provo, Utah. She received her master's degree in teacher education from Brigham Young University. While she is not currently engaged in formal research, her research interests include English language learners, immigration experiences, and the impact of school culture on teachers, students and student achievement. *Correspondence*: johanna_boone@hotmail.com

Jill Brown (BA, Grad Dip Ed. M.TESOL, PhD) is a senior lecturer in the Faculty of Education at Monash University, Melbourne, Australia. She started work at Monash after twenty-five years as an English language teacher in government secondary schools. She has extensive experience in teaching and supervising international students. Jill recently completed an international study of the ways in which children construct minority identity through drawings and is currently researching teacher work and identity in diverse contexts. She has also published on research student narratives as well as on second-language identity in narratives of study abroad. *Correspondence*: jill.brown@monash.edu

Cheryl Craig, PhD, is a Professor and Coordinator of Teaching and Teacher Education at the University of Houston, an official Asian-serving and Hispanic-serving research-intensive university that is the second most diverse higher learning institution in the United States. She is an American Educational Research Association (AERA) Fellow and a Lifetime Achievement Awardee for AERA's Division B (Curriculum). In 2015, she received the Michael Huberman Award for her Research Contributions to Understanding the Lives of Teachers. Currently, she is Executive Editor of *Teachers and Teaching: theory and practice* and sits on the editorial boards of *Reflective Practice* and the *International Journal of Education and the Arts.* She is the Past-Secretary (2009-15) of the International Study Association on Teachers and Teaching. *Correspondence*: ccraig@central.uh.edu

Ramona Maile Cutri is an Associate Professor of Multicultural Education at Brigham Young University's Teacher Education Department. Her research explores pre-service teacher candidates' identification of social privileges; the emotional work involved in multicultural teacher education; cross-class identities; and how technological integration can help engage pre-service teacher candidates intellectually and emotionally in the ethical, dispositional and pedagogical issues related to critical multicultural teacher education. *Correspondence*: ramona_cutri@byu.edu

Leslie Gauna is a full-time Visiting Assistant Professor at the University of Houston. She teaches bilingual education and English as a Second Language courses for teacher candidates and graduate students. She conducts qualitative research into teachers' language and cultural practices in the classroom. She has extensive knowledge and experience in teaching at all grade levels in multilingual schools with bilingual, dual-language and English as a Second Language programs in Texas. She has worked with migrant populations in urban school projects related to multicultural, bilingual, prevention of violence, gender and community participation issues both in the United States and in Argentina. She obtained her EdD in Curriculum and Instruction from U of H after completing a critical narrative inquiry study focusing on the narratives of first-year bilingual teachers who themselves had been raised as linguistically diverse students. *Correspondence*: lesliegauna@sbcglobal.net

Telma Gimenez holds a PhD from Lancaster University, UK and is an associate professor in the Department of Modern Foreign Languages at the State University of Londrina, Brazil. She supervises research at the postgraduate level and facilitates preservice teachers' courses. Her primary research focus is on educational policies and their impact on the lives of teachers and students in schools in a globalizing world. Her current research examines ways in which the developments in the field of English as a global language can be incorporated into teacher education programs. Dr Gimenez is a researcher funded by CNPq (Science and Technology Agency) and has published more than 100 publications in refereed journals, book chapters and conference proceedings. She served as a member of the Advisory Board of ALAB – Brazilian Association of Applied Linguistics (2014-15). *Correspondence*: tgimenez@uel.br

Penny Haworth, PhD, is an Associate Professor at the Institute of Education, Massey University, New Zealand. She teaches courses on learning/teaching English as an additional language, particularly for academic and specific purposes. She has led research projects in primary schools, adult education, teacher education, and a Ministry of Education–funded Early Childhood Education Centre of Innovation. As well as her interest in career trajectories of English language teachers, Penny's research includes teacher beliefs and change processes in linguistically and culturally diverse settings; student teacher efficacy in low socioeconomic settings; globalization impacts on literacy; and pedagogies for enhancing bilingual learning. Penny has served on Ministry of Education advisory panels for TESOL and literacy; she is a past regional chairperson and past national executive member of the New Zealand TESOL Association; and she has recently completed six years on the Executive Committee of the International Study Association on Teachers and Teaching. *Correspondence*: p.a.haworth@massey.ac.nz

Amanda Howard has spent many years working as an English language teacher, teacher trainer and lecturer in the Middle East and the UK. She gained her MEd TESOL from the University of Leeds in the 1990s and a PGCE from Melbourne University a few years later, followed by a PhD from the University of Warwick in ELT and Applied Linguistics. She has been continuously involved in postgraduate education for the last fifteen years and currently works as a freelance educator and researcher. Her interests cover observation and feedback in educational settings, teacher evaluation, teacher development and teaching young learners, and she has presented and written extensively on these topics. Her most recent publication has been a collection of papers entitled 'Teacher Evaluation in Second Language Education', co-edited with Helen Donaghue and published by Bloomsbury. *Correspondence*: amanda.howarduk@gmail.com

Hafdís Ingvarsdóttir is Professor of Education in the School of Education at the University of Iceland. She started out as a secondary school teacher but has been involved in teacher education for the last three decades. She was head of the teacher education programme at the university for a number of years. Her main research interests are teacher education and teacher growth with special emphasis on foreign language teaching and learning. Presently, she is involved in two main research projects: a nationwide project on the status and use of English in Iceland, and a project investigating pedagogical practices in upper-secondary schools. *Correspondence*: he@hi.is

Tomáš Janík is the head of the Institute for Research in School Education, Masaryk University, Brno (Czech Republic) and former editor-in-chief of *Pedagogická orientace*, one of the leading Czech academic journals on educational research. His research interests lie in the areas of instructional design and quality of instruction (video studies), curriculum, and teacher education. Together with his team, he carried out a large research study accompanying the implementation of the new curricular reform in the Czech Republic. *Correspondence*: tjanik@ped.muni.cz

Parussaya Kiatkheeree holds a PhD in Education from Massey University, New Zealand. She is a lecturer in teaching English in the Faculty of Education in Suratthani Rajabhat University (SRU), where she also serves as the director of the Association of Southeast Asian Nations (ASEAN) Studies and Development Centre. Her key responsibility in this centre is for building academic collaboration with the leading universities at both national and international levels. Her particular research focus is in the area of teaching English. She also has an interest in enhancing professional development for academic and support staff. In addition, she is responsible for the master's degree programme in Teaching English for Academic and Occupational Purposes. *Correspondence*: parussaya@yahoo.com

Stavroula Kaldi is an Associate Professor in Educational Studies in the Department of Primary Education at the University of Thessaly, Greece. She studied at the Aristotle University of Thessaloniki, Greece (BA) and at Sussex University, UK (MA & PhD). She has extensive experience in teaching and research in higher education and her research interests include project-based learning, cooperative learning, teacher education and teacher professional development. Her research is published in various refereed international journals, conferences and volumes. *Correspondence*: kaldi@uth.gr

Emmanuel Konsolas is an Assistant Professor in Teaching Methodology and its Applications at the Aegean University, Greece. He has a BA degree from the Department of Primary School Education of the Aegean University (Greece) and a BA degree in Philosophy, Pedagogy and Psychology from the University of Athens (Greece). He was awarded his doctorate (PhD) by the Department of Philosophy, Pedagogy and Psychology of the University of Athens (Greece). He has published more than 55 articles and has presented papers at international and Greek conferences.
Correspondence: konsolas@rhodes.aegean.gr

John McKeown, EdD, hails from Canada and is the director of the School of Foreign Languages at MEF University, Istanbul. He has served as a senior lecturer in English language teaching, as an assistant professor of education, and as school administrator and project manager. As Director of Academics for Mosaica Education, he led school reform initiatives in the Gulf States. He has lived and worked in Turkey for over 10 years and has held administrative, teaching and consultative positions there.
Correspondence: mckeownj@mef.edu.tr

Michael McMurray has been involved in the English-teaching field since 1980, teaching all levels and types of developmental as well as credit English courses in addition to ESL/EFL courses, including foundation program courses, ESP courses, and a host of continuing education courses. He has also served as curriculum designer for two internationally accredited foundation programs. His first 15 years were spent at community colleges in the Dallas area; since 1994 he has taught in the Arabian Gulf. *Correspondence*: mcmurray.m@gust.edu.kw

Eva Mináříková is a research assistant at the Institute for Research in School Education, Masaryk University, Brno (Czech Republic) and the associate editor of *Pedagogická orientace*, one of the leading Czech academic journals on educational research. Her research focuses on the use of video in preservice and in-service teacher education.
Correspondence: minarikova@ped.muni.cz

Stefinee Pinnegar is a teacher educator in the McKay School of Education at Brigham Young University. She is one of the founders of the Self-Study of Teacher Education Practices research movement. As Acting Dean of the Invisible College for Research on Teaching, she is concerned with developing arenas for conversations about teaching and learning research. She is most interested in what and how teachers know as teachers. She has published in the areas of teacher education, narrative, and self-study research and research methodology. *Correspondence*: stefinee@byu.edu

Michaela Píšová is an associate professor at the Institute for Research in School Education, Masaryk University, Brno (Czech Republic). She has conducted research on teachers and teacher education and has been one of the leading figures in designing and implementing innovations in teacher education in the Czech Republic in the last decade. Together with her team, she has carried out an extensive research study on expert teachers of English as a Foreign Language. *Correspondence*: pisova.mich@gmail.com

Tara Ratnam is an independent teacher educator and researcher from India. She received her PhD in English Language Teaching from the English and Foreign Languages University (EFLU), Hyderabad, India. She is the research advisor to the Indian Institute of Montessori Studies (IIMS), Bangalore, India. She pursues research on fostering teacher learning and change in reflective communities of inquiry focusing on the cultural, historical and institutional forces that mediate teachers' thinking and the resulting tension-laden path they negotiate. She is also keenly interested in the issue of diversity and in providing socially sensitive learning support to the culturally diverse student populations. Her theoretical perspective is interdisciplinary and includes the works of theorists such as Mikhail Bakhtin (philosophy of language), Lev Vygotsky (cultural historical psychology), William Perry (adult development) and Paulo Freire (critical pedagogy), among others. She is the Indian representative of the International Study

Association on Teachers and Teaching (ISATT). *Correspondence*: tararatnam@gmail.com

Pablo Silva Ríos, teacher of English, MA in Applied Linguistics, has taught students of all ages since 1993. Also, he has worked in curriculum design and in projects of assessment for learning at the Ministry of Education. He was a member of the team that wrote the standards for EFL initial teacher education in Chile. Currently, he is the director of the English Pedagogy Program at Universidad Alberto Hurtado.
Correspondence: psilva@uahurtado.cl

Nora M. Basurto-Santos holds a PhD in ELT and Applied Linguistics from Warwick University in the UK and an MSc in TEFL from Aston University, England. She has been a teacher trainer and has taught EFL and other subjects in the area of applied linguistics for over 30 years in the undergraduate and postgraduate programmes at the University of Veracruz, Mexico. She is particularly interested in doing research that involves fieldwork in different educational settings within the public sector. At present, she is a full-time researcher at the University of Veracruz and is a member of the Sistema Nacional de Investigadores – CONACyT. In the past 7 years, she, along with her colleagues from the Universidad Nacional de Colombia-Bogotá, has been involved in the organization of an international conference on research in foreign languages. She has many national and international publications and has been a keynote speaker at several international conferences. *Correspondence*: nbasurto@uv.mx

Phiona Stanley has degrees from Edinburgh, Sydney and Monash universities. She is a Senior Lecturer in Education at UNSW Australia in Sydney. She has worked in TESOL in Peru, Poland, Qatar, China, the UK and Australia, and as a teacher, CELTA trainer, director of studies, academic operations manager, and editor. Her research focuses on intercultural competence in educational contexts, particularly language education, and she is currently working on a book for Routledge on backpackers learning Spanish and interculturality in Latin America. *Correspondence*: phiona.stanley@unsw.edu.au

Ioanna Syriou is a secondary school principal in Athens. She has a Master of Arts in Education and is a doctoral candidate at the Aegean University. She is mainly interested in issues regarding innovative teaching practices in school, student assessment and school evaluation.
Correspondence: ioanna.syriou@gmail.com

Amira Traish is currently Foundation Program Coordinator of the English Language Centre (ELC) at the University of Sharjah in the UAE. She graduated from the University of Akron in May 2005 with a Master of Arts degree in Literature and a certificate in Composition. In 2014, she received her EdD in TESOL from the British University of Dubai. Her dissertation addressed the issue of use of the primary language (L1) to teach the target language (L2). She is interested in curriculum development, and her current target demographic for research and application in this field is young adult learners. She has facilitated curricular changes to the Foundation program at the University of Sharjah as well as the Community College. Sitting on the board of reviewers for Neem Tree Press, a London-based publishing company, Amira also reviews books for a number of regional publishers, applying her EFL/ESL expertise to assist them in achieving their objectives. *Correspondence*: amiratraish@gmail.com; atraish@sharjah.ac.ae

Liping Wei, EdD, is an assistant professor in the School of Education, Health Professions, & Human Development at the University of Houston-Victoria, USA. Her TESOL teaching experience has spanned both EFL and ESL contexts. Her research program mainly draws on narrative inquiry and teachers' reflective practices. She has wide research interests including ESL teachers' professional development, TESOL pedagogy, ESL teacher as researcher, international education, and multicultural education. Her current research interests centre on employing narrative inquiry to investigate the teaching experience of ELL teachers and the educational experience of linguistic minority students. She has published papers in various journals and presented her research internationally, nationally and regionally. *Correspondence*: weil@uhv.edu

Joanna W. Wong is Assistant Professor in the College of Education, California State University, Monterey Bay. She earned her doctorate at UC Davis in Language, Literacy, and Culture with designated emphases in Second Language Acquisition and Writing, Rhetoric, and Composition Studies. Her research interests include second-language writing, bilingualism, and teacher education to serve non-dominant populations. She draws on over 14 years of experience in urban elementary education for her research, teaching and professional development and has researched elementary bilingual writers' understandings, expectations and practices. She published an article on metalinguistic awareness as a resource for potential bilingual teachers in the *Bilingual Research Journal* and has a book chapter in press in *Second Language Writing in Elementary Classrooms* (ed. L.C. de Oliveira & T. Silva). She is currently a fellow with the National Council of Teachers of English Cultivating New Voices of Scholars of Color program. *Correspondence*: jowong@csumb.edu

Luxin Yang is a Professor at the National Research Center for Foreign Language Education at Beijing Foreign Studies University, China. She holds a PhD in Second Language Education from the Ontario Institute for Studies in Education, University of Toronto. Her research interests include foreign language teacher education, second language writing, and academic literacy development. She has articles published in such international journals as *Journal of Second Language Writing, Language Teaching Research, Language, Culture and Curriculum, System, Journal of English for Academic Purposes*. Since she returned to China in 2006, she has paid special attention to school EFL education in China and recently completed a national project on improving the quality of EFL teaching and learning at schools in China. She is now working with Dr Shijing Xu of University of Windsor, Canada on a large SSHRC (Social Sciences and Humanities Research Council of Canada) partnership grant project *Reciprocal Learning in Teacher Education and School Education between China and Canada. Correspondence*: yangluxin@bfsu.edu.cn, luxin_yang@163.com

Jianfen Ying is an associate professor in the College of Foreign Languages of Zhejiang Normal University, China. She is dean of the International Department of the college. She has been teaching English since 1997. In 2011 she won the honor of the 'Provincial Excellent Teacher' in Zhejiang Province. She was a visiting scholar at the University of Houston in 2014. Her research interests are English teacher development and learning community building. *Correspondence*: zsdyjf@zjnu.cn

Zhilian Zheng is an associate professor in the College of Foreign Languages of Zhejiang Normal University, China. She was vice-dean of the English Department from 2008 to 2014. She has been teaching English as a Foreign Language since 1985 in the college. She specializes in research on exploratory practice in the English curriculum as one of the main initiators of the RICH programme. Since 2002, her research interests have extended to teacher preparation, teacher training and exploratory practice. In 2012 she was named the 'National Excellent Supervisor for Postgraduates' in China. *Correspondence*: zheng66@zjnu.cn